ST GEORGE'S CHAPEL
WINDSOR CASTLE

Hugo Vickers
Photographs by Elizabeth Vickers
FOREWORD BY HRH THE DUKE OF EDINBURGH, KG

Stained glass in the Urswick Chantry.
The figures in the windows depict Christ, St Peter and four of the apostles.

First published in 2008 by The Foundation of the College of St George
The Cloisters, Windsor Castle, Berkshire SL4 1NJ

Designed and produced by The Dovecote Press Ltd
Stanbridge, Wimborne Minster, Dorset, BH21 4JD

ISBN 978-1-904-34957-0

Printed and bound in Singapore

All papers used by The Dovecote Press are natural, recyclable products
made from wood grown in sustainable, well-managed forests.

A CIP catalogue record for this book is available
from the British Library

1 3 5 7 9 8 6 4 2

Contents

Her Majesty The Queen and H.R.H. The Duke of Edinburgh, Garter Day 2007.

Foreword

WINDSOR CASTLE

St George's, the chapel within the Castle at Windsor, is an architectural marvel, but it is also the place of worship for all those who live in the Castle precincts, it is their, and our, parish church. It contains the remains of monarchs, together with many memorials to members of their families, and to many of their friends and loyal members of their households.

As the home of the Order of the Garter, it also honours many men and women who have given very special service to their country. This curious mixture of domestic and national functions gives St George's Chapel a very special character. Not least, it demonstrates the continuity of our national history. It has lived through all sorts of national dramas, but its core value as a place of Christian worship and memory remains as strong as ever.

The author tells a fascinating story, and his wife has added a wonderful store of images to go with it. Together they have produced a vivid account of this unique building, and of the community which it has served for so many centuries.

Introduction

My LOVE FOR ST GEORGE'S CHAPEL goes back to childhood. I was taken to Windsor Castle a few times on family outings when at prep school nearby – Scaitcliffe, at Englefield Green. Of those early outings I remember more of the castle than St George's Chapel itself. Yet two very early black and white photographs that I took of Windsor with my Box Brownie survive. One shows a guard in a sentry box on the parade ground, and the other shows the West Window of St George's Chapel. In 1965, when at Eton, I was photographed in one of the sentry boxes. That photograph also survives.

It was not until March 1964 that the fascination truly began. Elsewhere, I have related the story of

OPPOSITE PAGE The banners of the Knights of the Garter in the Quire, photographed from the Catherine of Aragon loft.

BELOW Two rather faded photographs from the author's collection. The first shows him in his school uniform in 1965, posed in a sentry box by the George IV Gate. He took the second in 1960, which is of an Irish Guard in the Lower Ward of Windsor Castle.

how Mr Owen, our headmaster at Scaitcliffe, took some of his senior boys to a performance of Bach's St Matthew Passion in St George's Chapel. This performance took place on 21 March 1964 and was sung by the combined choirs of St George's and Eton College Chapel, under the direction of Dr Sidney Campbell. We queued for a long time outside the South Door, and Mr Owen spoke of the history of the chapel, the Knights of the Garter, and the Royal Vault. I cannot explain why I became so fascinated by the concept of the Royal Vault lift in the centre of the Quire, which descended very slowly during a royal funeral, and how the dead King would slowly disappear from view.

Standing in that queue in 1964, I resolved that I wanted to know more about St George's Chapel. I was lucky to get into Eton the following September, and on my very first Saturday afternoon I went alone up the hill, paid my shilling, and began to explore. It was the first of a great many visits.

Such was my interest that I began to make a model of St George's Chapel at home. This became something of an obsession and I devoted almost all my free time to the adornment and peopling of this model. Eventually I moved it into an attic room at home and it expanded accordingly, presently occupying the whole room. It survived for many years afterwards until parts of it were ripped from the wall by some insensitive Rentokil operators, at a time when there was no one there to prevent them from doing so – or who much cared. Today only the fragile central part of the model survives, run-down, neglected. There are times when I consider restoring it, but that moment has not come.

I cannot explain psychologically the need to recreate a place in miniature. Perhaps it comes from a frustrated wish to 'possess' the real thing in some

way. There are many examples of such things happening. Cecil Beaton, for example, constructed a miniature theatre in boyhood, and went on to be a noted designer for stage and screen.

In my case, I can but claim that the faithful copying of the actual chapel with the banners of the Knights of the Garter and the heraldic stall plates led me to observe it with a keener eye than would otherwise have been the case. It meant that when at the real chapel I would be observing and noting; when at home I would recreate. And this applied not only to the fabric of the building, but also to those who peopled it. Since it was not possible to buy miniature figures to occupy my model, I was forced to make them myself. I made about 500 in the end, some emerging more realistic and successful than others. They were very detailed as to uniforms, robes, orders and decorations. These figures were all of living people. It has been a curious irony that I ended up friends of some of them in later life, and several of them have been the subject of biographies by me, while of the 500, many have appeared in the various books I have written. The little figures have survived in better condition than the original model.

I spent many happy hours in St George's Chapel,

ABOVE A view of Windsor Castle from the Long Walk in about 1960.

BELOW The stall plate of Edward, King of Portugal, KG (1435), an unusually large plate, nearly 16 inches long, made of copper. It depicts the arms of Portugal within a bordure of Castile.

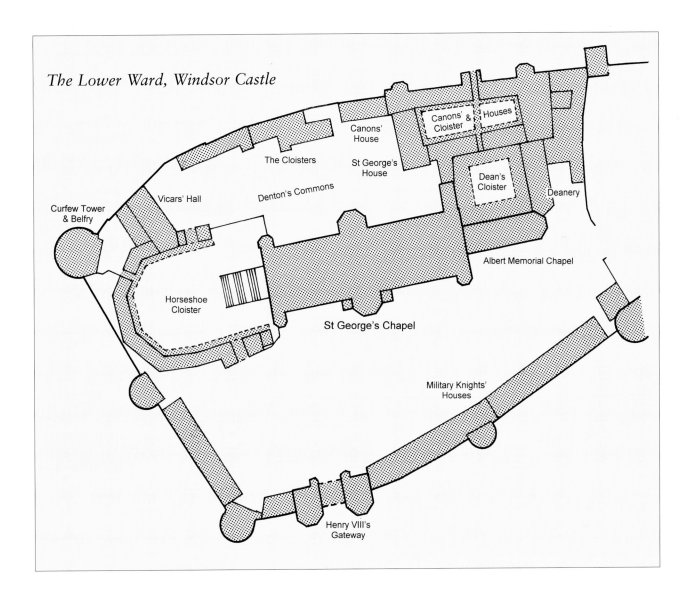

The Lower Ward, Windsor Castle

Curfew Tower & Belfry

The Cloisters

Vicars' Hall

Denton's Commons

Canons' House

St George's House

Canons' & Cloister

Houses

Dean's Cloister

Deanery

Horseshoe Cloister

Albert Memorial Chapel

St George's Chapel

Military Knights' Houses

Henry VIII's Gateway

while at Eton, visiting it virtually every Saturday and Sunday afternoon. In February 1966 I was invited to become one of the Eton guides in the days when the chapel was open for tourists on Sunday afternoons. The questions asked and the discussions with those that knew the chapel well, led to more discoveries. I was a chapel guide until December 1969, and during this time, showed all kinds of tourists around. The terrifying Governor of the Castle, Field Marshal Lord Slim, once brought a small group in; Queen Anne of Romania brought one of her daughters without admitting she was the girl's mother; and Lord Bridges, one of the Knights of the Garter, visited the chapel one Sunday afternoon to show his family his stall. There was the afternoon when the Queen and Queen Elizabeth came to the chapel to look at the King George VI Chapel then being built, and I was planted on the temporary door behind which the work had been going on. And of course there were the many from different lands who showed widely varying degrees of interest in differing aspects of the chapel and its life.

On Saturday afternoons I would talk to Roy Read, the Dean's Virger. I often wonder how different things might have been had he been

ST GEORGE'S CHAPEL, WINDSOR CASTLE / 12

OPPOSITE PAGE A view of the North Quire Aisle, looking into the North Nave Aisle, with the statue of King Leopold of the Belgians in the distance.

ABOVE The South Quire Aisle, with the tomb of Edward VII and Queen Alexandra on the left.

irritated by a stray question from me as to the location of Lord Palmerston's stall plate. He looked it up and in so doing unleashed a flood of further questions that continued for many years afterwards.

Sunday afternoons afforded us the chance to talk to the Canons, as there was invariably one of them in the chapel for a time each Sunday afternoon, and afterwards we had tea with the Dean, or one of the Military Knights and his wife. We could attend Evensong, and I was lucky to be allowed by the organist, Dr Sidney Campbell, to watch the service

from the Organ Loft. On certain occasions we were even treated to a glass of sherry before returning to school.

My father was a friend of Lt-Colonel 'Toddy' Hodgson, by then the longest serving Military Knight of Windsor. We watched the Garter procession from the roof of his house in June 1965 (I have never missed one since), and were planning to take tea with him in the autumn of that year, but he died, and on the day in question, we attended his funeral instead.

During those years I attended my first big service at the chapel – the Dedication of St George's House in October 1966 in the presence of the Queen and the Duke of Edinburgh, and a number of Knights of the Garter, including the 92-year-old Earl of Iveagh. And from the Organ Loft I watched the funeral

service of Princess Marina, the only time I ever saw the Duke of Windsor – on what proved to be his last ever visit to Britain, in August 1968.

On leaving school, the Dean of Windsor, Robin Woods, invited me to become a Lay Steward and I have continued to serve in that capacity since January 1970.

Some of the above might well suggest that when invited to write this book, I thought I knew quite a lot about St George's Chapel. The opposite is true. I have enjoyed finding out how much I did not know. This book has been a voyage of discovery for me, and the awful truth is that even at the end of it, there is surely an enormous amount that I still do not know, and that I will never know.

ABOVE St George's Chapel, the East Window, framed by the pipes of the organ.

OPPOSITE PAGE The present St George's Chapel owes its existence to Edward IV, who began its construction in about 1470. This portrait of the King and his Queen, Elizabeth Woodville, is in stained glass in the North Quire Aisle, opposite the King's tomb. Glass by Thomas Willement, 1845.

My aim is to tell the story through the people who have made the chapel what it is, and to throw light into previously dark corners, thus bringing the chapel to life through its past and its present.

HUGO VICKERS
April 2008

PART ONE

A ROYAL FREE CHAPEL

ONE

'St George for England!'

WHEN YOU enter St George's Chapel, you are entering a 'Royal Peculiar'. You are also entering one of the finest examples of late medieval architecture. This was not the first St George's Chapel. When Edward III founded the College of St George and the Order of the Garter in 1348, he took over a chapel originally built in the Lower Ward of Windsor Castle by Henry III in the thirteenth century, re-founding it in honour of the Blessed Virgin Mary, St George and St Edward the Confessor.

Originally the Manor of Old Windsor belonged to the Saxon Kings. We know that Edward the Confessor had a hunting lodge in Old Windsor which also served as the manor court. William the Conqueror raised the mound on which he built a motte and bailey castle, where the Round Tower and Middle Ward now stand, on account of its strategic position high above the river. The castle was completed before the Domesday survey of 1086. Henry I was the first king to build a residence in the castle, in the Upper Ward, and he held his court there for the first time at Whitsun 1110.

Henry II developed the castle, giving it stone curtain walls, the shell keep (Round Tower) on the motte, and first built a public great hall in the Lower Ward. He also developed the town of New Windsor around the market place and parish church, and almost certainly constructed the first bridge over the Thames to Eton.

OPPOSITE PAGE Gilebertus doors in the Ambulatory, the original door to the earlier chapel, now the Albert Memorial Chapel.

HENRY III (KING 1216-72)

Henry III loved Windsor Castle, and, although no great politician, he was an aesthete with an eye for beauty. Having rebuilt the eastern arm of Westminster Abbey and undertaken building work in the Tower of London, he set about improving the castle. He built the first chapel between 1239 and 1248 on the site of what is now the Albert Memorial Chapel. It was dedicated to St Edward the Confessor.

Some of this earlier chapel still exists, notably the west and north walls and the main door painted scarlet and dressed with exquisite gilded ironwork, the work of the craftsman Gilebertus. It is thought that these doors date from between 1247 and 1249, and that Gilebertus may have been the moneyer, Gilbert de Bonninton.[1] Originally there were three doors, a central west door and north and south doors leading into the galilee porch. The north wall of the original chapel is still visible in the Dean's Cloister, being the lower part of the original wall of that earlier chapel.

The scarlet exterior of the central door now serves as the interior of the double doors that are opened into the Ambulatory on royal occasions. Also surviving are six Purbeck columns and the arches of the narthex which now forms the vestibule.

EDWARD III (KING 1327-77)

In founding the College of St George in 1348, Edward III united the themes of chivalry with religious devotion, appointing the Knights of the Garter and then the Warden (later Dean), canons

ABOVE An early print of Windsor Castle. The River Thames is in the foreground and St George's Chapel on the skyline on the right.

RIGHT Edward the Confessor, King and Martyr (who reigned 975-979), holding a model of a chapel - a detail from the tomb of the Duke of Clarence, in the Albert Memorial Chapel.

and vicars of the College. He balanced the two elements of secular service and worship.

'St. George for England!' had been the war cry of the English soldiers, St George being been popular in the crusades of Richard I (the cry was given when fighting Saladin in the Holy Land). Edward III was covetous of the throne of France and adopted St George as his patron saint to represent this ambition.

Stalls were built in this chapel for both the Knights and the Canons. Knights' helms, crests and swords were attached to these stalls for the lifetime of each knight, and stall-plates affixed, some of which survived and were later moved to the new St George's Chapel.

The Order of the Garter is crucial to the College

of St George and St George's Chapel. Its establishment led directly to the foundation of the choir (by statute in 1352) to support the daily services of the College of St George, and of the poor knights (now the Military Knights of Windsor).

The Order of the Garter evolved from the Arthurian tradition. The idea of the Round Table, jousting, drawing around the King favoured and powerful figures as knights, all contributed to its creation. The 'Round Table' Tournament feast took place on 19 January 1344, pre-dating Crécy, and on this occasion the King attended with leading nobility, knights and esquires, and many valiant knights from overseas. The solemnity opened with a magnificent feast, followed by days of entertainment. Besides the men present, Queen Philippa and '300 of the fairest Ladies and Virgins, in their richest attire, all of noble and honourable families', feasted in the great hall of the Lower Wards, adding 'the greater lustre to this noble Assembly.'

To this feast is also dated the plan for a large circular space for jousting in what is now the Upper Ward of the castle. It was to contain a Round Table to seat some 300 knights. The diameter of the floor was to be 200 feet, and the circumference approximately 600 feet.[2]

After the victories at Crécy in 1346, and at the surrender of Calais in the following year, Edward III and his son, the Black Prince, returned to England to celebrate with a series of tournaments. The King crystallised his idea of an order of chivalry to include the new chapel, served by 13 canons and 13 priest vicars, with a Warden (the original title of the Dean), for all of whom accommodation was provided. There had been chaplains at Windsor before, but they depended on the King's will, being appointed and removed according to his personal whims.

There was also provision for poor knights, who

TOP RIGHT Edward III, wearing the Crown of England and with the crowns of France and Scotland on his sword.

RIGHT Prince Edward, the Black Prince from a sketch in Elias Ashmole's *The Order of the Garter*, 1672.

ABOVE The badge of the Order of the Garter.

RIGHT The sword of Edward III, which now hangs in the South Quire Aisle.

number of 'blue garters' in the wardrobe accounts over these years. Joan, the 'Fair Maid of Kent', later married the Black Prince.

Essentially the King created a way of demonstrating his respect to the knights who had served in battle with him, and of assuring their loyalty. Later it became a way to reward veterans who were no longer able to fight as in the days of their youth, and it was a relatively inexpensive way of rewarding loyalty. Edward III was in a good position to do this, as a noted warrior king with distinguished victories behind him. Honour was the main criterion for appointment, but inevitably the King sometimes appointed obscure English knights (such as Sir Walter Pavely) or foreign ones such as Sir Sanchet d'Abrichecourt or used the order for

were celibate and pensioned off from the wars. Their role was to represent the Knights of the Garter at services. Provision was made for 24 but until the Reformation there were never more than three at any one time. There were 24 Knights of the Garter (or 26 including the King and the Prince of Wales).

The Order is said to have acquired its curious name, the Order of the Garter, because Edward III was fond of ladies. At a ball in Calais held to celebrate the town's surrender in 1347 it was said that the young Joan, Countess of Salisbury, with whom the King was then in love, dropped her garter as she danced. The king retrieved the blue riband, and tied it on his own knee. When the courtiers laughed at the gesture, he remonstrated with them: 'Shame on him who thinks evil of it!' – *Honi Soit Qui Mal Y Pense*. This story was first related by the historian, Polidore Virgil about a century and a half later. Whether true or false, there were certainly a

patronage to reward the most powerful men in the land. There were 26 Founder Knights, comrades in arms to the King in his battles, most of whom had fought at Crécy, Calais or both:

1 King Edward III.
2 Edward, Prince of Wales (The Black Prince – son of the King).
3 Henry Plantagenet, Duke of Lancaster (the King's cousin, who had been at the siege of Calais, and governed Aquitaine).
4 Thomas Beauchamp, 3rd Earl of Warwick (who led the van under the Black Prince at Crécy).
5 Sir John de Grailly (who served under the Black Prince at Bordeaux and distinguished himself at Poitiers. He spent his last years as a prisoner, but his stall plate survives).
6 Ralph, 1st Earl of Stafford.
7 William Montacute, 2nd Earl of Salisbury.

Edward III and Queen Philippa from a stained glass window made by Willement, 1846.

8 Roger Mortimer, 2nd Earl of March.
9 John Lisle, 1st Lord Lisle of Rougemont.
10 Bartholomew Beauchamp Burghersh, 1st Lord Burghersh.
11 John Beauchamp, 1st Lord Beauchamp of Warwick (who had helped win the naval victory at Sluys in 1340).
12 John, 2nd Lord Mohun of Dunster.
13 Sir Hugh Courtenay.
14 Thomas Holand, 1st Earl of Kent.
15 John, 1st Lord Grey of Rotherfield.
16 Sir Richard Fitz-Simon.
17 Sir Miles Stapleton.
18 Sir Thomas Wale.
19 Sir Hugh Wrottesley.
20 Sir Nele Loryng (veteran of Sluys, 1340), and

The stall plate of Ralph, Lord Bassett, created a Knight of the Garter in 1368. This is the earliest stall plate to survive in St George's Chapel, and was one of those moved from the earlier chapel. The surviving stall plates of the Founder Knights mostly date from 1421.

whose stall plate survives.
21 Sir John Chandos (life-long comrade-in-arms of the Black Prince, veteran of Crécy and Poitiers, killed by the French at Lussac in 1369, and whose stall plate survives).
22 Sir James Audley.
23 Sir Otes Holand.
24 Sir Henry Eam.
25 Sir Sanchet d'Abrichecourt (of whom little is known, though his stall plate survives).
26 Sir Walter Paveley (who served in the Duke of Lancaster's fleet in 1351, and whose stall plate survives).

These Knights of the Garter were expected to attend a number of services at the chapel each year on St George's Day, or on the Sunday nearest to April 23rd.

In 1351 the Pope granted the new body of priests exemption from the jurisdiction of the Archbishop of Canterbury, and from the diocesan Bishop of Salisbury. This made St George's Chapel a 'peculiar'

and a 'royal free chapel', free from Episcopal jurisdiction. By 1355 there were two cloisters to the north of the chapel, the first of which had been built in the thirteenth century – the Dean's Cloister, and the Canons' Cloister, with dwellings for members of the College.

In 1351 Garter robes were made for the Knights, while the King's wife, Queen Philippa (of Hainault, who had successfully pleaded for the lives of the burgesses of Calais), received Garter robes in 1358, and her daughter Isabella in 1376, other ladies being accorded the honour later. Twelve Garter banners were ordered for the chapel, and ceremonies were held. These are the only two female appointments known to have been made by Edward III. Queens and Princesses, and other ladies were appointed Ladies of the Garter until the reign of Henry VII. Joan, Countess of Salisbury, was admitted in 1378, presumably by her son Richard II. Henry VII's queen was already a Lady, being the daughter of Edward IV. The only such appointment he made was that of his mother, Margaret, Countess of Richmond. All these ladies were issued with Garter robes and wore the Garter on their left arm, above the elbow. They did not have stalls or banners.[3] Ladies of the Garter were revived by Edward VII on the appointment of Queen Alexandra in 1901, and several queens and princesses have been admitted to the Order since, with stalls and banners.

Money was always a problem, Edward III's endowment consisting largely of appropriated churches, and bringing in £600 a year, a large sum in that century but nevertheless insufficient. Edward III died in 1377 and was succeeded by Richard II, during whose reign, in 1389, Chaucer was appointed Clerk of the King's Works. Though not responsible for Windsor Castle, he was granted the care of the old Chapel by special warrant. The reason for this was that the Chapel was on the point of collapse. This meant that any repairs were done at the expense of the Exchequer and not the Castle. Chaucer was charged to impress a great number of workmen into the King's service, and he ordered 101 tons of

A view of St George's Chapel from the Round Tower, showing the Albert Memorial Chapel in the foreground.

Stapleton stone from South Yorkshire and 200 cartloads of Reigate stone. All this arrived but was not put to use, and after two years Chaucer was relieved of his post.[4]

* * * * *

During the Middle Ages it became popular to endow chantries and several were endowed at Windsor. The basic requirement was that prayers and masses be offered for the good of the founders while alive, and their souls after their deaths. St George's Chapel remains one of the most important and ambitious medieval chantry foundations to survive and one of the only places where chantries were not abolished under Edward VI.

In 1399 Richard II was deposed by Henry IV, who usurped his throne, and almost certainly caused his subsequent murder. In 1413 Henry IV was succeeded by Henry V. During his reign, in 1421, his brother, John, Duke of Bedford, made a magnificent donation to the chapel, enriching the College with the grant of part of the property of Ogbourne, the richest of the seven Benedictine priories in England.

After the death of Henry V in 1422, the Lancastrian King, Henry VI, reigned until 1461, then ceding the throne to the Yorkist claimant, the nineteen-year-old Edward IV between 1461 to 1470, and reigning once more between 1470 and 1471, when he was probably murdered. He was then again succeeded by Edward IV, who was now safe in the knowledge that not only Henry VI, but also Henry's son, Edward, Prince of Wales had died in May 1471, the latter after the Battle of Tewkesbury.

EDWARD IV (KING 1461-83)

By 1475 Edward IV was entering the zenith of his reign. He was 33 years old; he had silenced his enemies, secured a pension for life from Louis XI of France, and was ready to indulge in the more enjoyable aspects of being a King. In the fifteenth century, Kings were expected to live extravagantly with many outward signs of richness to distinguish themselves from the common man.

Edward IV enjoyed luxury and fine clothes. In 1480 he ordered some 26 gowns, jackets and doublets, many in fine velvet, satin or cloth of gold. He bought plate and jewels and may have spent as much as £3,000 on a huge diamond and ruby ornament sent from Italy.

This was one of the periods of 'magnificently ostentatious piety, of lavish ecclesiastical building',[5] during which King's College Chapel at Cambridge was built, as was Eton College Chapel. It was also a time when men were obsessed by death, and in particular 'the progress of the soul from the cleansing fires of Purgatory to the bliss of Paradise through the performance of pious works by those

remaining in the world – above all by the offering of the Mass.'[6] Edward IV turned his thoughts to where he would lie after his death.

The King began to build on a large scale. He did not share Henry VI's taste for religious or educational establishments, and after spending money on necessary repairs for his castle at Calais and other fortresses damaged in recent fighting, he turned to his own residences, mostly those in the south east, though he spent some money on his residences at Nottingham and Fotheringay.

The King extended the palaces of Greenwich and Westminster; in 1475 he built a magnificent hall at Eltham Palace in Kent, which still survives and is considered on a par with Westminster Hall and the Great Hall at Hampton Court as one of the great royal halls of the Middle Ages.

St George's Chapel was his finest architectural achievement. Perhaps inspired by the collegiate church of Fotheringay (built by his father, Richard, Duke of York), or perhaps to rival Henry VI's chapel at Eton College, just down the hill, or King's College at Cambridge, he commissioned the building of a new chapel in the grounds of Windsor Castle, to be the new home of the College of St George, and the Order of the Garter (a particular interest of the King's and one of which he made considerable diplomatic use).

Edward IV did not replace Henry III's chapel. He began a new chapel at the west end of the old one, just separate from it. Not only did he aim to build a fine edifice but he planned to use it as a mausoleum for himself and his Queen and for members of the House of York. He took a particular interest in his own tomb, directing that a stone should be placed over his grave 'wrought with the figure of death, with scutcheon of our armour and writings convenient about the borders of the same remembering the day and year of our decease.' He wanted 'an image for our figure' and a chantry to be built nearby in which two priests would pray daily

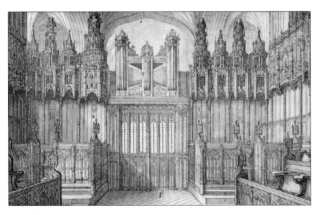

ABOVE An engraving by Wenceslaus Hollar of the Quire stalls, with the Sovereign's stall on the left and the Prince's stall on the right, from Ashmole's *The Order of the Garter* (1672).

RIGHT A detail of a Garter stall canopy, from a drawing by A. Buckler.

for the souls of himself, his wife, Elizabeth Woodville, and his ancestors.

In 1472 King Edward IV breathed new life into the Order of the Garter, which had gone through a quiet period in its history. He celebrated the Garter feast again, and created many new Garter Knights. He used the Garter as a political weapon to impress foreign kings and princes, choosing figures such as King Ferdinand I of Naples, the Duke of Milan, Charles, Duke of Burgundy, King Ferdinand of Castile, King John II of Portugal and Federigo, Duke of Urbino, commander of the papal troops (whose palace in Urbino is still extensively adorned with Garter badges), while for Englishmen election to the Order was very much in Edward IV's personal favour.

At the same time, in order to build St George's Chapel, he commissioned master craftsmen, stonecutters, carpenters, glass engravers and others from all over England. Richard Beauchamp, Bishop of Salisbury, Chancellor of the Order of the Garter, and from 1477 Dean of Windsor, oversaw the work and Henry Janyns was the master-mason. Stones, timber, tiles, shingles, glass, iron, lead and other material were ordered. The work was paid for by profits from baronial estates which had fallen into the King's hands during his minority. As the work

progressed, so the original building disappeared behind this new chapel. Work began in 1475 and two years later Thomas Chancellor was appointed controller of the works. Three years later so many stonecutters were being employed that the Chancellor of Oxford University could not find any masons to build the Divinity School. The Quire and side aisles were the first to be raised to their full height and roofed, albeit in timber. The quire stalls and canopies were finely carved, and finished in 1482/3. Between 1478 and 1483 the work cost £6,572, yet by the time Edward IV died in 1483, the chapel was by no means complete.

During the last years of his reign, Edward IV's greatest enemy was his brother, the Duke of Clarence, who was eventually accused of having 'violated the laws of the realm'. In 1477 he was arrested and imprisoned in the Tower of London. The following year he was put to death. By popular and Shakespearian mythology he was drowned in a butt which normally contained Malmsey wine.

In 1483 Edward IV was still a youngish man, enjoying the favours of three mistresses as well as his Queen. Two of his children, his third son, George (1477-9), and his daughter Mary (1467-82) (who had been destined to marry the Dauphin of France), had predeceased him and been buried in the chapel. In March 1483 he was at Windsor, returning briefly to Westminster on 25th. There he fell suddenly and violently ill. Various theories have been advanced – that he caught a chill on the Thames, that he was poisoned, that he was in a rage about the Treaty of Arras, or that he had succumbed to an ague or malaria. The only thing we know for certain is that he had grown overweight and unhealthy through overeating. He took to his bed. On 9 April 1483 he died a few days before his 41st birthday.

Edward IV's body lay naked to the waist for several hours in order that the various civic authorities could certify the death. After an elaborate lying-in-state in St Stephen's Chapel, Westminster, and a night lying in Westminster Abbey, the long, slow funeral procession made its way from Westminster to Windsor by way of

The tomb of Edward IV as seen in the North Quire Aisle.

Charing Cross and Sion Abbey, the coffin resting on a chariot covered with black velvet and pulled by six horses.[7] St George's Chapel was still unfinished but his marble tomb had been prepared for him and brought from abroad the year before. It was so heavy that it broke the crane that carried it. The King was laid to rest beneath it with great ceremony. The men of the Royal Household threw in their staves of office (today these are broken ceremonially at the monarch's funeral) – and the heralds surrendered their coats of arms.[8]

The King's will had stipulated elaborate plans for the tomb, including 'an image of our figure, which figure we will be of silver and gilt or at the least copper and gilt.'[9] This image was to be placed on the Tournai marble tomb. There was also to be a figure of death on the tomb itself. Originally the fine

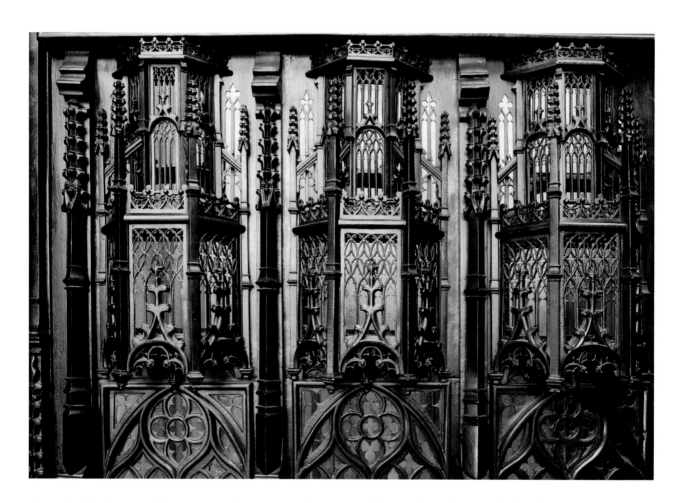

A detail of the John Tresilian gates on Edward IV's tomb, now in the sanctuary in the Quire.

ironwork gates of the tomb stood in the North Quire Aisle, but in 1790 the carver, Henry Emlyn, moved them to the other side – in the Quire itself – to the left of the High Altar. These were the work of the Cornishman, John Tresilian, and have been described as 'the last and finest piece of medieval decorative ironwork in England.'[10] Before the plunder of the chapel in 1642, these gates were apparently 'richly embroidered with pearl and gold, interwoven with Rubies',[11] just as were several accoutrements (the King's coat of gilt mail, covered with crimson velvet and bearing his coat of arms embroidered in pearls, gold and rubies, and his banner also bearing the royal arms) placed there at the funeral remained on the tomb until that looting.

When Edward IV died, the nave was not complete. Construction work continued until the Battle of Bosworth in 1485.

After Edward IV's death, his wife, Elizabeth Woodville, suffered an increasingly troubled and harassed widowhood. She finally died at Bermondsey in 1492, leaving instructions that her body 'be buried with the body of my lord at Windsor, without pompous interring or costly expenses thereabout.'[12]

On Whitsunday her coffin was taken by water during the night to Windsor, accompanied by a small group including 'Miss Grace', a bastard daughter of Edward IV. The bells did not ring on its arrival at the Chapel and a priest of the College, rather than the Dean, received it. She was buried 'without any solemn dirge done for her obit.'[13] The next day her three surviving daughters and others came to the chapel for the dirge. The day afterwards, Master Vaughan, one of the Canons, sang the Mass of Our Lady, and offerings were made by the family and courtiers, the Poor Knights, the Dean, Canons, Yeomen and Officers-at-Arms. Her son Thomas, Marquess of Dorset, offered a piece of gold, and paid for the funeral.

The actual burial place of Edward IV and Elizabeth Woodville was not discovered until 1789 when the Quire was being repaved. The stones covering the tomb had decayed. Workmen came across the skeleton of the King measuring six foot three inches, and, as was reported, beside his skull 'quantities of long brown hair which had fallen off. There were no traces of cerecloth, no rings or any other insignia and it seemed that the tomb had at some time been plundered.'[14] Two other coffins were also found – those of his children Prince George and Princess Mary. It was said that a lock of pale gold hair could be spotted through a narrow chink in the coffin, 'a touching remnant of departed beauty surviving the lapse of three long centuries.'[15]

In the reign of William IV an inscription was placed on the original Tournai marble slab, and the Windsor carpenter, Henry Emlyn, oversaw the rebuilding of the screen above it. One of those legendary American tourists observed the Roman numerals after the King's name, the last of which curves, and declared: 'There's Edward the 3rd - Junior'[16] *(see photograph on page 27)*.

The Rutland Chantry was built as a memorial to Edward IV's sister, Anne, Duchess of Exeter. She equipped this chantry for herself and paid for it. Some of the King's favourite symbols were crowned angels with sunbursts (a royal emblem), and some of these appear in the Rutland Chantry.

To Edward IV we also owe the Hastings Chantry, given so that his greatest friend, William, 1st Lord Hastings, KG (1462) could be near him in death as he had been in life. This chapel where he and Katherine, his wife (daughter of the Earl of Salisbury, and widow of William, Lord Harington) are buried is in the North Quire Aisle. Hastings's stall plate is still in the chapel.

Hastings was Edward IV's great ally. He had

The tomb of George Manners, 11th Lord Ros, and Anne, Lady Ros, daughter of Anne, Duchess of Exeter, in the Rutland Chantry. The tomb was restored between 1782 and 1793 and again in 1843.

accompanied him on his advance from Gloucester to London and on his expedition to the North, both in 1461. The King then appointed him Chamberlain of North Wales for life, Steward of various Lordships, Keeper and Constable of various castles, Master of the Mint and Grand Chamberlain of the Royal Household, Receiver of the revenues of the Duchy of Cornwall, and in 1471 Lieutenant-General of Calais. In the same year he was in command at the Battle of Barnet. He was the mediator in many truces with the Kings of Scotland, France and others. He accompanied the King to France in 1475.

Hastings was on less good terms with Queen Elizabeth (Woodville). After Edward IV's death, he veered between siding with Edward V and the Queen or Richard III. But despite being warned of the dangers, he attended a council in the Tower of London, where he was charged with high treason and immediately taken out and beheaded.

So he was brought forth into the greene beside the chappell within the tower and his head laid downe upon a long log of timber and there stricken off and afterward his bodie with the head enterred at Windsore beside the bodie of king Edward.'[17]

ABOVE Henry VI and Margaret of Anjou, part of a stained glass window by Willement, 1844.

LEFT The stall plate of Richard, Duke of York, KG (1475), the younger of the Princes murdered in the Tower of London.

The execution of Hastings is described in Shakespeare's *Richard III*. In the 1955 film of the play, Hastings was played by Alec Clunes. Elizabeth Woodville was played by Mary Kerridge, wife of John Counsell, Managing Director of the Theatre Royal, Windsor. In 1999 her funeral took place in the Chapel, yards from where that queen lies buried.

Edward V succeeded Edward IV as King, but he and his brother, Richard, Duke of York, (the Princes in the Tower) were murdered as boys, some say by the Duke of Gloucester, who succeeded as Richard III in June 1483. The fine Garter stall plate of the Duke of York is still in the Chapel today.

RICHARD III (KING 1483-85)

During his brief reign of two years, Richard III was engaged in many battles and political intrigues. He created only seven Knights of the Garter, but he did provide the Canons of Windsor with generous funds to continue the building work of St George's Chapel. At the quarterly obits, he is remembered as a benefactor of the Chapel, despite being responsible

for the execution of several other benefactors.

In 1478/80 the body of John Schorn, a reputed saint, was brought to the chapel. Some suggest that the Dean and Canons stole the body, which was later buried at the east end of the South Quire Aisle at Windsor, next to the Cross of Gneth. Schorn was a popular figure, who had been Rector of North Marston in Buckinghamshire from about 1282 until his death in 1314. Though a saintly man, he was never actually canonized. It is maintained that after a prolonged drought, he struck the ground with his staff and water capable of curing colds gushed forth as a perennial spring. He was also able to heal the ague and toothache and revive the drowned. Near his tomb was a boot which pilgrims put on to cure gout. At one time his popularity almost rivalled the shrine of Our Lady of Walsingham. Pilgrims flocked to St George's and placed money in an iron offertory box, similar to that which survives nearby for Henry VI. The tomb disappeared at the time of the Reformation.

Richard III was also responsible for transferring the mortal remains of Henry VI to the chapel.

King Henry VI is the earliest king (historically) to

lie in St George's Chapel, though this was not his first resting place. When he died suddenly in May 1471 he was buried in Chertsey Abbey. A.L. Rowse is one historian who has suggested that Richard III may have had a hand in the King's death – he had been 'done to death in the Tower on a night when we know Richard was there'.[18]

Richard III had his body moved to a spot on the south side of the altar, ironically close to the tomb of Edward IV, his victor, which is opposite on the north side. It is likely that Richard III was motivated by 'some kind of political interest' since many in England considered Henry VI a saint. As a result, Richard III made many public gestures of concern to his memory, including his religious and educational foundations. According to the historian John Rous, the King's remains were found to be 'incorrupt', despite not having been embalmed when first interred, and 'many miracles were wrought at his tomb.'[19] Henry VI's velvet hat was often placed on the heads of pilgrims to relieve headaches.

In November 1910 the site of Henry VI's tomb was investigated. A brick grave was discovered, containing a rectangular wooden chest. This in turn enclosed a smaller box made of oak, which contained 'a decayed mass of human bones, lying in no definite order, mixed with the rotten remains of some woven material in which they were wrapped.' After they had been examined, they were wrapped in white silk and placed in a new wooden box, and replaced in the wooden chest.

The poet, Pope, saw the irony in Edward IV and Henry VI lying so close to one another in death:

Here, o'er the martyr king, the marble weeps,
And fast beside him once-feared Edward sleeps.[20]

Next to this tomb there stands to this day an iron alms-box, probably made by John Tresilian soon after 1484, where pilgrims could leave their donations. It requires four keys to open it – so that the Dean and three Canons all needed to be present in order to insure that the money did not go astray. Recently (since the 1960s) two of the key covers have been lost.

Richard III was killed at the Battle of Bosworth in 1485 and the throne was taken by Henry VII.

The tomb of Henry VI in the South Quire Aisle.

The almsbox next to Henry VI's tomb, probably designed by John Tresilian.

of Richmond (mother of Henry VII) and was instrumental in the negotiation of Henry's marriage to Elizabeth, daughter of Edward IV, thus uniting the Houses of York and Lancaster. He became Henry's chaplain and confessor, and warned him of the machinations of Pierre Landois, chief minister to the Duke of Brittany. He accompanied Henry on his secret flight from Vannes. He was also present with him at the Battle of Bosworth.

He was rewarded with many appointments, including being Dean of York, and serving as envoy to the Pope. He was sent to Spain to negotiate the marriage between Prince Arthur and Catherine of Aragon. Many other important treaty negotiations followed, and in 1492/3 he was commissioned to invest Alfonso, son of the King of Sicily with the Order of the Garter. He became a Canon of Windsor in 1490, and in 1495 Dean. He also served

LEFT Henry VII and Elizabeth of York in stained glass, made by Willement, 1846.

BELOW An engraving of the Nave by Wenceslaus Hollar, 1663, looking towards the Bray Chapel.

HENRY VII (KING 1485-1509)

Henry VII's reign was more stable and he was therefore able to revive the Garter feasts in 1488, and to further advance the building work of Edward IV's chapel. He was impressed by all the pilgrims who visited Henry VI's tomb and considered being buried at Windsor himself. To that end he completely rebuilt the former chapel of Henry III as a new lady chapel. There was some legal discussion as to whether Henry VI had wanted to be buried in Westminster Abbey, but in the end he was left at Windsor. Henry VII finally decided that he should be buried in Westminster Abbey and had the new Lady Chapel built there for his tomb.

During his reign work on the new St George's Chapel continued under the enthusiastic leadership of Dr Christopher Urswick (1448-1522), a Canon who later became Dean of Windsor. Urswick came into royal circles as chaplain to Margaret, Countess

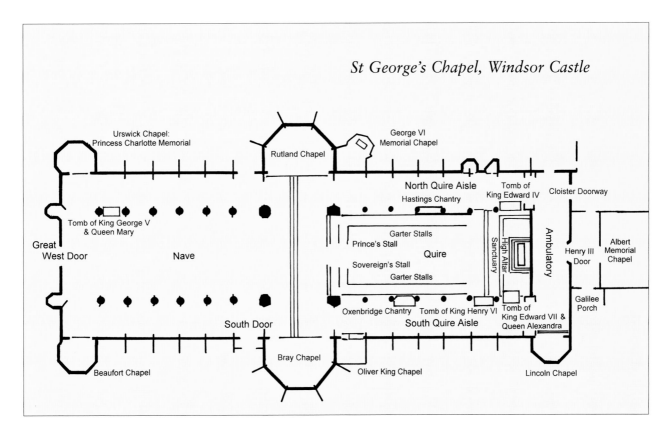

St George's Chapel, Windsor Castle

as executor to Margaret, Countess of Richmond, and was a close friend of Erasmus and More.

Urswick worked closely with Sir Reginald Bray over the completion of the building of St George's Chapel, and he rebuilt the Deanery. A chantry in the chapel bears his name, though later George IV appropriated it for the memorial to Princess Charlotte. Urswick is one of those recorded in the window over the door of the Albert Memorial Chapel, and his arms appear frequently in the chapel, like those of Bray.

Sir Reginald Bray, KG (1500), one of the most respected of the Chapel's benefactors, was a Tudor financier, a politician, statesman, and soldier who fought at home and overseas. He too began his work in the service of Margaret, Countess of Richmond, and was closely involved in the negotiations concerning the wedding between the future King and Elizabeth of York, daughter of Edward IV. It is said that it was he who retrieved the crown of Richard III on the field at Bosworth and placed it on the head of Henry VII. He was granted many properties, and when Prince Arthur married Catherine of Aragon, he was one of the trustees of the dower.

Sir Reginald Bray died in 1503, leaving large sums in his will for the completion of the Nave. It is rightly said that 'the chapel of St George at Windsor, and that of his royal master King Henry VII at Westminster, are standing monuments of his liberality and of his skill in architecture.'[21]

Under several Deans – Bainbridge, Hobbs and West – with money from Bray's Trustees, the nave vault was completed in 1506, and the vault of the quire between 1506 and 1508. A plan was formed to construct a lantern tower in the middle between the quire and nave, but this was eventually dropped during the reign of Henry VIII and that section was vaulted in 1528-9.

Bray's contribution went further than that. His numerous appointments and activities had made him a rich man. By a munificent bequest in his will, he enabled the Nave, which had been unfinished for twenty years, to be brought to completion and to its

LEFT The monument to Bishop Giles Thomson, Bishop of Gloucester, 1612, in front of what remains of the altar reredos in the Bray Chapel.

OPPOSITE PAGE The Nave seen from the West end of St George's Chapel.

reinstated him. He was later Bishop of Exeter, and of Bath and Wells. King died in 1503. He may have intended to be buried in this chapel, but a later Dean, Patrick Mitchell, discovered the record of his burial in Wells Cathedral.[22]

Henry VII himself was buried in his new Lady Chapel at Westminster Abbey, though at the time of his death, this was not quite complete.

HENRY VIII (KING 1509-47)

St George's Chapel was completed in the reign of Henry VIII. He loved Windsor, building the great gateway to the Castle. In his early days he took copious exercise, sang, danced and wrestled, while showing a deep fondness for music, playing the recorder and flute, and composing. Unlike his father, he was ostentatious, holding splendid Garter feasts, installing the Holy Roman Emperor, Charles V as a Knight of the Garter in 1522, when the Emperor came to Windsor in quest of an alliance.

Again, unlike his father, Henry VIII did not spend any money on St George's Chapel, which was completed in 1528, the final crossing vault being paid for by the Knights of the Garter. But Henry VIII provided in his will for the re-establishment of the thirteen Poor Knights as a proper Foundation.

Henry VIII turned to the Order of the Garter to show how vindictive he could be when displeased. Edward, 3rd Duke of Buckingham, KG (circa 1499), fell out with Cardinal Wolsey and was unfairly accused of listening to prophecies of the King's death, seeking to succeed to the crown, and even expressing an intention to kill the King. He was found guilty of treason, and deprived of his Garter in 1521. This was turned into an unpleasant ceremonial. The King came to a packed chapel and two men brought a ladder into the Quire, which was propped against the Duke's stall. One of the

full glory. For that reason, the hemp-bray, his heraldic device, is seen in many parts of the chapel.

At his death in 1503, Sir Reginald Bray was buried in the south transept, and a new screen bearing his heraldic arms, was built. This was assigned to him as his chantry.

The reign of Henry VII saw another side chapel (not a chantry this time) built by Dr Oliver King and now dedicated to his memory. King served Edward IV, Edward V and Henry VII as secretary. He was a Canon of Windsor and Registrar of the Order of the Garter from 1480. In 1483 Richard III sent him to the Tower of London on account of his association with Lord Hastings, but in 1485 Henry VII

The Oliver King Chantry in the South Quire Aisle.

heralds, Rouge Croix Pursuivant, climbed the ladder and declared the Duke a traitor. He then tore down the Duke's banner and flung it to the ground. The stall plate was wrenched from the stall and clattered into the aisle. The other achievements followed. Then Garter King of Arms stepped forward and proceeded to kick the fallen achievements down the Nave, out of the West Door of the chapel, down the steps, out through Henry's gateway, and thus out of the castle precincts.[23] The luckless Duke was then executed on Tower Hill.

For Queen Catherine of Aragon, Henry's first wife, the King converted the chantry chapel above Edward IV's tomb into a royal pew with windows, from which she could take part in the services of the Chapel in private and witness the Garter ceremonies. The Catherine of Aragon loft has been used not only as a private chapel, but also as a vantage point for many Queens to take part quietly in services in the chapel when they do not wish to sit in the Quire. Amongst these have been Queen Victoria at the wedding of her heir, the Prince of Wales in 1863 (see page 84) and the funeral of the King of Hanover in 1878; Alexandra, Princess of Wales (later Queen Alexandra) at the funeral of her son, the Duke of Clarence in 1892; and in the present reign, the Queen at the laying-up of the banner of Sir Winston Churchill in 1965. The western stone oriel window was made at the time of Edward IV, but the timber oriel window dates from the reign of Henry VIII. To this day there are some pomegranates carved around this window, it being the symbol of Catherine of Aragon.

It has been suggested that Henry VIII first spotted Anne Boleyn looking out of an upper window in the Dean's Cloister, when walking to St George's Chapel, though many dismiss this as a myth. That marriage ended with Anne's execution, Henry married his third wife, Jane Seymour in May 1536.

A carved pomegranate, the heraldic symbol of Catherine of Aragon.

The tomb of Charles Somerset, 1st Earl of Worcester, and his wife, Lady Elizabeth Herbert, in the Beaufort Chapel.

She gave him his only surviving son, later Edward VI, born on 12 October 1537, but as a result of his birth she died twelve days later at Hampton Court Palace, seemingly from septicaemia.

Her body lay in state at the palace for a fortnight, while Bishops said continuous masses in relays. A contemporary account related:

> The corpse [coffin] was put in the chair covered with a rich pall; and thereupon the representation of the Queen in her robes of estate, with a rich crown of gold upon her head, all in her hair loose, a sceptre of gold in her right hand, and on her fingers rings set with precious stones, and her neck richly adorned with gold and stones.[24]

Then on 12 November the body of the only queen that Henry mourned was conveyed in procession to Windsor, with the future Mary I riding behind as chief mourner, and the counsellors, bishops, nobles and courtiers following. The King himself did not attend, as was the custom of the day.

Charles Somerset, 1st Earl of Worcester, KG (1496), illegitimate son of Henry Beaufort, 3rd Duke of Somerset, and another benefactor of the chapel, fared better. He was raised by Henry VII, eventually becoming an Admiral. In 1490 he was sent to invest Emperor Maximilian with the Order of the Garter. As Vice-Chamberlain of the Household he arranged the ceremonial for the reception of Catherine of Aragon in 1501. When Henry VIII succeeded, the King appointed him Lord Chamberlain and he accompanied Princess Mary to France after her marriage by proxy to King Louis XII.

He presided over the arrangements for the Field of the Cloth of Gold in 1520, attended the Congress of Calais with Cardinal Wolsey, and was one of those who attested the Treaty of Windsor in 1522. When he died in 1526, he was buried in the polygonal chapel at the south-east corner of the chapel, later called the Beaufort Chapel.

Another internal chantry dates from this period – the Oxenbridge Chantry, in the South Quire Aisle. Canon John Oxenbridge was a canon at Windsor from 1509 until his death in 1522, and a generous benefactor of the Chapel. Above the door, his name is depicted as an Ox, the letter 'N' and a bridge over a stream.

Towards the end of 1546, three more wives having followed, it became clear that Henry VIII was gravely ill. Though only 55, he was unable to stand or walk, though he could still sit on his horse to watch the traditional slaughter of the hunt. He sent his sixth and final wife, Queen Catherine Parr to Greenwich for Christmas, while he remained at Whitehall. At the end of the year, he remade his will, and accepted that he should be buried in the chapel of his College at Windsor.

One of Henry VIII's last acts was to insure that Henry, Earl of Surrey, KG (1541) was executed (on 19 January 1547). Immediately after that, his health declined further. He sought repentance and eventually asked Archbishop Cranmer to come to him. The night was freezing, the rivers were frozen, and Henry was losing consciousness by the time Cranmer arrived. The King was able to squeeze his hand in repentance. He died at two in the morning on 28 January 1547. His death was kept secret for three days.

There had been various plans concerning the King's tomb. As early as 1518 Cardinal Wolsey had become involved in the design of a joint tomb for Henry VIII and Queen Catherine Parr, commissioning the Florentine sculptor, Pietro Torrigiano (who had designed the tombs of Lady Margaret, Countess of Richmond, and of Henry VII and his wife Elizabeth in Westminster Abbey) to work on it. Nothing came of this plan, but by 1524 Wolsey had commissioned the design of his own tomb by another Florentine, Benedetto da Rovezzano, and by 1529 the work was well advanced. From Benedetto he commissioned the 'white and black marble, with eight brazen columns around it and four others in the shape of candlesticks.'[25]

ABOVE Cardinal Wolsey, one time Canon of Windsor, and favourite of Henry VIII until his fall from grace.

BELOW The arms of Henry VIII surrounded by those of the Knights of the Garter, the centrepiece of the vaulting in the roof of St George's Chapel, denoting the chapel's completion in 1528.

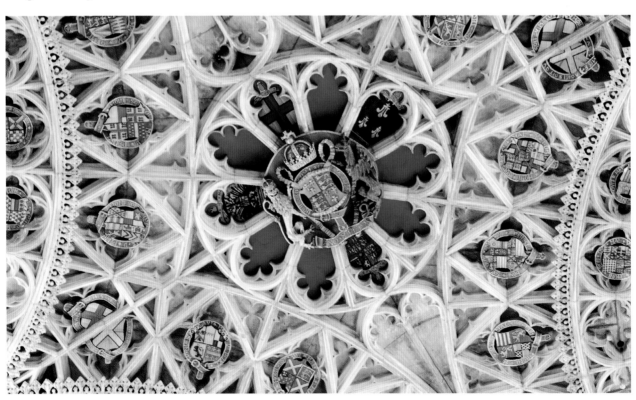

Henry VIII with his third wife, Jane Seymour, with his son, Prince Edward – later Edward VI (left) and his daughter, Elizabeth I (right) in stained glass by Willement, 1846, in the South Quire Aisle.

For many years it was asserted that Wolsey's tomb was to stand in the Lady Chapel. Wolsey was a Canon of Windsor from 1511 to 1514. During that time he would have seen the Tomb House as housing the tomb of Henry VI and Henry VII. As Professor P.G. Lindley has pointed out: 'It is hard to believe that even Wolsey could have been granted a building conceived as a royal shrine and burial chapel.'[26] In conclusion it is more likely that he planned to be buried in the Cardinal Chapel, Ipswich, or the projected Cardinal College, Oxford. In the end he was buried in an unknown grave in Leicester Abbey.

After Wolsey's fall from grace in 1529, Henry VIII plundered the Cardinal's tomb for his own use, removing any images that recalled or represented the Cardinal, but making full use of the remainder. All this work was undertaken at Westminster. Henry VIII's plans veered from using the Lady Chapel as a possible tomb house for himself to constructing an elaborate sarcophagus over the spot in the centre of the Quire where he is now buried, not unlike the tomb of his father, Henry VII, in Westminster Abbey. Initially nothing came of these plans due to Protector Somerset.

After Henry VIII's death in 1547, neither Edward VI or Queen Mary erected it. The tomb was moved from Westminster to Windsor in 1565, and in 1574 Elizabeth I commissioned an expensive model of it, but she did not move her father into this tomb. Thus the tomb remained in the Tomb House until 1645, when the bronze imagery was defaced in order to pay the Windsor garrison.

Nevertheless Henry VIII's was a splendid funeral. His body was conveyed to Windsor by chariot, his

OPPOSITE PAGE The six stone figures of the medieval and Tudor kings associated with St George's Chapel in niches on the outside of the south front.
TOP LEFT Henry III carrying a model of the earlier chapel.
TOP CENTRE Edward III. TOP RIGHT Edward IV
BOTTOM LEFT Henry VI. BOTTOM CENTRE Henry VII.
BOTTOM RIGHT Henry VIII.

The Lincoln Chantry in the south east corner of the Chapel.

waxen effigy lying on the top of the coffin, with the Imperial Crown on its head, under which was a nightcap of black satin, set with precious stones. The effigy was dressed in red velvet furred with miniver and powdered with ermine, and wearing the Collar of the Order of the Garter. Every possible accoutrement was attached, a sword at its side, diamond rings on the fingers, sceptre and orb. The funeral carriage was drawn by eight horses, trapped in black, adorned with escutcheons on which rode a child carrying a bannerole with the King's arms.

When this arrived at St George's Chapel, the effigy was first conveyed into the Quire, and then the coffin carried by sixteen yeomen with black staves in their hands. Queen Catherine Parr sat in the Catherine of Aragon loft and watched as the coffin was lowered into the vault beside the coffin of Jane Seymour.

In contrast to the grandeur of the funeral, the place of burial soon became obscure and indeed presently something of a mystery. Nor was a special monument created for Henry VIII.

EDWARD VI (KING 1547-53)
LADY JANE GREY (QUEEN 1553)
MARY I (QUEEN 1553-8)
ELIZABETH I (QUEEN 1558-1603)

The sole contribution of Edward VI and his 'protectors' was to discontinue the Garter feasts and to purge the Order of 'all papistical and superstitious practices'[27] in accordance with his strong Protestant sympathies. He redirected the Order to chivalric and charitable causes, focussing on education, and he appointed 13 Garter Knights, including Henry II, King of France. However, as previously stated, the chantries in St George's Chapel were never abolished.

Queen Mary restored her father's statutes in her quest to have things as they used to be. Her first Garter Knight was her husband, Philip II, King of Spain, who was installed as Joint Sovereign in 1554, but after her death in 1558, he resumed his place as one of the normal Knights, dying as late as 1598.

Elizabeth I is more generally associated with Greenwich, Richmond, Whitehall or Nonesuch than Windsor, though she built the Long Gallery in the Castle. She took part in certain Garter solemnities, not always at Windsor.

During her reign, Edward, 9th Lord Clinton, later Earl of Lincoln, died (in 1585) and was buried in the Lincoln Chantry in the south east corner of the chapel with his third wife, Lady Elizabeth Fitzgerald, and his children by earlier marriages. In

A detail of a Garter procession in the twentieth year of the reign of Elizabeth I. The Queen is at the end of the procession. Drawn by Thomas Hawes, former Rouge Croix Pursuivant. From Ashmole's *The Order of the Garter*, 1672.

1534 Lincoln's first wife was Elizabeth, widow of Lord Talboys, a well-known mistress of Henry VIII and the mother of his illegitimate son, Henry Fitzroy, Duke of Richmond (whose birth had confirmed Henry in the inability of Catherine of Aragon to produce a healthy son). Very much in Henry VIII's favour, Lincoln was one of those who received Anne of Cleves when she arrived to be the King's fourth wife. He survived many political vicissitudes, being created a KG by Edward VI in 1551, witnessing the will of Edward VI by which the doomed Lady Jane Grey briefly took the throne. He served as Lord High Admiral to Edward VI, Queen Mary (supporting the Spaniards at St Quentin) and Elizabeth I, serving her equally as prominently. Just as he survived through four reigns, he managed to maintain good relations with such diverse figures as Somerset, Northumberland and Burghley.

His widow, Lady Elizabeth Fitzgerald, one time lady-in-waiting to the future Mary I, and later to Queen Catherine Howard at Hampton Court, was celebrated in verse as 'the Fair Geraldine' by the Earl of Surrey (executed by Henry VIII). She was buried beside Lord Lincoln in 1589.

Elizabeth I received many overseas visitors at the Castle. One of them, a certain Count Frederick Mompelgart, later Duke of Württemberg, greatly annoyed her by requesting to be made a Knight of the Garter following a visit to Windsor in 1592, at a time when she was not there. On his return home, the Duke bade his German secretary write of how impressed the Duke was by the pleasing ceremonies and music in St George's Chapel, of the voice of a particular solo-boy, of the attentions given to the Poor Knights, and by the banners and shields of the Knights of the Garter which inflamed him with the desire to be one of them. Elizabeth I finally gave way to the Duke's blandishments and gave him the Garter in 1597. He was invested in November 1603, the Queen having died the previous March.

Elizabeth I was succeeded by King James VI of Scotland, whom she had appointed as a Knight of the Garter in 1590.

TWO

The Years of Neglect

JAMES I (KING 1603-25)
CHARLES I (KING 1625-49)

T HE FIRST TWO Stuart kings did not alter the structure of St George's Chapel. James I's primary interest in Windsor was the hunting, while Charles I preferred to adorn his other palaces with his wonderful collection of pictures, some of which, most notably the Van Dyks, are now in the State Apartments. In 1607 James I did, however, commission a bird's eye view of the castle from John Norden, the earliest detailed plan of the castle in existence (*see following page*).

James I presided over Garter installations, most notably in 1615 when Thomas Erskine, Viscount

Charles I and Queen Henrietta Maria, depicted in stained glass between his sons, the future Charles II (left) and the Duke of York – the future James II (right). An 1849 window by Thomas Willement.

Labels on the drawing:
Parte of the Litle Parke:
The Garden plott graunted by Patent
Timber yarde
Litle Parke
Lodginges for the Howshold
Pryme Lodginges
Penye Lodginges
The gallery
Tennys Courte

John Norden's 1607 bird's-eye view drawing of Windsor Castle from the north. Norden's view shows St George's Chapel with blue roof and pinnacles on the extreme right. Between the walls and what is now the Albert Memorial Chapel are the Dean's and Canons' Cloister. The Horseshoe Cloister is to the right of the chapel, described as 'Petite Canons' Lodgings'. Not all the buildings between the Cloisters and the 'Bell Tower' still survive.

Fenton, later Earl of Kellie (a Scotsman), and William, Lord Knollys, later Earl of Banbury (an Englishman), vied to outdo each other with three hundred followers each, the Scottish contingent being deemed to have won the day being 'generally better apparelled, with many more chains of gold and better horses by means of the King's and

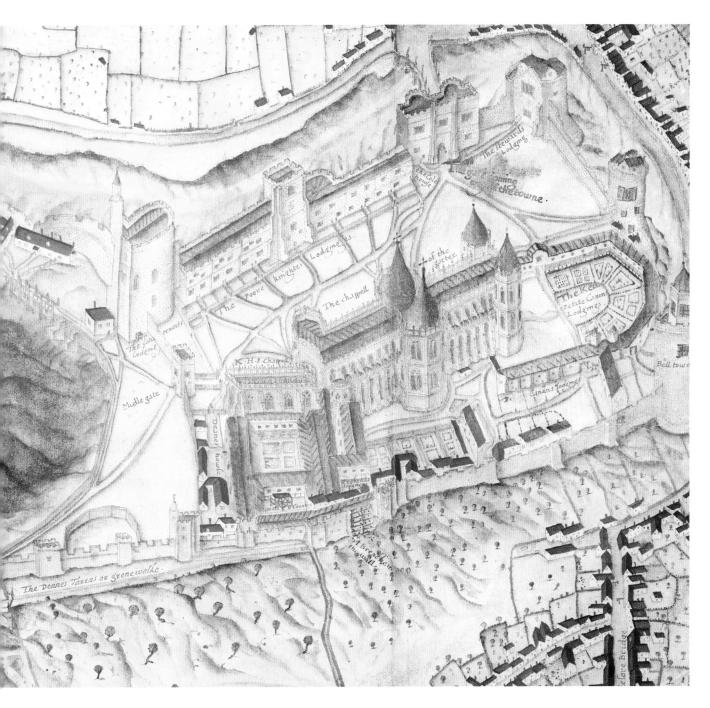

Prince's stables.'[1]

In 1618 he took the unusual step of appointing as Dean of Windsor, Marco Antonio de Dominis or Gospodivtch, a Roman prelate who had defected to Britain in 1616, having fallen out with the Pope when 500 crowns were taken annually from his archbishopric. During his four years at Windsor he quarrelled with his Canons, imposed higher rents on the tenants of the Chapter and finally absconded with the then considerable sum of £1,700. He returned to Rome in 1622, was arrested and died in 1624. His body was disinterred and burnt as a heretic.

Charles I presented St George's Chapel with a

ABOVE Dean Christopher Wren, Dean of Windsor 1635-59, wearing the robes of Register of the Order of the Garter. Portrait by an unknown artist. Dean Wren was the father of the architect, Sir Christopher Wren.

BELOW The Register of the Order of the Garter, one of the items saved during the ransacking of Windsor Castle. From Ashmole's *The Order of the Garter* (1672).

magnificent baroque service of altar-plate, executed by Christian van Viernan, a Dutch craftsmen lured by him from the Netherlands. While Charles I was on the throne, a better remembered cleric arrived – John Hales, from Eton, who was also Regius Professor of Greek at Oxford and considered as one of the finest scholars of his day, who wrote a famous tract on Schism. He was appointed a Canon in 1639, the year after he became Archbishop Laud's chaplain. Along with Dean Christopher Wren, he was ejected in 1642 and died at Eton in 1656. John Aubrey wrote well of him in *Brief Lives*, describing him as 'a prettie little man, sanguine, of a cheerful countenance, very gentle, and courteous.'[2]

Charles I ocasionally retreated to Windsor before, during and after the Civil War. The castle was occupied by parliamentary forces in October 1642 following the Battle of Edgehill. It only narrowly escaped the fate of other royal residences when a Parliamentary bill to sell off its lands for ready money was narrowly defeated. Nevertheless, St George's Chapel then entered the sorriest phase in its otherwise remarkably positive history.

Christopher Wren (father of the architect, Sir Christopher Wren) was Dean of Windsor from 1635 to 1659, a year before the Restoration, though unofficially from around 1642 when the College of St George was abolished. One Captain Fogg demanded the key of the Treasury from the Dean and Canons, threatening to pull the whole place down over their heads. Wren and his Canons refused, so Fogg broke it open and plundered it. Dean Wren attempted to hide some of the chapel's treasures, but only managed to save a few volumes of records (including the Register of the Order of the Garter) and the great sword of Edward III (now in the South Quire Aisle).[3] But they lost everything else and the Deanery was ransacked.

Colonel John Venn, the Governor of the Castle, recommended that Cromwell turn out the Dean, Canons, Minor Canons, and others who belonged to the chapel, and the order was given. But they were allowed to take their possessions after they had been searched. Venn made the Deanery his headquarters and for some weeks sheltered his

horses in the Nave.4 He began to remove much of value in the chapel to turn it into money. He carried off Edward IV's coat of mail, 'and his surcoat of crimson velvet, embroidered with gold and pearls, and decorated with rubies which had hung over his burial-place from the time of his funeral.' Venn tore up the seats of the Poor Knights, and other woodwork, spoiling the painted windows and the organ. Charles I's magnificent plate was looted from the chapel. The gold and silver that was found was sent up to London to be coined into money.

The 1448 Canons' Chapter House, a large detached north-south building to the north of the north-east end of the chapel was destroyed. So was the west end of the Canons' Cloister (the site where St George's House now stands). The other fourteenth and fifteenth century Canons' houses survived. Cromwell's men also ransacked the Tomb House, but the Dean and Canons hid the great marble sarcophagus that Henry VIII had planned to use for his tomb. Deemed to have no intrinsic value, it lay hidden and neglected for 150 years. When Nelson died at Trafalgar in 1805, and St Paul's Cathedral became his burial place, the sarcophagus

The Dean's Cloister showing the window in which Anne Boleyn is said to have first been spotted by Henry VIII. Photograph taken from the walk used by Queen Victoria between the Deanery and the Catherine of Aragon loft. After the occupation of the Castle in 1642 the Canons' Chapter House and the west end of the Canons' Cloister were destroyed.

at last found a home and became the base of Nelson's tomb, which it remains to this day.

There had been four huge candlesticks destined for each corner of Henry VIII's tomb. These were sold to the Bishop of Ghent when he visited England and survive today in the Cathedral of St Bavon in Ghent. In the late 1920s King George V and Queen Mary had two copies made and these stand either side of the High Altar in the Quire in memory of their respective parents, King Edward VII and Queen Alexandra, and the Duke and Duchess of Teck, both couples having been married in the chapel, and both couples being buried in the Royal Vault.

At this time went the fine funeral accoutrements of Edward IV, the organs were destroyed, and painted windows smashed. The Commonwealth took over, prisoners were taken, the College of St

George abolished and the Canons forced from their houses. In the next years Renaissance candlesticks were sold, a huge bronze statue of St George removed and almost certainly melted down, and the unfinished enamels originally destined for Wolsey's tomb likewise sold.

Charles I is best remembered at St George's Chapel for his extraordinary burial. In July 1647 he was taken to Windsor as a prisoner for two days, the bells being rung on his arrival, as by well-honed custom. He was several times imprisoned there, notably at Christmas 1648 when he was there for three weeks before his fateful journey to Whitehall and his beheading on 30 January 1649.

The next problem was where to bury the King. Charles I had never expressed any wishes on this matter, nor had anyone dared discuss it with him in his lifetime. The obvious choice was Henry VII's Chapel within Westminster Abbey, but this request was denied on the grounds that 'infinite numbers of peoples of all sorts' would be drawn to it. The next choice was Windsor and to this Parliament gave their assent, authorising Sir Thomas (Theo) Herbert, Groom of the Bedchamber to the King, and his constant companion in the last days, and Captain Sir Anthony Mildmay, another staunch supporter, to bury the King there, by an order dated 7 February.

The body of Charles I, covered by a black velvet pall, was then conveyed in a hearse from St James's to Windsor, followed by four coaches. Herbert and Mildmay presented the burial order to Colonel Bulstrode Whitelocke, the Governor. First the King's body was taken to the Deanery and laid on a long table and then to his former bedchamber in the castle. They then inspected St George's, considered and rejected the tomb house as not being in the chapel, and began to contemplate the tomb of Edward IV in the North Quire Aisle. But then the Duke of Richmond, the Marquess of Hertford, the Earls of Southampton and Lindsey and William Juxon, Bishop of London, arrived and they took the initiative. In a contemporary account:

They in like manner viewing the Tomb House, and the Quire, one of those Lords beating gently upon the Pavement with his Staff, perceiv'd a hollow sound, and ordering the Stones and Earth thereunder to be removed, discover'd a descent into a Vault, where two Coffins were laid near one another, the one very large of antique form, the other little, suppos'd to contain the Bodies of King Henry VIII and Queen Jane Seymour, his Third Wife, and Mother of King Edward VI of whom in the Year 1537 she died in childbed … the Velvet Palls that were over them seemed fresh, albeit laid there 130 Years and upwards.

The Lords agreeing that the King's Body should there be interr'd (being about the middle of the Quire, over against the Eleventh Stall upon the Sovereign's side) they gave order to have the King's Name, and Year he dyed, cut in Lead, which whilst the Workman was about, the Lords went out, and gave the Sexton order to lock the Chapel Door, not suffering any to stay till further notice.[5]

The sexton thought he had cleared the chapel, but a soldier hid, and when no one was looking, got into the vault, cut a piece of the pall over Henry VIII's coffin, made a hole in the coffin and stole a bone.

The body of Charles I was then carried in a solemn little procession from his bedchamber to St George's Hall and then to the Chapel under the cover of darkness. Though the sky was 'serene and clear' as the cortège came into the open air, it suddenly began to snow and by the time the procession reached the Great West Door, the black velvet pall was white with snow, which many deemed significant, white being 'the colour of innocency.'

The Quire was in some disarray and the altar bereft of ornaments. The Bishop of London, was about to read the burial service but the Governor of the Castle forbade it, having been issued with an order to that effect. The King's body was simply laid in the vault beside Henry VIII, and his soul quickly commended to God. At some point before the vault was closed, one of the noblemen asked that the coffin be opened. The King's face was clearly discerned by the small group, including the sexton. Thus full proof of burial was assured. The coffin bore an inscription in lead 'King Charles – 1648', the velvet pall was thrown over it, and the tomb closed. The small party dispersed.[6] At that point the tomb was unmarked, and it was William IV who placed the inscription over the vault in 1837.

The burial was not entered in the St George's Chapel register, though the vicar of the Windsor Parish Church recorded in his register: 'Feby.9. King Charles in the Castle.'[7]

In 1696 the vault was again opened for the burial of a stillborn son of Queen Anne. By 1813 the exact spot where Charles I was buried had become uncertain. By mistake the vault was accidentally knocked into during the construction of George III's new Royal Vault. The Prince Regent then decided to use this as an opportunity for establishing where Henry VIII, Jane Seymour and Charles I were lying. Thus on 1 April 1813 the vault was opened in the presence of the Prince and the surgeon, Sir Henry Halford, who made a square opening in the coffin of King Charles. There was the king's head, with one eye wide open, the other gone, and a black ribbon round his throat. As he took the head out, the surviving eye turned to dust before their eyes. Halford observed:

> On holding up the head to examine the place of separation from the body, the muscles of the neck had evidently retracted themselves considerably: and the fourth cervical vertebra was found to be cut through its substance transversely, leaving the surfaces of the divided portions perfectly smooth and even, an appearance which could have been produced only by a heavy blow, inflicted with a very sharp instrument.[8]

An additional discovery made during the opening was that Henry VIII's coffin appeared to have been beaten in, exposing a skeleton. Halford removed some relics from the body of Charles I – the neckbone, a tooth, a piece of the beard (cut by the executioner's axe), and some hair from the back of his head. These were taken with permission for examination, and were preserved at Wistow Hall, Sir Henry's Leicestershire seat.

In the chapel that day, was a carpenter's boy, who grew up to be an official of the chapel. Years later he told the portrait painter, William Powell

The slab above the grave of Henry VIII, Jane Seymour, Charles I and an infant child of Queen Anne, in the centre of the Quire.

Frith, that Henry Halford had actually dropped the head, as it was so greasy he could not hold it. After they closed the tomb, a tiny relic of the King was found on the chapel floor. The carpenter's boy wore it in a locket on a waistcoat chain from that day on.[9]

In 1888 another Sir Henry Halford, grandson of the surgeon, presented a casket containing these relics to the Prince of Wales (later Edward VII) at Marlborough House. The Prince informed Dean Davidson of their existence and the suggestion was made that these relics should be reunited with the king. Queen Victoria agreed on condition that no one entered the vault or disturbed the coffin.

After evensong on 13 December 1888 the vault was again opened, some stones and bricks being lifted to make an aperture of eighteen inches. The Prince of Wales arrived alone, a long coil of magnesium wire lit the narrow chamber and the Prince stooped down and lowered the casket onto the coffin of the executed King. By 9.30 pm, the vault was finally closed for the last time.

Dean Bruno Ryves, Dean of Windsor from 1660 to 1677 and a strong Royalist. The original of this portrait is at Woburn Abbey. Ryves presided over considerable restoration at the chapel following the return of Charles II.

In 1928 a London solicitor produced what appeared to be the stall-plate of Charles I. It was offered to Canon Dalton, who declared it a forgery, so Sir Owen Morshead took it into the Royal Library. Later opinion verified the plate as genuine and in 1950 King George VI commanded that it be placed in a stall, S3 on the Sovereign's side, next to that of his brother, Henry, Prince of Wales, and his son, Charles II.

THE COMMONWEALTH (1649-60)

During the Civil War and the period of the Commonwealth, Windsor Castle was a garrison and prison and much damage was done, though less to the chapel itself, due to the orders of Parliament. In the summer of 1648, General Fairfax insisted that the garrison be properly maintained, and life in the Castle became more settled.[10]

St George's Chapel remained in some disorder until the Restoration in 1660, but accounts of how much it was plundered vary and some are now considered to be exaggerated. During this unhappy phase, the diarist, John Evelyn, and his wife, visited the Castle. He did not give an altogether negative account of what confronted him. On 8 June 1654 he recorded:

> We din'd at Windsor, saw the Castle and Chapell of St George, where they have laied our blessed Martyr King Charles in the vault just before y alter. The church and workmanship in stone is admirable. The Castle itself is large in circumference, but y rooms melancholy and of ancient magnificence.'[11]

CHARLES II (KING 1660-85)

Charles II's Restoration led to restoration in every sense. The squatters were thrown out of the castle and the Governor, Bulstrode Whitelocke replaced by Lord Mordaunt, soon to be replaced in turn by Prince Rupert of the Rhine, prematurely aged and retired.

When the King and his friends entered St George's Chapel on their return to Windsor, unlike Evelyn, they looked round in horror, hardly recognising the place. At first it seemed impossible that they could revive the chapel from the damage wrought by Cromwellian soldiers but at once the King gave orders that it should be done, and gradually they succeeded. Some say that Charles II was happy to spend lavishly on the castle, but bothered little with the appearance of its chief ornament, St George's Chapel, allowing it to remain in its neglected state, and that he cared more for the building of Cumberland Lodge, and Cranbourne Lodge, in the Great Park.

In fact Charles II directed considerable energy towards the chapel. Bruno Ryves, Dean of Chichester, was installed as Dean of Windsor on 3 September 1660. Restoration work was undertaken in the chapel, new rafters and ironwork were introduced into the ceiling of the Cloisters and a garden placed there, the Canons' houses were restored and rebuilt in the 1660s and 1670s and a new canonical residence was built in Denton's Commons.[12] Christopher Wren carried out the first detailed survey of the fabric of the chapel in 1682 before its first major restoration. The King's Beasts on the chapel roof were broken and Wren recommended their complete removal and replaced

ABOVE 23 The Cloisters, traditionally the home of the organist and containing the choir's practice room.

RIGHT Charles II in the robes of the Order of the Garter, following his Restoration, from Ashmole's *The Order of the Garter* (1672).

with pineapples. The Beasts were duly removed, but the pineapples were not placed there.

Charles II also gave significant plate to the chapel, including 'a pair of plain-gilt flaggons, bought with the money collected from the Knight-Companions, weighing 150 ounces',[13] as well as candlesticks, basons, chalices and covers. The musical services were re-introduced, and the place quickly put into order again, though like previous monarchs, the grave of Charles I remained unmarked. The statesman and historian, Edward Hyde, 1st Earl of Clarendon claimed: 'The confusion was so great that at the Restoration none could point out the exact position of the grave.' But it would seem that the new King made very little effort to locate the grave. Had he wished to, he

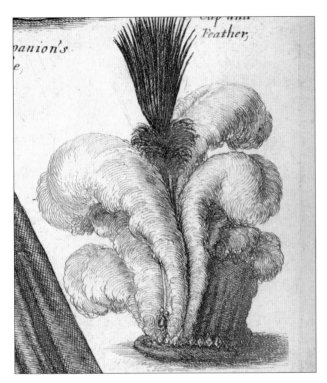

Two illustrations from Ashmole's *The Order of the Garter* (1672). The one on the left is of a Garter bonnet, at the time of Charles II, the one above of the Garter, with its motto: *Honi Soit Qui Mal Y Pense*.

could have consulted an eyewitness, Sir Thomas Herbert, whom Charles II had rewarded with a baronetcy and who did not die until 1682. Some concluded that the King had 'no desire to discover the exact resting-place of his father, or to erect a mausoleum to his memory.'[14]

Charles II commissioned drawings from Sir Christopher Wren to convert the former tomb house and Lady Chapel into a memorial to Charles I, but this did not happen.

The ceremonies of the Order of the Garter were revived with yet more pomp and splendour than before. Charles II had continued to appoint Garter Knights while in exile, and within a year of his Restoration, he had brought the Order of the Garter back to its former glory. He quickly filled the Order to its full complement and great feasts were held in the tapestry hung St George's Hall.

In 1670 the gravy alone for the three days of celebration was made from 249 lbs of beef, 74 lbs of bacon, four cases of veal, two cases of mutton, a case of pork, ten dozen pullets, nine dozen sheeps' tongues, eighteen dozen sweetbreads, seven dozen marrow bones and much more besides. 12,000

prawns were eaten, as were 1,500 crawfish, 136 large lobsters, 118 large crabs, 400 scollops, twelve quarts of oysters, sixteen barrels of pickled oysters, 8 lbs of caviar, and a multitude of other delicacies, including 2,000 eggs and 6,000 asparagus sticks.[15] The feast cost nearly £2,395.

For this feast the King sat on a dais in his robes as Sovereign of the Garter. There was a Chapter and a mighty procession for the installation of new Knights in St George's Chapel, the King, following the Knights and Heralds, walking under a long canopy.

* * * * *

In February 1665 Samuel Pepys visited Windsor by coach and called for Dr William Child, organist of the chapel since 1636. As Pepys recorded:

Childe came to us, and carried us to St George's Chapell; and there placed us among the Knights' stalls (and pretty the observation that no man, but a woman may sit in a Knight's place, where any brass plates are set); and hither come cushions to us, and a young singing-boy to bring us a copy of the anthem to be sung. And here, for our sakes, had this anthem and the great service sung extraordinary, only to entertain us. It is a noble place indeed, and a good Quire of voices. Great bowing by all of the people, the Poor Knights particularly, to the Alter. After prayers, we to see the plate of the Chappell, and the robes [banners] of Knights in being, which hang up over the stalls. And so to other discourse very pretty, about the Order. Was shewn where the late [King] is buried, and Henry the Eighth, and my Lady [Jane] Seymour. This being done, to the King's house. . .[16]

Charles II had decreed that under the Garter robes, the under garments should be of cloth of silver to make a more grave and stately appearance. Two years later John Evelyn told Pepys that this had led to a shocking incident:

He did tell me of the ridiculous humour of our King and the Knights of the Garter the other day, who, whereas herefore their robes were only to be worn during their ceremonies and services these, as proud of their coats, did wear them all day till night, and then rode into the Parks with them on. Nay, and he tells me he did see my Lord Oxford [KG 1660] and the Duke of Monmouth [KG 1663] in a hackney-coach with two footmen in the Parke, with their robes on: which is a most scandalous thing, so as all the gravity may be said to be lost among us.[17]

Matters appeared calmer when Evelyn witnessed a chapel service in 1670:

One of the Canons preach'd, then followed the offering of the Knights of the Order, according to custom; first the poore Knights in procession, then the Canons in their formalities, the Deane and chancellor, then his Majestie (the Soveraine), the Duke of York, Prince Rupert, and lastly, the Earle of Oxford, being all the Knights that were at Court.[18]

Charles II fell ill at Whitehall in February 1685 and was incoherent when Thomas Howard was buckling the Garter below his knee. He died on 6 February and was buried in Westminster Abbey.

JAMES II (KING 1685-8)
WILLIAM III & MARY II
(jointly KING & QUEEN 1689-94)
followed by WILLIAM III
(KING 1694-1702)

The short reign of James II made no positive impact on the chapel, other than that he gave over the former tomb house and Lady Chapel to Roman Catholic use, commissioning Verrio to paint a handsome ceiling, ornamenting and painting the walls and causing the mass to be said there publicly. But it soon deteriorated, particularly after James II's departure.

In the early 1700s, Joseph Pote, the bookseller and printer, visited the former tomb house. His impression was not an encouraging one:

Pity it is, that this Chapel, which might be an Ornament, should be suffered to run to ruin, and stand as a mark of public Resentment, for being once employed in a service disagreeable to a Protestant people; but certain it is, since that Prince's reign, it has been entirely neglected, tho' the care and repair of it is peculiar to the Crown, being no Appendage to the Collegiate Church.[19]

An organ was restored to St George's Chapel, brought from Winchester, and the Quire paved in the black and white squares still in place today. The paving was paid for by the same Dr William Child who had been dragooned by Pepys into helping him on the day of his visit. Pote related the story:

Dr. Child having been organist some years to the K(ing's) Ch(apel) in K(ing) Ch(arles) 2nd's time, had great arrears of the salary due to him to the value of about 500 which he and some of our Canons discoursing of Dr. Ch(ild) silted and said he would be glad if anybody would give him 5 and some bottles of wine for; which the Canons accepted of and accordingly had articles made with hand and seale. After this King James 2 coming to the Crown paid of his Br(other)'s arrears; which much affecting Dr. Child, and he repining at, the canons generously released their bargain on condition of his paving the body of the Choir with marble which was accordingly done as commemorated on his grave-stone.[20]

James II was driven out of England in the so-called 'Glorious Revolution' and was succeeded by King William III and Queen Mary II (the eldest of four daughters of James II).

Queen Anne, whose favourite residence was Windsor Castle.

QUEEN ANNE (QUEEN 1702-14)

Both William and Mary were buried in Westminster Abbey. Queen Anne, the next of Mary's sisters became Queen on 8 March 1702. Windsor Castle was soon her favourite residence. Here, in what is now the Print Room, she received the news of the Duke of Marlborough's victory at the Battle of Blenheim. She had actually lived in the Queen's Lodge opposite the South Terrace and so, effectively since the days of Charles II, the castle had been neglected and fallen into disrepair.

It is not every British monarch who has cared for the castle or improved it, not to mention St George's Chapel within the great castle walls. Although the Sandby brothers produced beautiful watercolours of Windsor Castle from the mid 1750s onwards, this neglect was destined to continue until the reign of George III.

THREE

'A scene of lightness and graces'

GEORGE I (KING 1714-27)
GEORGE II (KING 1727-60)
GEORGE III (KING 1760-1820)

THE FIRST TWO Hanoverian Georges did not bother with Windsor, and it was not until Queen Charlotte encouraged George III to live there that the castle enjoyed a revival. Queen Charlotte had loved Windsor since she first saw it soon after her marriage. In due course, every summer George III and his queen settled into the Queen's Lodge, the princes living on the south side of the castle, and the princesses in Burford Lodge (renamed Lower Lodge), the former home of Nell Gwynn at the end of the garden of the Queen's Lodge.

At first the King only stayed there when it was too late to return to Kew after a day out hunting, but gradually he fell for the place, relishing its informality and the relaxed life that it was possible to live there.

George III allowed visitors to enter Windsor Castle freely. He felt at ease when in the castle. He enjoyed meeting visitors informally in a way that was not possible in London. In the evening he and Queen Charlotte would stroll arm in arm along the North Terrace. He could be seen in the town, browsing in the local bookshop or watching Windsor boys playing cricket. He gave the parish church the old organ from St George's and founded the theatre in 1793, regularly attending plays there.

The King and his family first worshipped at St George's in August 1776, with their elder children, walking from the Queen's Lodge to the South Door, where they were greeted by the Dean and Canons and the Poor Knights. George III sat in his stall, the

The Quire of St George's Chapel in about 1832.

Prince of Wales and 12-year-old Prince Frederick (later Duke of York), both Garter Knights, in theirs. For the sermon the Royal Family came into the Nave and faced west towards the congregation. Later the Royal Family tended to use the Royal Closet, where the King and his family could attend the services, just as Catherine of Aragon had done in a previous century. In 1785 the staircase in the vestry was added to provide easier access.

Burial within the chapel became a feature of the King's reign. William, Duke of Gloucester, was a

55 / 'A SCENE OF LIGHTNESS AND GRACES'

FIELD MARSHAL AND
COMMANDER IN CHIEF.

BORN 24ᵗᴴ MAY 1736;
DIED 29ᵗᴴ JAN. 1820.

BORN 19ᵗᴴ MAY 1744;
MARRIED 8ᵗᴴ SEP. 1761.

FROM HIM PROCEEDS A GEM
TO LIGHTEN ALL THIS ISLE.

King George III and Queen Charlotte, a stained glass window in the North Quire Aisle, by Thomas Willement, 1852. Also depicted are two of the King's sons. On his left, Frederick, Duke of York (1763-1827), and on the Queen's right, Edward, Duke of Kent (1767-1820), father of Queen Victoria. The King and Queen and those two sons are interred in the Royal Vault.

younger brother of the King (and third son of Frederick, Prince of Wales). Of all his brothers, he was the most like George III in temperament, and the King relied on him somewhat. He served in the army (which he hoped to lead), insisted on correct etiquette being observed and possessed a certain dogged intelligence. A man of inflexible habit, when still young he fell in love with a widow eight years his senior, Maria Countess Waldegrave, a niece of Horace Walpole, with three daughters by her first husband. As a young widow she had taken lodgings in Windsor Castle, and so alluring was she that the Dean of Windsor noticed that rather more Eton boys than usual attended services when she was

there. The Duke of Gloucester married her secretly in 1766, and later, after much discussion and argument, had her recognised as Duchess of Gloucester. This family is buried in a special vault near the Sovereign's stall, known as the Gloucester Vault.

When the Duke's younger daughter, Princess Caroline (1774-75), died at the age of nine months, the Duchess complained that the King would not allow the child to be buried in the royal vault in Westminster Abbey. This new vault was the solution. The Duke himself (1743-1805) was buried there relatively privately, as later on his wife Maria (1739-1807), their son William, 2nd Duke of Gloucester (1776-1834), their elder daughter, Sophia (1773-1844), and many years later, Mary (1776-1857), widow of the 2nd Duke of Gloucester, herself the fourth daughter of George III. Mary, Duchess of Gloucester was accorded a Victorian memorial in the South Quire Aisle outside the Oliver King Chantry, while the Gloucester Vault is unmarked, as was the original fate of the Henry VIII vault and the tombs of Henry VI and Edward IV.

Sir William Chambers advised the King that he needed to spend large sums on the restoration of the castle, but besides establishing rooms for himself and his family overlooking the North Terrace, which were finally ready by 1804, he preferred to devote his money and energy to St George's Chapel, which had been neglected for over a century. Francis Pigott, son of the former organist, described it in 1786 as:

> this elegant and neglected Gothic chapel, perhaps the first in the world for beauty and splendour, but dirty, and disregarded to such a degree, as to become a nuisance to the eye, and a reproach to the sextons, who, I am told, receive daily handsome donations for shewing it, yet are regardless to the greatest degree of shame, not so much as dusting the monuments, or washing the chapel.[1]

Some of the monuments were cracked and tied up with string. The College of St George was in no better state. The minor canons were either under-employed or bad readers, at least one was superannuated, another unfit for duty and one deemed 'at times so mad as to be capable of making a worse use of the Book than that of reading the service ill out of it.'[2]

Neither the Nave or Quire was in a good state, and in due course the King spent all his money on the Quire. In 1786 George III introduced new categories to the Order of the Garter. Sons of the Sovereign could become Knights of the Garter in addition to the 24 Companions, and in 1805 he further extended the Order so that lineal descendants who may be elected could also be additional members. In 1831 George IV decreed that such lineal descendants should be Extra Knights. In the twentieth century certain of these, such as the Earl of Athlone (KG 1928) and Earl Mountbatten of Burma (KG 1946), though lineal descendants were included in the 24. Foreign Sovereigns were also appointed from time to time, which became more of a feature in Queen Victoria's reign, and is a practice which continues to this day.

To accommodate these the Garter stalls were

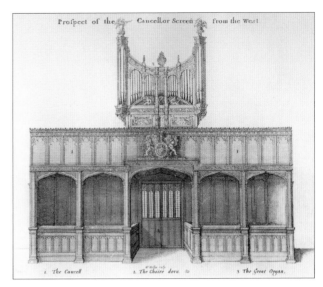

The stalls in the Nave under the organ loft.

reorganised so that the achievements of more Knights could be accommodated. Previously the stalls had alternated – knight – canon – knight; now the stalls nearest the altar were all assigned to Garter Knights, and two new stalls, perfect replicas of the fifteenth century ones, were added on each side at the end nearest the altar. These stalls were decorated with scenes from the King's reign, such carving being a feature of the lower stalls.

Henry Emlyn, carpenter, builder and architect, attached to the chapel from 1761, oversaw the work, which was funded by the Privy Purse so that 'all [should be] made in accord, which, as it had been put up at different times, was not the case at present.'[3]

The altar was replaced and a reredos installed. A painting of the Last Supper by Benjamin West hung above the altar.

The King gave the chapel a new organ with a new case. He commissioned a new stained glass window at the East End from his favourite artist, Benjamin West, an impression of the Resurrection, in one of the central windows of which, the King's young son, Prince Octavius, was depicted amidst cherubims and seraphims. The King paid for the window, with contributions from Knights of the Garter including the Stranger Knights. As work on the window progressed, Fanny Burney, celebrated novelist and

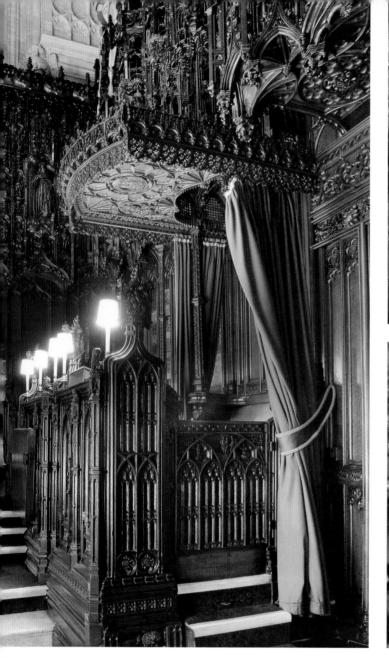

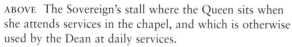

ABOVE The Sovereign's stall where the Queen sits when she attends services in the chapel, and which is otherwise used by the Dean at daily services.

ABOVE Details of some of the carvings on the door of the Sovereign's stall, carved by Henry Emlyn. The top one is thought to represent Edward III feasting with a group of Knights of the Garter. The lower one shows George III inspecting a design for a window with stalls and banners to the left. The date 1790 is carved below the King.

second Keeper of the Robes to Queen Charlotte, was taken to see it. The artist met her in the chapel. She observed:

> The subject is the Resurrection. The Guiding Angel is truly beautiful in it, but our Saviour is somewhat too earthly; He seems athletic as an Hercules, and rather as if He derived His superiority from strength of body than from influence of divinity. The window itself was not yet to be seen.

Mr. West, whom I had once met at Sir Joshua Reynold's, was exceeding civil, showing the cartoon himself, and explaining his intentions in it. He spoke of the performance with just such frank praise and open satisfaction as he might have mentioned it with, if the work of any other artist; pointing out its excellences, and expressing his happiness in the

execution --- yet all with a simplicity that turned his self-commendation rather into candour than conceit. 4

ABOVE A contemporary print of St George's Chapel and the Lower Ward with the Round Tower in the background. Note the fence and line of trees along the south front.

The window was finally put in place in 1786. When Fanny Burney met Boswell in the chapel in October 1790, she noted that by then it was 'repaired and finished by the best artists at an immense expense, which was now opened after a very long shutting up for its preparations'.5 The restoration cost £20,000 in total, the King contributing all but £5,800 (which the Chapter paid).6

George III was also responsible for the Organ screen with its beautiful fan vaulting underneath it. He also commissioned carved oak stalls for himself and his family when they came to the Nave to listen to the sermons. These wooden stalls were later removed.

The restoration work attracted many visitors, well known and otherwise. One who saw it was the feminist writer, Mary Wollstonecraft, who spent summers in Windsor with one of the Canon's daughters. She was impressed:

When I first saw it the pillars within had acquired, by time, a sombre hue which accorded with the architecture; but now it all bursts on the view at once; and the sublimity has vanished before the brush and broom, for it has been white-washed and scraped till it is become as bright and neat as the pots and pans in a notable house-wife's kitchen – yes, the very spurs on the recumbent knights were deprived of their venerable rust.7

Another was Horace Walpole, who came with General Conway in October 1791. He too was impressed, though he did not care for 'several tawdry pictures by West of the history of the Garter'8 in the state apartments:

St George's Chapel, that I always worshipped, though so dark and black that I could see nothing distinctly, is now being cleaned and decorated, a scene of lightness and graces. Mr Conway was so struck with its Gothic beauties and taste, that he

King George III, wearing the Windsor uniform, on the terrace of the castle, where he frequently walked in the evenings. Painted by Peter Edward Stroehling in 1807.

Christ is a poor figure, scrambling to heaven in a fright, as if in dread of being again buried alive, and not ascending calmly in secure dignity: and there is a Judas below, so gigantic, that he seems more likely to burst by his bulk, than through guilt. In the midst of all this solemnity, in a small angle over the lower stalls, is crammed a small bas-relief, in oak, with the story of Margaret Nicholson, the King, and the Coachman, as ridiculously added, and as clumsily executed, as if it were a monkish miracle. Some loyal zealot has broken away the blade of the knife, as if the sacred wooden personage would have been in danger still.[9]

Not long after the restoration work was complete, George III suffered his first serious illness. For a time all was still well, and when a Garter Chapter was held at St George's Chapel in September 1787, it was reported:

His Majesty, first bending in reverence of the solemn nature of the place, walked up in the middle of the chapel, repeating this reverence at the half-way distance from the Altar, at which arriving, he knelt and deposited upon it a golden ingot.[10]

A witness was in awe of the dignity and splendour of the ceremony:

Through the whole, the most awful stillness of attention prevailed, and the minds of the spectators received a mingled impression of august dignity, pious awe, and tender ecstasy, that constituted an intellectual gratification of the most delightful and interesting kind.[11]

Fanny Burney, frequently at the chapel, noted in 1788: 'I ventured once more to the cathedral [as it was often called], to join in the public prayer . . . Dr. Duval [Canon of Windsor] preached a sermon, from Job, very applicable and very well, all exhorting to trust in God, however hopeless in man.'[12]

From this illness the King made a full recovery for some years. A decade later, Fanny Burney again attended a service, inspired by the wish to see the King in chapel:

After the service I got a glimpse of the good King, in his light-grey farmer-like morning Windsor uniform, in a great crowd, but could not even obtain that glance of the Queen and Princesses. The day was

owned the Grecian style would not admit half the variety of its imagination. There is a new screen prefixed to the choir, so airy and harmonious, that I concluded it Wyatt's; but it is by a Windsor architect, whose name I forget. Jarvis's window, over the altar, by West, is rather too sombre for the Resurrection, though it accords with the tone of the choirs; but the

charming. The chapel is admirably repaired, beautified, and a new west window painted on glass. All was cheerfulness, gaiety, and good humour, such as the subjects of no other monarch, I believe, on earth enjoy at the present.[13]

In 1804 the King moved into his new apartments overlooking the North Terrace. He liked to live a Spartan existence, in a room which rarely saw the sun and where there were no carpets – the King believing that these harboured dust. Whereas he was happy, Queen Charlotte was less so. 'I have changed', she wrote 'from a very comfortable and warm habitation [Kew] to the coldest house, rooms, and passages that ever existed.'[14]

Before he descended into his long final illness, the King began to take a new interest in the Order of the Garter. When the Knights of the Garter arrived for the investiture and installation ceremonies on 23 April 1805, they found a new grand staircase which the King thought more appropriate to the ceremonial. A magnificent luncheon was served to the Knights, and eighteen tables were spread with food in the castle yard. The King obtained a baron of beef apparently weighing 162 lbs. While it was being roasted, he was forever heading to the kitchen to watch the process of basting, spicing and browning.

Then came the installation ceremony in St George's Chapel at which one observer, Charles Knight, a lad of fourteen (later the author of a guide to Windsor, and a Mayor of the Borough) who had been allowed to witness the event from a castle parapet, had mixed feelings about the ceremony:

> The old King marched erect; and the Prince of Wales bore himself proudly ... but my Lord Salisbury [KG 1793], and my Lord of Chesterfield [KG 1805], and my Lord of Winchilsea [KG 1805], and half a dozen other lords – what a frightful spectacle of fat, limping, leaden supporters of chivalry did they exhibit to my astonished eyes![15]

The King wore the (then) purple robe of the Order and its cap but on his head he had put an enormous powdered periwig, which rolled in a multitude of curls and was so extraordinary that it became the subject of some mirth. One account

described it as resembling 'a huge spherical mass of snow, descending between the shoulders of an inverted cone,' adding that 'the appearance was not improved by the pressure of a heavy cap and plume'.[16] Underneath it, the King's face was 'unusually red and anxious' and gave 'an immediate impression' of insanity.[17]

In chapel the King rolled up the printed service sheet and used it to beat time with the music. He directed the attention of his trainbearers to points of interest in the service. When Sir Sydney Smith, who seemed unable to decide where to sit and took up a position immediately in front of the King's stall, the King gave him several taps on the back of the head with his scroll, and he swiftly retreated to a seat next to the Duchess of Rutland.

In 1804 George III commissioned the excavation of the Royal Vault under what is now the Albert Memorial Chapel. This was accessed by a lift under a slab in front of the high altar in the Quire. At the appropriate moment in the funeral service, the coffin descends into the ground and is then taken along an underground passage into the vault itself. In 1873 Queen Victoria built stairs in the Ambulatory for easier access to the vault by the living.

It is more normal in the present reign for a royal coffin to be taken for burial at Frogmore as soon as the funeral service is over. Thus the coffin is carried down through the Quire and the Nave to the Great West Door, and the Royal Family follow it onto the steps. It then leaves by hearse for Frogmore. The last time a coffin descended into the Royal Vault during the service was the funeral of Princess Andrew of Greece in 1969.

George III was prompted to build the Royal Vault by his wish that his family should be buried at Windsor, and the first to be buried there was his daughter, Princess Amelia, who died in 1810, just before the Royal Vault was completed. Though a lively girl, she had suffered indifferent health since childhood. She was sent to Weymouth for a tubercular condition, with her father's ADC, Col the Hon Sir Charles FitzRoy, in attendance. Unfortunately she fell madly and hopelessly in love

A rare photograph of the Royal Vault, taken by Sir Benjamin Stone in the late nineteenth century, depicting royal coffins behind grilles.

with him, a situation he accepted with sedate resignation, but without discouraging her. Inevitably her attachment to him was noticed. When Queen Charlotte was informed, she did nothing, referring to it as 'this unpleasant business.'[18] The love turned to obsession, the poor princess anxiously consulting the terms of the Royal Marriages Act of 1772 for a way forward. Her sole comfort was that her brother, the Prince of Wales, had promised to allow the marriage when he came to the throne. Meanwhile, she regarded herself as married in spirit, and from 1804 signed her letters AFR (Amelia FitzRoy). Eventually Queen Charlotte intervened, Princess Amelia's health declined, and she was moved to Windsor where she died at the age of 27 on 2 November 1810.

Before the funeral on 13 November, the Prince of Wales was vexed as to whether he and others should wear the Garter collar at the service. The Dean discovered that it was against the statutes of the Order of the Garter to wear collars after sunset. Princess Amelia's remains were deposited in a temporary vault in what was called the East Aisle, intended to be the entrance to the Royal Vault, then being constructed under the Tomb House. The death of Princess Amelia finally tipped the King into his second illness. 'The agitated and anxious mind of the King sunk beneath the shock.' From this illness he did not recover.[19]

The new Royal Vault was ready by 1813, though the underground tunnel was still being constructed. The vault was hewn out of the dry chalk and matched the size of what is now the Albert Memorial Chapel above it, about 15 feet below ground, 70 feet long, and 28 feet wide. Receptacles were created either side to hold the coffins, formed by Gothic columns of an octagon shape in Bath stone, and supporting four shelves in Yorkshire stone. It was said that each side could hold 32 bodies, there were five niches for the reception of bodies, and in the middle 12 low tombs for the Sovereigns. The work was undertaken by James Wyatt.

As noted, it was at this time that the vault containing Henry VIII, Jane Seymour and Charles I was accidentally discovered, Edward IV and Elizabeth Woodville having been discovered some years earlier.

At the same time, the chapel above was much altered, the ceiling by Verrio, commissioned by James II, removed in favour of a more appropriate Gothic roof, and at the end of the reign of George III the plan was to use the former Tomb House for Garter Chapter meetings.

On 23 March 1813 George III's sister, Augusta, Duchess of Brunswick (1737-1813), mother of Caroline, Princess of Wales, died at her London home in Hanover Square, 'a melancholy specimen of decayed splendour', as one visitor described her.[20] She was the first to be buried in the Royal Vault, on 31 March 1813.

George I had been buried in Hanover, George II and Frederick, Prince of Wales in Westminster Abbey, but from now on the Kings and Queen of England and for a century or so senior members of the Royal Family would largely be buried at Windsor. Inevitably, from now on, some of the great

moments in the chapel's history concerned the burial of kings and queens, princes and princesses, when the focus of the nation's grief rested on Windsor.

As for King George III he was but rarely seen. In his new apartments in the castle he spent his twilight years in a state of mental instability over which the historians are still divided – whether mad, a sufferer of porphyria, or the victim of infections or toxic processes. He spent his days alone in three rooms (including what is now the Print Room). He wore a blue dressing gown with the Garter star attached to it, played the harpsichord, occasionally growing a long beard, and was visited regularly by his doctors, who despaired of finding a cure. As Hilaire Belloc wrote years later:

> They murmured, as they took their fees,
> There is no cure for this disease.[21]

The King slept in what was described as an officer's

George IV and his daughter, Princess Charlotte of Wales, in stained glass in the North Quire Aisle by Thomas Willement, 1854.

camp bed, with a simple mattress, one bolster, but no pillow.

On 5 February 1811 the King's son, the future George IV, assumed the position of Regent of the United Kingdom and acted on behalf of the King for the rest of his life.

* * * * *

At that point, the Prince Regent was heir to the throne, to be followed by his daughter, Princess Charlotte, born in 1796. Curiously, considering that George III and Queen Charlotte had fifteen children, she held the unique position as their only legitimate grandchild all her short life. Had she lived, she would have succeeded to the throne in the

The funeral of Princess Charlotte in the Quire of St George's Chapel in 1817. A hand-coloured lithograph, painted by Thomas Sutherland, after Charles Wild, and after James Stephanoff. First published 1818.

place of William IV and Queen Victoria.

Princess Charlotte had not been to St George's Chapel until 1811. Seeing it for the first time, she wrote: 'It is quite beautiful & I am enchanted with it, the organ is uncommonly fine & I confess I was much affected at hearing it, as well as seeing the place where poor Amelia lay.'[22] However, Princess Charlotte annoyed her grandmother, Queen Charlotte, by talking to the Maids of Honour between the prayers and the sermon.

In 1816 Princess Charlotte married Prince Leopold of Saxe-Saalfield-Coburg, the handsome German prince who later became King Leopold I of the Belgians, and Queen Victoria's 'Dear Uncle Leopold'. But, on 5 November 1817, following a labour of fifty hours, she gave birth to a stillborn male infant, and the following day she herself died.

After a sad procession from Claremont, the princess's funeral cortège arrived at Windsor at 2 am on 17 November, and her body lay in state in Lower Lodge. That evening, the funeral procession made its way to St George's, lit by flares, and to the solemn beat of drums. The widower, Prince Leopold, who for days before had clung disconsolately to her bonnet and cloak, and other members of the Royal Family were present, but as Prince Regent, Princess Charlotte's father stayed away. Absent members of the Royal Family sent empty carriages, the nineteenth century way of being represented on such occasions. A special porch, festooned in black, had been erected over the South Door, through which the procession entered the chapel. There was much black drapery within the chapel, creating 'a suffocating atmosphere, like a black cave.'[23]

There was evidently a certain lack of decorum in the proceedings, the undertakers in attendance being noticeably the worse for alcohol. Princess Charlotte was lowered into the Royal Vault, and her stillborn child, in its silver coffin, was placed at her feet on the following day.

Into the Urswick Chantry, the Prince Regent caused one of the most unusual monuments to be placed to his daughter. Designed by Matthew Wyatt, in white marble, it showed mother and child being directed to Heaven by the angels, while her draped body lay below attended by veiled mourners. As Olivia Bland wrote: 'It combines neo-classical serenity with baroque shock tactics in a manner peculiar to the Romantic period.'[24] At this time the memorial screen erected by Dean Urswick was removed: it was replaced in the restoration of 1920-30.

A year later Princess Charlotte's grandmother, Queen Charlotte, died at Kew Palace, to which she had retreated to live, and she too was buried in the Royal Vault on 2 December 1818. Fanny Burney, wrote sadly:

> The Queen, the exemplary Queen, was this day interred in the vault of her royal husband's ancestors, to moulder like his subjects, bodily into dust; but mentally, not so! She will live in the memory of those who knew her best, and be set up as an example even by those who only after her death know, or at least acknowledge, her virtues.[25]

This time the Prince Regent was present, weighed down by his large mourning cloak and no less than four collars of orders of chivalry, including the Garter collar, which he insisted on wearing.

After Queen Charlotte's death in 1818, the care of the King was consigned to his second son, Frederick, Duke of York.

Following Princess Charlotte's death, the royal Dukes, the younger sons of George III, were urged to marry as there was a lack of heirs in the next generation. In 1818, William, Duke of Clarence, the third son, married Princess Adelaide of Saxe-Coburg-Meiningen, who gave birth to two short-lived daughters – of whom the younger, Princess Elizabeth (1820-21) is buried in the Royal Vault. In the same year, Edward, Duke of Kent, the fourth son, married Princess Victoria of Coburg, and produced the future Queen Victoria in 1819. Again in the same year, Adolphus, Duke of Cambridge, the seventh son, married Princess Augusta of Hesse-

The white marble memorial to Princess Charlotte of Wales in the Urswick Chantry, the work of Matthew Wyatt (1778-1862), son of James Wyatt, Surveyor-General to George III. It was paid for by subscription (limited to a shilling per person) and unveiled in 1824.

Cassel, and produced Prince George, 2nd Duke of Cambridge, later Commander-in-Chief of the British Forces, and two daughters, one of whom, Princess Mary Adelaide became Duchess of Teck, and the mother of Queen Mary, wife of George V.

Of the other sons, the second, the Duke of York, was married but childless. The fifth, the Duke of Cumberland, had married in 1815, Princess Frederica of Mecklenburg-Strelitz. He later became King of Hanover, and had one son – the blind King George V of Hanover. The sixth son, the Duke of Sussex, married twice, but both times in contravention of the Royal Marriages Act of 1772. Two further sons had died young.

Two royal deaths followed in quick succession in 1820. Edward, Duke of Kent (1767-1820), did not long survive his marriage and the birth of his daughter. At a time when it was clear that George III was dying, the Duke had retreated to Sidmouth, in Devon, partly to save money and partly on account of his wife's health. Though he himself enjoyed robust health, he was struck down by a bad cold, following a rainy walk. This became pneumonia and on 23 January he died. His body was brought back to Windsor, lay in state at Cumberland Lodge, and on 12 February was laid in the Royal Vault, the occasion marked with full military honours, but no music in deference to his father, George III, who had died a mere six days after the Duke, on 29 January, and lay unburied.

Half a century later, in 1874, a sarcophagus in memory of the Duke of Kent was placed in the Nave by Queen Victoria. At first it stood outside the Beaufort Chantry, but was later moved between the pillars, where the Prince Imperial's memorial now stands. In 1953, it was moved again, to the Royal Mausoleum at Frogmore.

There was an interesting sequel to George III's death in his rooms at Windsor Castle. The King used to hear the stamp of the guards' feet on the North Terrace and invariably went to the window to watch them pass. The ensign in command would give 'Eyes Right' and the King would raise his hand in acknowledgment. After he died, the ensign was so certain that he saw a bearded figure at the window that he automatically gave the traditional command. The ghostly figure raised its hand as the King had done in life. The ensign was Sir William Knollys. He became Comptroller to the Household of Edward VII when he was Prince of Wales. He told the story to King George V, who in turn told it to his librarian, Sir Owen Morshead.[26]

Though the King had not been seen in public for many years, his death ended a reign of nearly sixty years. His body was placed in a handsomely adorned coffin of Spanish mahogany and covered with a pall of rich Genoese velvet of royal blue, and certain people were admitted to the State Apartments by ticket to view it. Near the head was a rich star of the Order of the Garter, and the Royal arms of England, 'beautifully executed in dead gold'.

The Lying-in-State took place at Windsor, the crowd weaving its way through the castle and through the State Apartments, all hung with purple velvet until they reached the Audience Chamber, lit with twenty double branches on silvered escutcheons, each containing two wax lights. Here the King's body lay. A contemporary account described the scene:

> Here a mournful splendour was thrown over the scene by a profusion of wax lights displayed in rows on each side, and at the end of the room. A temporary throne was erected, richly hung with black cloth, under which the coffin was placed, on a platform ... The throne, steps, and footstool, under the organ gallery, where the picture of Handel is placed, were covered with black. There were Yeomen in black and heralds in tabards, four Gentlemen Ushers, four Pages, two Grooms of the Great Bed Chamber, ten Gentlemen Pensioners, all in deep mourning.

On the evening of the internment, the cavalry lined the High Street and Park Street. Huge crowds gathered and some were admitted to the castle by ticket.

Inside St George's Chapel, platforms had been erected to house a larger congregation than the Chapel could normally hold, notably 100 Eton boys (the King having held Eton in high esteem). Above the entrance to the Royal Vault (where there was a lift to lower the coffin into the ground) a magnificent canopy of purple had been erected, topped by a crown and cushion: 'This kind of canopied temple, or baldaquin, had a very imposing effect.' Extra branches of candles were added to the stalls of the Knights of the Garter to better light the chapel, while extra wax lights hung from special chandeliers. So full was the chapel that 94 distinguished mourners observed the funeral from the Organ Loft.

Street liners took up their positions, the procession formed in St George's Hall, and the Duke of York, as chief mourner, took up his position at the head of the coffin, accompanied by the Dukes of Clarence (the future William IV), Sussex, and Gloucester, and Prince Leopold (future King of the Belgians and widower of Princess Charlotte). By tradition the new King, George IV, stayed away because in those days it was deemed unpropitious that the monarch should in any way associate himself with death. At 9pm the sound of Handel's 'Dead March' from *Saul*, the occasional trumpet sound, and the minute guns indicated that the splendid procession had begun its last journey.

> The evening was dark, but the torchlights produced the finest imaginable effect. While they displayed the personages engaged in the solemn ceremony, they cast a bright light on the countenances of the observing multitude, and brought to view, with all the magical appearance of castellated scenery, the venerable towers, and battlements, and pinnacles of that combination of edifices, which mark and recall to us the days and the works of our progenitors. The pride and pomp of monarchs, who have slept for centuries, seemed called up by artificial lights, in the decaying testimonials of their greatness, to lend the rich and mellow tints of their antiquated abode to the obsequies of a King, the length of whose reign far exceeded theirs, and, without their aid, excited recollections as solemn as the remotest of them all.

In due course the procession reached St George's Chapel, led by the Poor Knights, and followed by a host of distinguished figures – judges, generals, bishops, Privy Counsellors, and peers. Then came

ABOVE The slab covering the lift that leads down into the Royal Vault, and a detail of the slab.

FOLLOWING PAGES The Quire today.

peers bearing the banners of the Union, of St George, of Scotland, Ireland, Hanover and Brunswick. Amongst the pallbearers was the great Duke of Wellington, victor of Waterloo. The canopy was held over the coffin by the Marquesses of Stafford and Cholmondeley. When the coffin appeared, the choirs began to sing, and the coffin entered the chapel to the anthem: 'I know that my Redeemer liveth!'

The service ended with the funeral anthem composed for Queen Caroline, George III's grandmother, in one portion of which just the voices of the boys were heard – 'a masterpiece of delicious enchanting harmony'.

As the Dean read the prayer which accompanies the lowering of the body into the grave, the coffin gradually disappeared from view, 'without hands, and as if it had been mysteriously withdrawn by some supernatural power'.

The nonagenarian, Sir Isaac Heard, Garter King of Arms, who but two years later would himself rest beneath a stone in the Ambulatory of the chapel, read the late King's titles, and the procession retreated from the chapel in more or less the order in which it had entered. Later thousands were admitted to the chapel to see the coffin and 'its splendid paraphernalia, as it lay in the entrance to the Royal Vault'. Thus ended 'the most awful and magnificent ceremony which any British subject now living ever witnessed in this country.'[27]

The Royal Vault received the Duke of Kent on 12 February 1820, and King George III on 16 February. Just before that, on 11 February, the coffins of two of George III's sons, Prince Alfred and Prince Octavius were brought from the vault in Westminster Abbey, and placed in the Royal Vault. It was noted that 'The Hearses did not arrive until ½ past 2 o'clock in the morning.'[28]

GEORGE IV (KING 1820-30)

The new King was no great lover of religion, often preferring to shoot than to attend Divine Service. Nor were his relations with the Chapter at Windsor at all amicable.

The funeral of Princess Charlotte in 1817 had caused new tensions between the Chapter and the Royal Household. The then Prince Regent had moved the Dean and Canons from their stalls and made them sit behind the Poor Knights, because he had been offended when they had excluded his pages and principal gentlemen from the chapel on the night of her funeral.[29] When a dispute arose about the Canons and their right to walk on the Terrace at Windsor, a privilege they claimed from the days of Charles II, the King demanded that the Prime Minister explain to him 'in the most scrupulous manner, what real power the King has over the Dean and Chapter of Windsor, for a more offensive and troublesome set of individuals to the King personally it is impossible to imagine.'[30]

In 1816, soon after becoming Regent, he had appointed as Dean Hon Henry Lewis Hobart, youngest son of 3rd Earl of Buckinghamshire. In so doing he honoured the known wish of his father, though, disliking him intensely, he made it clear that the Dean should absent himself whenever the court was in residence. Nevertheless Hobart presided over the chapel until 1846.

While George IV did much to enhance the look of Windsor Castle, he made little contribution to the life or look of St George's Chapel.

Inevitably there were more royal funerals in the chapel. When the Duke of York died in January 1827, the King sent Sir William Knighton, his physician and later Private Secretary and Keeper of the Privy Purse, down into the Royal Vault in order to select a 'desirable spot' to place the Duke's remains as near as possible to his father, George III.

A man with a torch climbed down the ladder that led to 'this gloomy abode', next went Sir William, while another man held the ladder from above. They then walked about 100 yards along a subterranean passage, finding the coffin of George III on a block of marble, facing east, with Queen Charlotte to the right of him, while his daughter, Princess Amelia was to the left of the King and Prince Edward (who died early) on the right of the Queen. On the other side of the Queen was another deceased young prince. In a niche to one side were Princess Elizabeth, short-lived daughter of the future Queen Adelaide, at whose birth Sir William had assisted, Princess Charlotte and her baby (the Princess's heart in an urn), the old Duchess of Brunswick and the Duke of Kent, father of Queen Victoria. Knighton recorded:

It is quite out of my power to describe to you the imposing and solemn situation in which I found myself – in the dead of night, with a single torch in my hand, in the bowels of the earth, with my late King and Queen and their dead family, all of whom I believed had at that moment a spiritual existence. I felt as if the Almighty was present and almost imagined that the spirits of the departed were also before me.[31]

The Duke of York could not lie in state at Windsor because there was too much construction work going on, and no suitable state room available. George IV did not attend the funeral, remaining in his chamber with Knighton (as ever) in attendance. He was lucky. He was spared a dismal occasion, as Sir Robert Peel related to his wife. As they approached Windsor, they saw many drunken people on foot, and closer in the military presence, foot guards lining the route, and 'the horses of the cavalry, mourning at least as well as a great part of the human attendants in the ceremony.'[32] At Windsor, Peel, the Duke of Wellington and others were shocked to observe Lord Westmorland, uninvited, in his Garter robes, which was contrary to regulations.

At about eight o'clock in the evening the group was marshalled into one of the aisles. Peel was not impressed by what he saw:

> Opposite this door the canopy was stationed, borne by six dukes. The canopy, supported by six slender poles, looked exactly like the top of a servant's bed without curtains, save that there were six instead of four. In this cold aisle, on the flags without a mat or piece of green baize to cover them, we all waited, the Dukes of Clarence, Sussex and Gloucester among the rest, three-quarters of an hour, to the imminent danger, I should think, of old men like the Chancellor, just recovered from a fit of illness. He took my advice, and put his cocked hat under his feet, and stood on the silk which was put round it. Perhaps the Duke's illness, the Duke of Wellington I mean, was caused by his standing in this cold aisle.
>
> The Duke of Clarence did not act the part of Chief Mourner very decorously. He spoke to everyone very much as usual. I heard him inquire from Lord Hertford how many head of game he had killed at Sudburn. An odd question, considering that he was waiting in momentary expectation of his brother's corpse. . .[33]

The coffin arrived, was placed under the canopy and moved off in procession. The next problems were the bitter cold and the almost complete darkness. 'It was in no way, excepting the attendance of the soldiers, more impressive than the funeral of a private gentleman.' It was 'so miserably cold that all comfort during the service was at an end.'[34] The chandeliers Peel dismissed as 'little dirty, trumpery wooden contrivances' and the service was badly read by Dean Hobart, who may well have derived some satisfaction from presiding over these proceedings. Peel concluded: 'The organ loft was the place for a spectator who was indifferent to darkness and to the blast of every wind of heaven.'[35] As the mourners left the chapel in no particular order, Canning observed to Peel: 'Such a procession and such a ceremony, if offered at the theatre, would be hissed as contemptible.'

Worse was to follow. The Dukes of Wellington, Sussex and Montrose and Lord Rosslyn all caught bad colds, and Wellington was criticized for not having adorned his London home, Apsley House, with any outward signs of mourning. Canning, whose further cynical comment was that 'whoever filched the cloth or the matting from under our feet in the aisle, had bets or insurances against the lives of the Cabinet',[36] went down with rheumatic fever and was forced to spend some weeks recuperating at Brighton. Lord Liverpool suffered a stroke from which he never recovered, and Rt Rev George Pelham, Bishop of Lincoln, died.

* * * * *

Three years after the Duke of York, George IV followed him into the Royal Vault, after his death in the castle early on the morning of Saturday 26 June 1830. His funeral took place on 15 July, a fine day which many made a public holiday. The general public behaved in a somewhat unseemly manner as they queued for the Lying-in-State, only becoming reverential in the presence of the coffin.

For the actual procession, the Poor Knights led the way. As the procession set off and the first minute gun sounded, the carpenters were still busy constructing the canopy over the Royal Vault. The wood shavings were still in evidence on the floor.

The Times was particularly critical of the proceedings. The deceased King was little regretted amongst the visitors in the streets of Windsor: 'The only sign of mourning which is visible is their dress. There is no affectation of grief in the countenance – no sound of lamentation in the street.'[37] The new King, William IV, decided to act as Chief Mourner to his brother, but was criticised for his demeanour in the chapel, 'talking incessantly and loudly to all about him, so that the most frivolous things were heard.'[38]

On account of the long procession from London, the service did not start until 10 o'clock at night. *The Times* correspondent was no happier about what he found in the chapel itself:

> When the Royal Body appeared, not a single mark of sympathy was exhibited, but an intense curiosity was expressed to see the present King as mourner. This curiosity was all but disappointed, for His Majesty not having the ostentatious presence of some of the branches of the Royal Family, was not easily discerned, and was besides almost hidden by a numerous retinue of supporters . . .
>
> The Duke of Cumberland [fifth son of George III] was quite as visible as any person could wish, nor was the grave presence of Prince Leopold [widower of Princess Charlotte] difficult to be discovered. The Duke of Wellington, being small in person, was not perceptible to the anxious eye of the spectators, but they had an opportunity of expatiating on the portly appearance of the Duke of Buckingham. [Richard Grenville, 1st Duke of Buckingham and Chandos, the only duke created by George IV]
>
> We cannot dismiss this portion of the solemnity without stating, in the most emphatic terms, that nothing could be worse managed than this branch of the ceremonial, as far as regarded the spectators – no small part of any public pageantry. [39]

William IV took his place in a large chair covered in black velvet near the entrance to the Royal Vault. The service lasted two hours, by which time it was midnight, and near the end, the body of George IV descended just two feet below the level of the aisle, on its way into the Royal Vault. At this point, while an anthem was being played, William IV stomped out, with a peremptory nod to the Earl Marshal.

WILLIAM IV (KING 1830-37)

The day after George IV's death was a Sunday. One of the congregation, Miss Margaretta Brown went to St George's, noting: 'No name was mentioned for the new King, as there is a doubt which he means to be – Henry IX or William IV.'[40]

There was soon a more sober regime in the castle. King William IV, as the Duke of Clarence chose to be styled, liked to attend chapel at St George's with Queen Adelaide and members of the Royal Household. Queen Adelaide asked the Chapter to reserve some seats for her dressers, and these were allocated to the south side of the altar.

On one Sunday in August 1834, while the King was in the Royal Closet about to receive the holy sacrament, a 'gross and infamous outrage' occurred in the chapel, when a 'person named Miller' insulted a certain Mr Legh, a partner in the firm, Ramsbottom & Co. The insult was overheard by Legh's son, who remonstrated with Miller. Miller responded by striking the son with his walking stick so hard that it broke in two. A scuffle ensued and Miller was knocked down. The matter was investigated by the Attorney-General, and it was noted that Miller was fortunate: 'By an old law of Henry VIII, which is not repealed, an outrage of this description was tried at the Castle, the Lord Steward of the Household presided as judge, and the delinquent was punished by having his right arm chopped off! The head cook of the King's household performed the operation ...'[41]

The King and Queen had no surviving children, but they were surrounded by FitzClarences, the offspring of the King and the actress, Mrs Jordan. They also had two of the King's young nephews, Prince George of Cumberland (later King of Hanover) and Prince George (later 2nd Duke) of Cambridge, with them frequently. The King appointed both these cousins Knights of the Garter in 1835. Also at the castle was a niece of Queen Adelaide, Princess Louise, Duchess of Saxe-Weimar.

She had been born in Ghent in 1817, the elder
daughter of Duke Bernard of Saxe-Weimar and his
wife Ida. She died at the castle in 1832, aged 15. For
her a new vault was constructed in the North Quire
Aisle, near the Vestry and there she was buried.

In the same year the memorial to Field Marshal
the 3rd Earl Harcourt, GCB (1742/3-1830), was set
up in the North Quire Aisle. The Harcourts had
been inner members of the Household of several
generations of Hanoverian Kings and Queens. Lord
Harcourt's father, the 1st Earl, attended King
George II at the Battle of Dettingen, was Governor
to the Prince of Wales (later George III) from 1751
to 1752, and Ambassador to Mecklenburg-Strelitz
when the King married Princess Charlotte in 1761.
He then served as Queen Charlotte's Master of the
Horse from 1761 to 1763 and as her Lord
Chamberlain from 1763 to 1768. The tradition
continued, his son, 2nd Earl, serving as Master of
the Horse to the Queen from 1790 until his death in
1809.

The 3rd Earl was the 2nd Earl's younger brother.
He had been in his father's suite when Queen
Charlotte travelled to London. He succeeded his
brother as her Master of the Horse, serving from
1809 to 1818. In his early life he had commanded
the troop which captured the American General
Charles Lee in 1777, returning to England to great
acclaim. He was Deputy Lieutenant of Windsor
Castle, and also Deputy Ranger of Windsor Great
Park from 1806 until his death. He and his wife
were 'on terms of close intimacy' with the Royal
Family. The *Dictionary of National Biography*
wrote of him: 'His court duties during the King's
first illness in 1787 were of a very close and
confidential character, and Mrs Harcourt was
selected to attend the Princess Caroline, wife of
George IV, on her wedding journey to England.'[42]

At the Coronation of George IV in 1821,
Harcourt bore the Union Standard, and was created
Field Marshal. He died at the age of 87, on 17 June
1830 at his home, St Leonard's Hill, Windsor, which
he had purchased from Prince William, Duke of
Gloucester (brother of George III).

A memorable event in the reign of William IV

Statue to Field Marshal 3rd Earl Harcourt, GCB, sculpted
in 1832 by Robert William Sievier (1794-1865). Originally
destined for Stanton Harcourt Church in Oxfordshire, it
was placed in the North Quire Aisle on the instructions of
King William IV. Sievier also designed a monument to
Harcourt in St Andrew's Church, Clewer.

was the summons issued by the King to the
widowed Duchess of Kent and her young daughter,
Victoria, to attend his 71st birthday celebrations in
August 1836. During the visit the King and Queen
took the Duchess of Kent and Princess Victoria,
then aged 17, to the Royal Closet for morning
service. The young princess displayed an early sign
of later morbidity in her journal:

The Cathedral [as they still called it] made me rather
sad. The thought and knowledge that beneath the
very stones we were walking on, lay so many near

me, in eternal sleep, including my poor dear Father, and that so many more will be placed there, who are now in health and strength, must make one pensive and serious and melancholy.[43]

The visit ended badly. In a speech at his birthday dinner, attended by a hundred guests, William IV launched a virulent attack on the Duchess of Kent, declaring that he hoped he would live nine months more and thus prevent the Duchess becoming Regent – a woman 'surrounded by evil advisers and who is herself incompetent to act with propriety in the station in which She would be placed.' This caused a 'terrible scene', following which the Duchess removed her daughter from Windsor the next morning.[44]

King William IV succeeded in living until Princess Victoria came of age on 24 May 1837. Only a month later, on 26 June, he died at Windsor, and was succeeded by his 18-year-old niece.

The King's funeral was again at Windsor. Much disappointment was felt by those who missed the Lying-in-State, while others found the heat in the chamber where his body lay most oppressive. The atmosphere was more 'sedate and grave'[45] than at the obsequies for George IV, and pictures not only of King William and Queen Adelaide, but also the new young Queen Victoria adorned the windows of the trades people of Windsor.

The night before, the opportunity was taken to move the remains of a stillborn daughter of Ernest Augustus, Duke of Cumberland (fifth son of George III), who had lain in the Royal Vault of Westminster Abbey since 1817. Her father was a younger brother of William IV and the Duke of Kent. The child would have been closely in line to the British throne, as the Duke of Cumberland was heir presumptive until Queen Victoria married and had children.

At the death of William IV, the Crowns of Great Britain and Hanover separated for the first time since 1714, on account of the Salic Law, which prevented a woman from succeeding to the throne of Hanover. Therefore the Duke of Cumberland, the next brother in line, became King Ernest of Hanover.

A photograph of the Lower Ward of Windsor Castle in Victorian times by Roger Fenton (1819-69). In those days, there was a large porch at the entrance to St George's Chapel known as the Galilee Porch.

FOUR

Queen Victoria

QUEEN VICTORIA
(QUEEN 1837-1901)

Soon after the death of William IV, Queen Victoria arrived at Windsor and attended morning service at St George's at 11, but did not get back to her apartments until 1.30, after 'a very bad sermon by the Dean [Hobart].'[1] Queen Victoria was put off attending further such services by their length and the long sermons, combined with the bitter cold of the Royal Closet. There were further hazards to relatively public worship. One Sunday in November 1838, a 'stranger of gentlemanly appearance' seated himself near the royal pew and began to kiss his hand and make 'sundry other movements' to the point that he was asked to leave. When he refused to do so, he was removed by force. As he was taken away, he looked up to the Queen and exclaimed: 'Your Majesty, you see I am arrested in the church, in the reign of Victoria!'[2]

For whatever reason, Queen Victoria decided to worship either at the Royal Chapel at Royal Lodge, or later in the private chapel in the State Apartments, after its consecration in 1843.

Queen Victoria inherited Henry Hobart as her first Dean and had five more Deans in her long reign.

HON HENRY HOBART (DEAN 1816-46)

Henry Hobart was born in 1774, the youngest son of the 3rd Earl of Buckinghamshire. He was a man of great character, whose principal interests were breeding dogs and tortoises and was long remembered at Windsor for decrying the obit service as 'rank popery' adding 'but we have to use it to keep our property'.[3] Hobart was no more a favourite of Queen Victoria than he had been of George IV's. In 1841 he offended her by congratulating her on the birth of the future Edward VII and on thus 'saving us from the incredible curse of a female succession.'[4]

Dean Hobart presided over the funeral of Queen Victoria's aunt, Princess Augusta (1768-1840), second daughter of King George III, who died ,unmarried, at Clarence House, London, on 22 September. This was an affair as elaborate as any recent royal funeral, with special porches and platforms being erected, a procession from the South Door to the West End and up the central aisle to the Quire.

In advance of the funeral, workmen opened the Royal Vault for the first time since the burial of William IV in 1837. A correspondent gleaned some idea of the state of the vault, noting:

> Upon entering the Royal Vault yesterday there was scarcely any dampness manifest, nor was there any effluvium perceptible of an offensive nature, although it had been closed for upwards of three years. Many of the coffins, with their splendid appointments and rich embellishments, appeared nearly in the same state that they were in when placed there.'[5]

In the faintly glimmering candlelight, the correspondent concluded that the embellishments on William IV's coffin had not survived as well as that on the coffin of George III, the coronet being fine, but the velvet cushion on which it sat 'nearly eaten away, apparently by mildew', and the tassels

The baptism of Albert Edward, Prince of Wales, by
William Howley, Archbishop of Canterbury, in the Quire,
25 January 1842, painted by Sir George Hayter.

wholly rotten and lying on the ground.[6] On the
appointed day Princess Augusta's coffin descended
into the Royal Vault.

Hobart was Dean when the windows giving light
to the Quire were altered. The clerestory windows
at the East End, which had been covered over with
tin plate at the time that the Benjamin West window
had been put up, were now opened. Dark glass by
Charles Forrest was placed in the two openings next
to the east end, and the next four windows were

RIGHT The Great West Window. The entire window was rearranged in the 1840s by Thomas Willement, an early Victorian specialist in stained glass. The banners either side of the door were designed by the painter Thetis Blacker (1927-2006), who also designed an altar frontal (*see pages 35 and 36*).

glazed 'in rich and powerful colours' by Thomas Willement.[7] This had the effect of brightening Benjamin West's east window. It also alleviated the very real problem of people tripping on the steps up to the altar in indistinct light.

The stonework of the Great West Window was entirely renewed and the glass rearranged. In 1767 one of the Canons, Dr John Lockman (later Dean), had collected all the ancient glass to be found in and around the chapel and placed it in the Great West Window. For some years this window had bulged inwards to the point that George IV's architect, Sir Jeffry Wyattville, had wanted to repair it. But he had proved too busy and so in 1841 the Dean and Canons instructed Edward Blore to take out all the valuable stained glass and the interlocking stonework and rebuild it. At that time the West Window was a mess, *The Times* correspondent noting:

> There is little doubt that the ancient parts of the stained glass in the grand western window, now vilely mixed up with common glazier's patterns, were formerly in the window over the altar ... The figures possess considerable merit, but they have evidently been very ignorantly put together.[8]

Where there had been gaps these had been filled with stained glass of glaring orange or purple, whose only merit was to light the chapel in particular ways at sunset, when it showed the architecture to fine advantage. The words of warning were heeded and Thomas Willement was commissioned to rearrange the glass, retaining the ancient glass, and where necessary commissioning new and more appropriate stained glass to harmonize with the old.

The Quire stalls were restored to their original state, 'for repeated varnishings and a long accumulation of dirt had rendered the high beauty of the carvings nearly invisible.'[9]

On 22 October 1842 the Chapel reopened for divine worship. The effect was judged a huge success, and *The Times* correspondent alerted his readers to a narrow escape for the window:

> It is not generally known, that it was at one time intended to throw the whole of this window into one immense opening, and to fill it by a colossal subject of the Crucifixion, from a design by West. This work had been very far advanced by Forrest at the time of his death, and, with gratitude be it said, lies still in an

unfinished state in the stores of the Dean and Canons. The result of the same kind of (what the improved taste of the present age calls) profanation at the east end of this chapel will be a powerful warning, while it remains in existence, to those ill-judging persons who may wish to give stained glass a character and self-importance so inconsistent with its own true and intrinsic beauty when judiciously and tastefully applied.[10]

The correspondent also approved of the considerable amount of new heraldic glass in the windows of the South Quire Aisle.

The organ, some of whose keys were by then over fifty years old, was restored by Robert Gray and some of the keys replaced. It was also re-ornamented. The Chapter also ordered a complete clean of the chapel, which involved restoration of the wood carvings, and of the alabaster and marble monuments in the side chapels. The ceilings of Nave and Quire were cleaned, immense scaffolding being constructed in the chapel. Gothic screens hiding the Beaufort and Lincoln chantries were removed and the stonework restored to its rich, natural colour. When they tackled the Catherine of Aragon loft, they discovered it was not stone, but once layers of paint and whitewash had been removed, that it was of carved oak. This was stained and varnished. It now matched its only known counterpart – in Lincoln Cathedral. Some heraldic bosses on the vaults were newly cut and others newly emblazoned with the arms of Kings and Knights of the Garter, under Willement's supervision.

A huge sixteenth century brass lectern was discovered by the Dean, lying dilapidated amongst some rubbish in a vault beneath the chapel. It was restored and polished and placed in the centre of the Quire, where it remained until well into recent times. The chapel was thrown open for two days in September 1843, free of charge, for anyone who wished to see it, and two days later Dr George Elvey played the magnificently restored organ.[11]

But there remained one problem, as the ever-vigilant *Times* correspondent pointed out:

It would be as well, perhaps, if, amongst all the improvements which have been effected in connexion with the chapel, some improvements were to take place in the behaviour of the men who show the public over the building. Their great incivility, which has been often loudly complained of by the public (inhabitants of the town as well as visitors), from whom they exact large fees, as showmen, is of the most rude and bearish character, and is deserving of the severest castigation.[12]

While Hobart was Dean, Queen Victoria was crowned and she married. Her wedding to Prince Albert of Saxe-Coburg and Gotha took place at the Chapel Royal, St James's Palace, on 10 February 1840. During her reign the Dean buried Princess Sophia of Gloucester in the Gloucester Vault on 10 December 1844.

Dean Hobart himself died on 8 May 1846, and perhaps history does not adequately credit him with the restoration carried out towards the end of his years at Windsor. He was succeeded within a month by Neville Grenville.

HON NEVILLE GRENVILLE (DEAN 1846-54)

(George) Neville Grenville was the third son of 2nd Lord Braybrooke, and came to Windsor, having been Master of Magdalene College, Cambridge, and Rector of Hawarden, County Flint, the parish of William Gladstone. He was born in 1789. In 1816 he married Lady Charlotte Legge, daughter of 3rd Earl of Dartmouth, KG.

It fell to him to bury Queen Adelaide, widow of William IV. She died at Bentley Priory, Middlesex, on 2 December 1849. She left instructions that her 'mortal remains be conveyed to the grave without any pomp or state.' She wanted 'as private and quiet a funeral as possible.'[13] The Archbishop of Canterbury officiated at the service, Queen Victoria, and some Royal Family and Household were in the chapel and she was duly reunited with William IV.

Dean Grenville died on 10 June 1854.

HON GERALD WELLESLEY (DEAN 1854-82)

Gerald Wellesley was one of the most influential Deans in the history of the College of St George, and relations between the Queen and the College improved in 1854 with his appointment. It would be possible to write about Queen Victoria without mentioning Dean Wellesley, but not possible to write about the Dean without mentioning her. He had a strong and positive influence on the Queen. He used his position as Dean to great advantage and his personal relations with the Queen were very close. She held him in high esteem as 'the last of her husband's old friends and the most intimate of all' and when he died after 33 years of friendship, she described his loss as 'irreparable'.[14] Dean Davidson wrote of him: 'Dean Wellesley had been among the most trusted of her friends.'[15] Randall Davidson's biographer credited Wellesley with instilling into her 'a character and possibilities all its own'.[16]

Hon Gerald Valerian Wellesley was the third son of Henry Wellesley (later 1st Lord Cowley), and a nephew of the great Duke of Wellington. He was born in 1809 shortly before his mother, a daughter of 1st Earl Cadogan, eloped with Lord Paget, later 1st Marquess of Anglesey (to whom she bore three sons and three daughters). This was a huge scandal at the time, and since Gerald was born in the early months of his mother's love affair, his paternity was questioned, though the Wellesleys accepted him without question as his father's son. Custody was granted to his father, though he was largely brought up by the Duchess of Wellington.

Young Gerald progressed from Rottingdean to Eton, where William Gladstone was in the next-door room and became a friend (though the Dean, try as he did, was unable to guide Gladstone in his dealings with Queen Victoria). After Trinity College, Cambridge, he was ordained, became Chaplain at Stratfield Saye, the Hampshire seat of the Wellingtons, from 1836 to 1854. Having been appointed Domestic Chaplain to Queen Victoria in 1849, he came to Windsor as Dean in 1854. From 1870 he served as Lord High Almoner. In 1856 he married Hon Magdalen Robinson, daughter of 6th Lord Rokeby.

Dean Gerald Wellesley, Dean of Windsor from 1854 to 1882. He was one of Queen Victoria's most trusted friends. Portrait by Heinrich von Angeli (1840-1925).

Wellesley had many royal duties. He examined the Prince of Wales (later Edward VII) rigorously before his confirmation in St George's in 1858. He was not a frequent attender at services in St George's, but he was a conscientious and admirable Dean. He fought battles with the Lay Clerks and the Military Knights, the latter group failing to attend daily services with regularity. He solved that problem by abolishing compulsory attendance, which threatened their continued existence, though Edward VII reinstated compulsory attendance at Sunday Mattins. He visited all the livings owned by the College in the West Country in 1858.

Queen Victoria suffered two serious bereavements in 1861. On the morning of 16 March 1861, her mother, the Duchess of Kent, died of cancer at Frogmore, with the Queen holding her hand. The Royal Vault was a temporary resting place for her until the Kent Mausoleum, planned by the Duchess, was ready at Frogmore. Her coffin was placed in the Nave before dawn on the day of the funeral, and she rested in the Royal Vault until that August.

Yet more serious was the death at Windsor of the Prince Consort on 14 December, leaving the Queen

OPPOSITE PAGE View of the Albert Memorial Chapel with the Prince Consort's memorial in the foreground and the Duke of Clarence's tomb in the centre.

LEFT The Prince Consort's effigy by Sir (George) Gilbert Scott (1811-78).

BELOW LEFT 'The Sorrowful Queen' – a depiction of Queen Victoria on the front of the Prince Consort's memorial, photographed by Sir Benjamin Stone in 1899.

utterly bereft and in a state of perpetual mourning until her own death in 1901. Dean Wellesley was present when Prince Albert died, recalling 'the fervent kiss' the Queen gave him, 'the look of despair as she suffered herself to be led away' and 'her loud sobs as she went off to her solitary room'.[17]

The Prince Consort's funeral took place on 23 December and he remained in the Royal Vault until 18 December 1862, when he was transferred to the Royal Mausoleum at Frogmore.

Following the Prince Consort's death, Queen Victoria transformed the former Tomb House and Lady Chapel into a memorial to the Prince Consort, restoring and refurbishing it between 1863 and 1873. She commissioned Sir George Gilbert Scott to produce a new painted roof and stained glass windows. Favouring the works of French artists, she commissioned Baron Henri de Triqueti (1804-74), who had worked for Ferdinand Philippe, Duc d'Orléans in France, to decorate it internally with his particular technique of engraved marble with coloured marble in the incisions. The mosaics of the ceiling and west wall were by the Venetian, Antonio Salviati (1816-90). The result was a completely restored chapel in the neo-Gothic style, covered with costly mural decorations, inlaid with precious stones and marbles. The cenotaph for Prince Albert was also designed by Triqueti, the work being completed in 1873. Thus the Albert Memorial Chapel, as it was now called, became one of the more elaborate of the multitude of memorials to the Prince Consort that Queen Victoria planted across the land – all of them contrary to her late husband's instructions as declared in his will.

* * * * *

The sculptured reredos by Sir (George) Gilbert Scott behind the High Altar – another memorial to the Prince Consort.

of the Prince of Wales, his lack of church going and the Princess of Wales's disinterest in Low Church services due to her inability to hear them on account of her deafness. He was protective of Prince Leopold, the young haemophiliac prince, and involved in numerous discussions over his education, particularly encouraging the prince in his wish to go to Oxford and how to tie this in with his mother's demands. He advised over the marriages of the Queen's daughters and intervened over her bad relations with his friend, Gladstone.

Dean Wellesley did not approve of the idea of the Mausoleum at Frogmore, fearing that this would detract from St George's Chapel as the place for royal burials, with the attendant ceremonial. Instead he favoured the Albert Memorial Chapel as both memorial and final resting place. The problem was to find a private route of access for the Queen to the chapel from the State Apartments. The architect, George Gilbert Scott, was prepared to bring the Queen via the Moat Garden and then across the Upper Ward by means of a well-lit covered bridge – reminiscent of the Bridge of Sighs in Venice. Fortunately Queen Victoria rejected this elaborate scheme.

Dean Wellesley presided over a number of memorials to the Prince Consort at St George's. His death provided the Dean and Canons with a long awaited opportunity to get rid of Benjamin West's East Window and to turn this into a memorial to Prince Albert.

Scott had designed the framework for the memorial to Queen Victoria's aunt, Princess Mary, Duchess of Gloucester in the South Quire Aisle in 1859. Now he was asked to create a sculptured reredos for the sanctuary. Wellesley then told Queen Victoria that he sought a window 'corresponding with the magnificent one in the West, which should contain the Prince's arms (if not his likeness) with emblems of immortality.' He developed this plan to include compartments illustrating the virtues and actions of the Prince Consort.[18] The window was begun by Clayton & Bell in 1862 and was in place in time for the wedding of the Prince of Wales in March 1863. The window did not emerge as

In widowhood the Queen relied more and more on Wellesley, to the point that no appointment, be it to the See of Canterbury, to the Premiership or to the Household, was made without the Queen consulting her Dean. When he himself was offered the See of Canterbury, he declined out of modesty. He advised the Queen over the various peccadilloes

magnificent as the West Window, but all the 52 lights had an early to mid fifteenth century character.

* * * * *

The Quire and High Altar photographed from the Organ Loft.

The wedding of the Prince of Wales and Princess Alexandra of Denmark, March 1863, with Queen Victoria in the Catherine of Aragon loft. Painting by William Powell Frith (1819-1909).

The wedding of the Prince of Wales (later Edward VII) on 10 March 1863 to Princess Alexandra of Denmark was the greatest wedding ever celebrated in the chapel. Queen Victoria was still grieving deeply. The day before the wedding she took the young couple to the Mausoleum so that they could be close to the earthly remains of the Prince Consort and pronounced a blessing on them on his behalf. She witnessed the service from the relative privacy of the Catherine of Aragon loft. One of the guests, Lady Augusta Stanley, described her: 'Most beautiful Her expression was, tho' more drawn and pinched than usual.'[19]

Queen Victoria asked the ladies to wear muted colours in mauve, lavender or light blue, which proved extremely effective. The Prince of Wales himself wore the robes of the Order of the Garter, the Garter Knights being in their stalls, most notably Lord Palmerston. Mr Gladstone was also seated in a Garter stall, Benjamin Disraeli in a row in front but opposite.

For the occasion a vast anteroom had been built over the west steps leading to the Great West Door. Lady Augusta Stanley thought these temporary rooms 'fitted up with the greatest taste'. She spotted figures such as Thackeray in the Nave, and continued:

The poor Princesses wept as they saw their Brother's advance without his Father ... Prince William of Prussia [the future Kaiser] improved the occasion to aggravate and set his small uncles at defiance, and managed to get the Cairn gorm out of the head of his dirk, and to pitch it to the other side of the Choir for the sake of an excitement! I will not attempt to describe the ceremony only to say, that there was a solemnity and feeling about it that could not but thrill thro' one. His look to His Mother while waiting for the Bride, and Hers to Him, the reverent attitude of the Bride and Bridegroom and all, and the beautiful reading of the Service were most affecting. The Music was also very impressive, and when all was ended, the joyous look with which, recovering from her feelings and emotion, the Bride took his arm and walked down the Nave, returning the greetings, were most heart-moving.[20]

After the ceremony the Queen left via the Deanery and hurried back to the State Apartments to welcome the young couple at the door. Queen Victoria had a posed wedding group photograph taken of the bride and groom and immediate family surrounding a bust of the Prince Consort.

There were five more royal marriages in the chapel during Queen Victoria's reign – Princess Louise to the Marquess of Lorne (later 9th Duke of Argyll) 1871; Prince Arthur, Duke of Connaught to Princess Louise of Prussia, 1879; Princess Frederica of Hanover (elder daughter of King George V of Hanover) to her late father's ADC, Baron Alfons von Pawel Rammingen, 1880; Prince Leopold, Duke of Albany to Princess Helen of Waldeck and Pyrmont, 1882; and the unfortunate union of her granddaughter, Princess (Marie) Louise of Schleswig-Holstein (daughter of Princess Christian) with HH Prince Aribert of Anhalt, 1891.

* * * * *

Other royal events presided over by Dean Wellesley included the burials of Princess Mary, Duchess of Gloucester (daughter of George III), in May 1857, in the Gloucester Vault. Into the Royal Vault went Prince Frederic of Schleswig-Holstein (infant son of Prince and Princess Christian), who died at Frogmore, only eight days old, in May 1876; the blind King George V of Hanover in June 1878, and the infant, Victoria von Pawel Rammingen (daughter of Princess Frederica of Hanover and thus granddaughter of King George V of Hanover), born

Sir Benjamin Stone's wonderfully atmospheric photograph of St George's Chapel from the Round Tower in Victorian times.

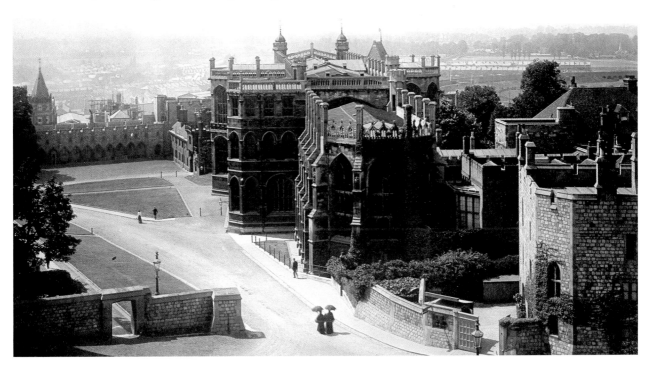

at Hampton Court, and dead after 22 days, in March 1881. That funeral was conducted partly alongside the steps to the Royal Vault, and then the mourners descended by foot into the vault for the last part of the service. Her mother, Princess Frederica of Hanover (1848-1926) was also buried in the Royal Vault when she died in Biarritz in 1926, an old agreement made by Queen Victoria being honoured.

King George V of Hanover (1819-78) and his family were buried in the chapel because he was a Prince of Great Britain. He was the only son of Ernest, Duke of Cumberland, and therefore a first cousin of Queen Victoria. Because of the Salic Law, which meant that the Crown of Hanover could not go to a woman, his father had succeeded William IV as King of Hanover in 1837, and he had succeeded him as King in 1851. He was blind, having lost one eye in childhood and the other in a later accident in which he was swinging a cord around on the end of which was a gold acorn. This hit his eye, inflamed it and he lost the eye. Until the birth of Princess Victoria, the Princess Royal in 1841, George V of Hanover was heir to the British throne.

In 1866 he refused to remain neutral in the Austro-Prussian war, as a result of which Hanover was annexe by Prussia. His last years were spent in exile in Austria, though he frequently visited Paris, where he died in June 1878. At first it was agreed that he would be buried in the Hanover family vault at Herrenhausen, but when conditions laid down by the King's son were not agreed, Queen Victoria offered St George's Chapel instead. The night before the funeral his coffin rested near the Urswick Chantry, containing the memorial to Princess Charlotte, and was then buried relatively privately, with Queen Victoria in the Royal Closet. A feature of the service was a rolling bier, pushed by invisible men, hidden by the folds of the Palls.

After the service the Queen allowed members of the Royal Household to go down into the Royal Vault to pay their respects. Queen Victoria then commissioned her nephew, Count Gleichen (1833-91), the former Prince Victor of Hohenlohe-Langenburg, son of Princess Feodora of Leiningen,

Queen Victoria's half-sister (by her mother's second marriage), to undertake a monument. This remains in a lesser form than the original, near Princess Charlotte's memorial in the Urswick Chantry.

As the Queen's reign continued, so she frequently visited the coffins of departed members of the family in the Albert Memorial Chapel and the Royal Vault. She refused to allow fresh flowers in the vault so that wreaths had to be artificial.[21]

There were other less obvious burials and monuments placed in the chapel on Queen Victoria's instructions. One such was Alamayu, Prince of Abyssinia (son of Emperor Teweodros II of Ethiopia), who died aged 18 at Headingley, near Leeds in 1879. Queen Victoria was fond of him and allowed him to be buried next to St George's Chapel

His was a terrible story. In 1867 Queen Victoria failed to answer a letter from the Emperor, upon which he took offence and imprisoned several British residents in Ethiopia, including the Consul. In retaliation, an army of 12,000 under the command of Sir Robert Napier, was sent from Bombay to rescue the British nationals. Napier stormed the fortress of Magdala in April 1868, at which the Emperor shot himself dead in the mouth.

The Empress was dying and asked Captain Speedy of the Indian Army, described as 'a red-bearded 6'6" gentle giant of a man'[22] to look after her son. Speedy took him to England, and gave him what Queen Victoria described as 'kindly, judicious and almost maternal care.'[23] Alas he was no scholar and failed to learn to read, so Robert Lowe, Gladstone's Chancellor of the Exchequer, removed him from the kind Speedy, made him a ward of the British government and consigned him to the care of Dr Thomas Jex-Blake, first at Cheltenham, and later at Rugby. He was then allowed to enter Sandhurst without taking the exam. He did not like the Royal Military College, but he liked Cyril Ransome, his military tutor. Sadly he then contracted pleurisy, from which he died.

Queen Victoria commented in her journal: 'It is too sad! All alone in a strange country, without a single person or relative belonging to him . . . His was

ABOVE The effigy of the Prince Imperial by Sir J. Edgar Boehm (1834-90), on his cenotaph, now in the Nave. Until recently this memorial was in the centre of the Bray Chantry.

RIGHT The memorial to King Leopold I of the Belgians, sculpted by Sir J. Edgar Boehm in 1878. It stands outside the Urswick Chantry. Queen Victoria caused it to be placed there, and it bears the inscription: 'her maternal uncle, who was as a father to her, as she was to him a daughter'.

BELOW The cenotaph of Dean Gerald Wellesley in white Carrera marble in the North Quire Aisle. Again the work of Sir J. Edgar Boehm. Gladstone had composed an inscription in Latin, but in the end an English one by Dean Charles Vaughan (1816-97), Master of the Temple, was used.

no happy life, full of difficulties of every kind.' [24] On the brass memorial placed near the Urswick Chanry by Queen Victoria, near the outside burial spot, is the inscription: 'I was a stranger and ye took me in.'[25]

Queen Victoria had also been fond of the Prince Imperial, heir to the throne of France. Meeting him at Camden Place, Chislehurst, shortly after the death of Napoleon III, she described him as 'a nice little boy, but rather short and stumpy.'[26] Queen Victoria had enjoyed good relations with his parents, Emperor Napoleon III and particularly his wife, Empress Eugénie, who later lived at Farnborough Hill, and came frequently to Windsor. The Prince Imperial pleaded to be allowed to serve in the Zulu War after being turned down by the Duke of Cambridge, Commander of the British Army. Because Queen Victoria and Empress Eugénie intervened, he was allowed to go as an observer and he sailed to South Africa.

During a skirmish in Zululand on 1 June 1879, he tried, in an act of bravado, to leap into the saddle of his horse, but the girth gave way and he was hurled to the ground. He turned to face the Zulus, firing at them with his revolver but caught his foot in a hole, and fell over. The enemy rushed towards him and killed him brutally with their assegais.

The Prince Imperial was buried first at Chislehurst, and later at St Michael's Abbey, Farnborough, where today the Emperor and Empress and their son lie buried in the crypt.

There was some confusion over a memorial to the Prince. A public appeal raised £2,000 and the Dean of Westminster agreed the monument could be placed in the Henry VII Chapel in Westminster Abbey. To this the French Government protested. There was an unpleasant debate on the issue in the House of Commons. Queen Victoria went to St George's Chapel in November 1880 and settled on the Bray Chantry as the best place for the memorial. In 1881 it was placed there.[27] Empress Eugénie had been upset by the controversy but went to see the memorial:

> I have been glad to see the beautiful monument and the place where it stands. The Queen, who feels that those who suffer and, what is rare, had the courage to show her feelings, has completed the work of those that by affection for my dearest child wished a durable monument for him.[28]

In 1950 George VI approved the removal of the Duke of Kent's memorial to Frogmore. This was done in 1953. In the 1980s the Prince Imperial's memorial was moved to the place where the Duke of Kent's memorial used to be between two pillars in the South Nave Aisle.

Outside the Urswick Chantry there is a memorial to King Leopold I of the Belgians, who died in 1865, by Sir Edgar Boehm, and near to it a memorial tablet to the blind King George V of Hanover.

In the last year of his life Dean Wellesley was present at the wedding of Prince Leopold, Duke of Albany to Princess Helena of Waldeck and Pyrmont, on 27 April. It was a magnificent occasion, the packed chapel filled with 'the costliest costumes and the most diverse uniforms, ablaze with jewels, and brilliant with the insignia of every order of chivalry.'[29]

* * * * *

From the mid sixteenth century the College of St George had ranked after Westminster Abbey and Canterbury Cathedral as one of the richest foundations in the country, owning considerable estates then valued at over £1,500,000, many of which had come from ancient bequests in medieval times. But in 1867 an Act of Parliament enabled the Ecclesiastical Commission to appropriate their land and their stock under Order in Council. Compensation was made in an annual grant of £14,400 a year, which was thought at the time to put the finances of the College on a sound footing for ever. The annual sum soon proved inadequate. This was to cause Dean Wellesley's successors considerable trouble in the twentieth century.

It was said that Wellesley was the only person of whom the Queen was in awe.[30] He impressed the choirboys too, the young Walford Davies recalling that: 'he had a deep, rolling, resonant way of reading the Communion Service. He always stood at the North End of the Communion Table, where we could (as Decani choristers) clearly see his stern, rugged face and feel something like awe at the sight.'[31]

The Dean, whom the Queen described as 'tender-hearted' beneath a 'rough exterior',[32] died on 17 September 1882 and was buried under a chestnut tree in the graveyard at Stratfield Saye, at a service attended by the Prince of Wales, Mr Gladstone, the choir of St George's and several Military Knights.

On 1 December 1884 Queen Victoria, Princess Beatrice, Princess Christian and the Duchess of Edinburgh were present when a memorial to him was unveiled in the North Quire Aisle – a recumbent figure in Carrara marble, designed by Sir Edgar Boehm.

GEORGE HENRY CONNOR (DEAN 1882-3)

Dean Connor was a short-lived incumbent of the Deanery, who was installed on 10 November 1882, but died on 1 May 1883. He had been a much-respected Vicar of Newport on the Isle of Wight for nearly thirty years, and as such had been involved in the religious life of the Queen and the Prince Consort when they were at Osborne House. The Queen wanted him because he was one of those who remembered the Prince Consort, and was thus part of what she called the pre-1861 life, and it was her son, Prince Leopold, who invited him to be Dean. She wrote of 'his upright, kind and sympathetic nature', and how she 'felt he was no stranger.'[33]

In those days Windsor was considered to be an appointment of 'dignified ease' but Connor wondered how much there would be of 'what was called the *otium cum dignitate*' in his new post.[34] He had been a good parish priest, but in retrospect it was clear that he could not bring to the office what the Queen required.

Walford Davies remembered him too, 'with a very gentle face and manner. He seemed always to wear his Garter blue ribbon (which Dean Wellesley did only on Sundays); so his face and the bright ribbon are quite inseparable in my memory.'[35]

As it happened, there was no time for him to make an impression. He preached but once in the chapel, though several times to Queen Victoria in her Private Chapel. He managed to attend the christening on 26 March 1883 of Princess Alice of Albany, Prince Leopold's daughter, who was born on 25 February that year (and lived until January 1981): she was thus christened by Dean Connor, the 55th Dean and buried by Bishop Michael Mann, the 62nd Dean in a span of nearly a century. A few weeks later Connor was dead. The Queen mourned his loss: 'Alas! I have now lost almost all of those who were associated in any way with my altered and saddened life since Decr. 61.'[36]

RANDALL DAVIDSON (DEAN 1883-91)

Randall Davidson had been Chaplain to Archbishop Tait for six years and his son-in-law for four. He came to Queen Victoria's attention when Tait died on 3 December 1882. Within a few days Davidson had held the Queen's attention with an account of the Archbishop's last hours. The Queen met him in December 1882 and took to him at once,

Randall Davidson, Dean of Windsor 1883 to 1891, seen here as Bishop of Winchester (1895-1902), and wearing the robes of Prelate of the Order of the Garter. A photograph given to the Deanery by his widow.

noting that she 'was seldom more struck than I have been by his personality . . .'[37]

Presently he was passing on the late Archbishop's thoughts about his successor as Primate, which led to the appointment of Edward Benson. Queen Victoria then summoned Davidson to Osborne in January 1883 and began to confide in him.

When Dean Connor died, she asked the new Archbishop of Canterbury for Davidson, commenting that 'the only thing that might be said against his appointment is his youth. But surely that is a fault which recedes quickly . . .'[38] In Davidson, she commended his charm of manner, and his knowledge of society and the clergy.

Davidson accepted the call and was installed on 25 June 1883. He was not only Dean of Windsor but also Domestic Chaplain. In no time he had stepped into Gerald Wellesley's shoes as her advisor on church and other matters.

The funeral of Prince Leopold, Duke of Albany on 5 April 1884. The coffin had just descended into the Royal Vault. Sir Albert Woods, Garter King of Arms, pronouncing the styles and titles of the deceased prince. In those days there were screens to the right of the High Altar.

Born in 1848, he became Dean at the young age of 35. His health was never strong due to a shooting accident at Muirhouse in 1866, when a friend and he were out pursuing rabbits and his friend's gun accidentally went off, peppering his back with shotgun pellets at close range. He was an invalid for many months but two years later he won a cup at racquets at Oxford.

Davidson was a sound man. He never failed to complete a task, and his workload was immense. He found himself presiding over rather an elderly Chapter, and was soon a force of energetic change, tackling long-neglected problems such as the repair of the chapel roof, in particular the vaulting in the Nave, and the mullions of the windows in the clerestory.

In 1883 the question of the vaulting of the Nave provoked some controversy in the offices of the Society for the Protection of Ancient Buildings. They were concerned that the medieval vaulting was to be pulled down and replaced, whether or not this was necessary, and recommended that a committee should decide, not a particular individual.[39] Five years later the arms of twelve

Knights of the Garter were put into windows in the North Nave Aisle, and the tapestry of the 'Supper on the way to Emmaus' was hung on the wooden panels that then occupied the south side of the Quire altar (where Edward VII's tomb now is). The tapestry, originally given to Windsor by Lady Mordaunt in the reign of Charles II, was said by Canon Dalton, with his habitual conviction, to be a copy of a painting by Titian in 1509. In this case, Christ's head was based on Emperor Charles V of Austria, uncle of Catherine of Aragon, and the two disciples variously based on Philip II of Spain (his son) and Cardinal Ximenes (Prime Minister to King Philip II).[40]

Dean Davidson updated the fire precautions and addressed the chapel's heating problems. He introduced ladies' bible classes, and turned the Deanery into what Walford Davies called 'a choristers' paradise'. Even so some criticized his youth and one not so young Minor Canon was overheard referring to him as the 'Boy Dean'.[41]

Besides his duties in Chapter, he soon became a close spiritual advisor to Queen Victoria. By this time she was spending two months at Windsor from mid-February, some weeks after Easter, a month in June or July and part of the autumn there, from November until after 14 December, the anniversary of the death of the Prince Consort. Because the Prince Consort had died at Windsor and was buried at Frogmore, the Queen developed a special bond with the place.

Davidson soon had to help her through two crises, the first one the complicated and sensitive issue of her reaction to the death of John Brown, the Scottish ghillie to whom the Queen had become close, a matter which even this very sensitive advisor found hard to cope with. Brown had died in May 1883, just before Davidson arrived at Windsor. The second bereavement was as serious, but at least more conventional – the death of Prince Leopold, Duke of Albany, her fourth son.

Prince Leopold was another victim of haemophilia, and had died after a fall in Cannes in March 1884. He had expressed a wish to be buried in St George's Chapel, but Queen Victoria did not wish her son to lie in the 'gloomy, cold, dark' Royal Vault, so his coffin was transferred to the Albert Memorial Chapel, in June 1885. His sarcophagus depicts him in the uniform of the Seaforth Highlanders, the work of the sculptor, Sir J. Edgar Boehm.[42]

The Dean and his Sovereign often discussed death and grief, and even addressed the question of life beyond the grave. She told him that she had not been impressed by one senior cleric who consoled her when she became a widow, telling her: 'Henceforth you must remember that Christ Himself will be your husband.'[43] This she dismissed as 'twaddle'.

Davidson found himself confronted by a Sovereign who had almost made a virtue out of grieving. She was widely criticized for making servants bring hot water into the Prince Consort's bedroom each night, and keeping the Duchess of Kent's sitting room at Frogmore as she had left it. Davidson concluded that no one had ever suggested she give counter orders, and she never thought to do so, therefore these traditions continued. The Queen often received him in Prince Albert's room and so he talked to her frequently with the hot water steaming away in the background.

Most times they got on well, but there was one rift when he dared to suggest that she did not publish a further edition of her Highland journals. He did not entirely spell out his reasons, but he feared she would write extensively about John Brown, and that this would not serve her well.

When he preached to her in the Private Chapel or at Osborne, he was bidden to mention recent happenings at court, demises etc. He continued to advise her on church appointments, and was closely involved in issues concerning the marriages of her daughters. At the time of the Golden Jubilee in 1887 he and his wife entertained five present or future Sovereigns to tea at the Deanery, and when he left Windsor to become Bishop of Rochester in 1891, the Queen herself took tea with him at the Deanery to bid him farewell.

Even then the closeness did not cease. Queen Victoria insisted that he preach to her each May and

The tomb of Prince Leopold, Duke of Albany in the Albert Memorial Chapel. The effigy is by Sir J. Edgar Boehm.

at the Mausoleum on 14 December. She appointed him Clerk of the Closet, and thus a member of the Household. He conducted the funeral of the Duke of Clarence in 1892 (the Archbishop of Canterbury being away), was present at the wedding of the Duke of York (the future George V) to Princess May of Teck, and was acting chaplain to the Queen on one of her visits to Cimiez in the South of France. When he became Bishop of Winchester in 1895, Osborne, on the Isle of Wight, then fell within his diocese. Queen Victoria told him she wanted him to succeed Archbishop Benson at Canterbury when Benson collapsed and died during morning prayers at Hawarden Castle, staying with Gladstone, but other church figures thought him too young. Thwarted, the Queen refused to allow him to be appointed Bishop of London, ostensibly on health grounds.

Davidson was present at St Paul's for the Diamond Jubilee in 1897, wearing the robes of Prelate of the Order of the Garter. He was at the Queen's bedside when she breathed her last at Osborne, and a key figure at her funeral at St George's.

When he was appointed Archbishop of Canterbury in 1903, Princess Beatrice wrote to

ST GEORGE'S CHAPEL, WINDSOR CASTLE / 92

ABOVE Dean Philip Eliot, Dean of Windsor from 1891 to 1917. He lived a humble life despite the grandeur of the court.

OPPOSITE PAGE Two watercolours dated 1870 by A.Y. Nutt, who went on to be Chapel Surveyor from 1873 to 1912. The top one is of Denton's Commons, the lower one shows the south gateway to the Horseshoe Cloister, very much as it is today. St George's Chapel would be to the left.

congratulate him and said it was what her mother had always hoped for him. From a different point of view, the Duke of Argyll, husband of Princess Louise, wrote: 'I have always said you are one of the very few preachers who prevent me from falling asleep.'[44]

Albert Baillie, his chaplain at Rochester and a later Dean of Windsor, wrote that in his early days he was 'generally classed as a second-rate man who had gained prominence through court favour, but that by the time he left Rochester to be Bishop of Winchester, Canon Brooke declared: 'We are losing our Bishop who is certainly the greatest saint the Church of England has produced since the

Reformation, and perhaps in all time.'[45]

And so it was that this young chaplain who had caught Queen Victoria's attention in 1882, went on to be present at the death of Edward VII in 1910, to crown George V in 1911, and deal with the numerous ecclesiastical, political and diplomatic pressures that being Archbishop involved, until his retirement in 1928. He died peacefully on 25 May 1930.

PHILIP FRANK ELIOT (DEAN 1891-1917)

Randall Davidson naturally recommended his successor as Dean to the Queen. He noted that the Queen 'was in a tremendous fuss about it.'[46] There was even an idea of dividing the roles – having a Dean of Windsor and a Domestic Chaplain. In the end, one of the Canons was chosen, largely since, as his second wife, he had married Mary Pitt, a much-liked Maid of Honour to the Queen.

Eliot was born in 1835, so he was thirteen years older than his predecessor. He had a high reputation as a pastor, and had established a new parish at Bournemouth, to which he returned whenever possible. He was deemed both Christian and evangelical. He was an honorary Canon of Winchester and after his marriage to Mary Pitt, he was appointed a Canon at Windsor, dividing his time between Bournemouth and Windsor.

Eliot never succeeded in establishing the same rapport with Queen Victoria as had been enjoyed by Davidson, partly because she still relied on Davidson. He found the Queen monosyllabic when he dined with her, and sometimes came away complaining about the cold and the discomfort of his court dress, rather than the interest of the occasion.

As Domestic Chaplain he had to preach in the Private Chapel. The first time he preached, Queen Victoria noted that the service had been performed 'by the new Dean Eliot, who preached very nicely and reads very well.'[47] He did not approve of the Queen and her guests playing cards on Sundays and never took to court life.

Hardly had he become Dean than he faced two problems – one caused by the 'spread of Oxford Movement doctrine and ritual at the chapel'[48] and the other the perennial problem of the discipline and duties of the Military Knights. Ritual was such an issue in those days that Bishop Edward King had been tried for sacrilegious practices in church in 1890.

The Military Knights had been a problem for many centuries. There was a problem when some of them wanted to trade from their houses. There was a battle with Colonel Francis Maude, VC, whom the Dean would not promote as he was a discharged bankrupt. Maude declared he would petition the Lord Chancellor, and then he offended Queen Victoria by writing an article for the Christmas edition of *Home Chat*, which revealed details of life in the Queen's Household. Eliot called all the Military Knights in and read the letter from Sir Arthur Bigge expressing the monarch's displeasure. This kept them in order for the rest of the Queen's reign.

In the days of Wellesley and Davidson, the Dean was in permanent residence, while the Canons were little more than an advisory body. This worked well since they had dominant personalities. Dean Eliot did not, and as a result the College of St George ceased to be a 'truly corporate community.'[49]

During the last decade of Queen Victoria's life, there were yet more royal burials. Prince Albert Victor, Duke of Clarence, elder son of the Prince of Wales, was second in line to the throne. In 1891 he became engaged to Princess May of Teck, to the delight of the Queen, but he succumbed to pneumonia at Sandringham and died in a state of delirium on 14 January 1892. Had he lived, the Duke of Clarence would have become King in succession to his father, Edward VII. His funeral took place in the chapel, after which the coffin was returned to the Albert Memorial Chapel.

The Duke of Clarence was buried in the most splendid tomb in the centre of the Albert Memorial Chapel, where the base of the proposed tomb of Henry VIII had once stood.

Within days of the Duke's death, the Prince and Princess of Wales summoned Alfred Gilbert to Sandringham, because he had been a pupil of Boehm's and commissioned him to design a tomb suitable to the role the young Duke would have held had he lived, a role which Queen Victoria described as 'the greatest position there is'. While at Sandringham, Gilbert designed what he called 'the ensemble of the entire monument'.[50] On his return to London he locked himself in his studio for four days. During that time he produced a wax model of the Duke, recumbent on a sarcophagus, with a kneeling angel bearing a wreath of victory above his head, and a putto at his feet. The Prince of Wales inspected the work twice, and on 6 March Gilbert showed it to Queen Victoria at Windsor. She pronounced it 'beautiful'. [51]

Gilbert was pleased to discover that his concept for the tomb matched Henry VII's tomb in Westminster Abbey by Pietro Torrigiano, the Florentine sculptor, whose work had inspired Wolsey in planning his own tomb. Gilbert noted that the Princess of Wales wished her son's remains to 'rest in mid-air. The kneeling angel at his head, supporting the elaborately wrought crown, as a canopy over the figure, is symbolic of the promise of Eternal Life, the crown representing the twelve-gated City spoken of in the book of Revelation.'[52]

The effigy was made in mixed media, Gilbert even using aluminium, which was unusual. It depicts the Duke of Clarence with white marble face and hands, wearing the uniform of Xth Hussars, made of bronze and brass. This was inspired by the tomb of Queen Victoria's father, the Duke of Kent, at that time in the nave of St George's Chapel, where the Prince Imperial's cenotaph now rests. As Gilbert had never seen the Duke of Clarence in life, he worked from photographs and a watercolour by William Simpson of the corpse, surrounded with flowers, and Canon Dalton, the Duke's tutor, helped with advice. Clarence's cloak and the angel above his head are made of aluminium.

The body of the Duke of Clarence was moved into his tomb in March 1893, when the tomb was still far from complete. In due course, his effigy was

placed there and surrounded by a grille in polychromed bronze and aluminium, with angels and saints. For these, Gilbert revitalized the lost wax technique, which enabled him to create the complex and especially fine small statues.

In July 1898 Queen Victoria personally placed the ivory and aluminium cast of the St George on the tomb, thus in effect dedicating it.

All this took Gilbert a long time to create, taking him away from more lucrative commissions. For a time while at work on the tomb, he lived in the Henry III Tower, which gave his creditors the idea that he had acquired a fortune. They harassed him and he was finally declared bankrupt in 1901. Then Edward VII lost patience with him when he foolishly sold versions and replicas of four of the figures or 'working models' as he called them for £1,600.

A detail of the tomb of the Duke of Clarence, who died in 1892, showing the Duke's effigy above his tomb, with an angel, bent over in sorrow, holding a crown on high over his head. The work of the sculptor Alfred Gilbert (1854-1934), and the central tomb in the Albert Memorial Chapel.

Gilbert retreated to Bruges, leaving five of the niches in the grille empty. He was finally commanded to return home by a slightly mistrustful George V in 1926, and the missing figures were added to the tomb as late as March 1928. In the end the tomb had taken 36 years to complete.

One of the saints on the tomb is The Virgin, placed there partly to recognise that the chapel used to be a Lady Chapel, and partly to represent the figure of Queen Alexandra, mourning. St Edward the Confessor was based on the painter, George

The figure of St Elisabeth of Hungary on the side of the Duke of Clarence's tomb. St Elisabeth was an ancestor of the Prince Consort, and is thought to have the face of Nina Cust, one of 'The Souls', and a friend of Alfred Gilbert.

Watts, and St George on Burne-Jones. The figure of St Elisabeth of Hungary is thought to have the face of Nina Cust, wife of Harry Cust and one of 'The Souls' – the well-known social group, including politicians and intellectuals, whose interests were primarily artistic.

St Elisabeth is there because Queen Victoria wanted to recognise her as an ancestor of the Prince Consort, she having been the wife of the Landgrave of Thuringia. St Catherine of Egypt is certainly

based on Violet, Duchess of Rutland, also a 'Soul'. Both Violet and Nina Cust were patrons and friends of Gilbert.

The result was one of the most magnificent royal tombs ever, described by Gilbert's biographer, the art historian, Richard Dorment as 'a neo-Gothic extravaganza.'[53]

* * * * *

After a suitable interval for mourning, Princess May was re-engaged to the next in line, the Duke of York (later George V). Her parents both died before Queen Victoria and they too were placed in the Royal Vault – Princess Mary Adelaide, Duchess of Teck (first cousin of Queen Victoria, and a granddaughter of George III) in 1897 and Prince Francis, Duke of Teck in 1900.

The Queen also placed a memorial in the Bray Chantry to Prince Christian Victor, her grandson, who died in Pretoria from fever during the South African War, in 1900.

A seemingly happier occasion was the wedding in July 1891 of Princess Christian's younger daughter, Princess Victoria of Schleswig-Holstein (later Princess Marie Louise) to Prince Aribert of Anhalt. The Dean commented that at the dinner on the Sunday night: 'The music was certainly beautiful, and I think it was such a good idea of the Queen to have this Sacred Music for all her foreign guests on Sunday evening, instead of their playing cards, etc.' He thought the wedding itself 'magnificent as a scene . . . the whole of St George's filled from end to end with men in magnificent uniforms and ladies in magnificent dresses.'[54] Unfortunately the marriage was not a success, the groom proving less than satisfactory as a husband, and the princess was soon back to share the spinsterhood of her elder sister. As Princess Helena Victoria and Princess Marie Louise, they were frequently at Windsor in the next half century.

The long reign of Queen Victoria came to an end at Osborne on 22 January 1901, with her family around her, and the faithful Randall Davidson there to give them support. A few days after her death Walter Parratt brought some of the men and boys of

On a winter day as gloomy and damp as this photograph by Sir Benjamin Stone suggests, the cortège bearing the coffin of Queen Victoria arrived at the West Steps.

the choir from Windsor to Osborne to sing hymns and anthems in the little chapel, which all the Royal Family present much appreciated.[55]

Back in St George's Chapel, Dean Eliot compared Queen Victoria favourably to some of her predecessors: 'Their most devoted subjects could never have affirmed they were wise. They thought foolishly; they spoke foolishly, they acted foolishly.' He pointed out that this had all ended with the Queen who entirely understood the role of a constitutional monarch, and had thus made 'democratic ideas and democratic institutions entirely compatible with perfect loyalty to the Throne.'[56]

The Queen's coffin was brought over the Solent in the Royal Yacht, a scene that Randall Davidson described as 'beyond question the most solemn and moving of which I have ever had experience.'[57] The funeral in the chapel on 1 February was very late, if not as late as Hanoverian services, because the horses pulling the coffin breaking their traces at Windsor station.

Queen Victoria's coffin rested in the Albert Memorial Chapel awaiting burial. The 8th Duke of Northumberland was on guard in the chapel and recalled: 'It was so full of flowers that the walls were completely covered. Some of the officers fainted from the scent during the night.'[58]

Three days later a further solemn procession followed the coffin to the Mausoleum at Frogmore. In the Mausoleum, the grave was open and the coffin of Queen Victoria was placed next to that of the Prince Consort. The Royal Family filed across

the platform to pay their respects. Three generations of future kings were there. Davidson described the scene:

> The King [Edward VII] came first alone, but, instead of simply walking by, he knelt down by the grave. Then the Queen [Alexandra] followed, leading the little Prince Edward [the future Edward VIII] by the hand. She knelt down, but the little boy was frightened, and the King took him gently and made him kneel down beside him, and the three, in perfect silence, were there together, a sight not soon to be forgotten.[59]

ABOVE The heavily scented wreaths in the Albert Memorial Chapel after Queen Victoria's funeral. The Dean's Cloister was also filled with extravagant wreaths and floral tributes. Photographed by Sir Benjamin Stone on 3 February 1901.

BELOW By the end of the nineteenth century St George's Chapel was very much on the tourist route for visitors to Windsor. This photograph of a group of them was taken by Sir Benjamin Stone on the West steps of the Chapel in May 1900. Sir Benjamin is the bearded figure, second left.

FIVE

Restoration and Renewal

KING EDWARD VII did not take a particular interest in St George's or make a noticeable mark, though he had been baptised and married in the chapel. Following the death of Queen Victoria, the atmosphere at Windsor changed. The new King kept his courtiers mainly in London, so the College of St George lost its regular interaction with the Court. Inevitably this had an isolating effect.

The King did attend two royal weddings in the Chapel. On 10 February 1904 Prince Leopold's daughter, Princess Alice of Albany married Prince Alexander of Teck (brother of the future Queen Mary). They were later better known as the Earl of Athlone and Princess Alice, Countess of Athlone, and for some years lived in the Henry III Tower, the Earl being Governor of Windsor Castle from 1931 until his death in 1957. In old age Princess Alice could be seen dipping under the rope to lay some

A portrait of Edward VII in Garter robes by Harold Speed (1872-1957), painted in 1905.

Princess Alice, Countess of Athlone, the last surviving granddaughter of Queen Victoria, photographed by the author, at the Royal Windsor Horse Show in 1967.

flowers on the tomb of her father in the Albert Memorial Chapel.

The other wedding was that of Princess Margaret of Connaught to Crown Prince Gustav Adolph of Sweden on 15 June 1905. She was the grandmother of the present King of Sweden. She died of peritonitis in 1920.

Edward VII effected a welcome change when, in 1905, he transferred 'the control and discipline' of the Military Knights by letters Patent from the Dean and Canons to the Governor and Constable of the

From left to right Bishop Alfred Barry (Canon of Windsor and son of the architect Sir Charles Barry), Canon John Dalton, KCVO, CMG, whose presence loomed over the College of St George from 1884 to 1931, and Dean Eliot. A photograph by Sir Benjamin Stone.

Castle.[1] Nevertheless they remain to this day a part of the College of St George. Two years later he put their affairs further in order by commanding their regular attendance at Sunday Mattins, obit days and certain other occasions. He changed their uniforms to include the white sword belt. After these changes everyone was happier.

Dean Eliot still had many years to serve, though now his duties were principally to the chapel and not as domestic chaplain. He was responsible for enriching the chapel services. In 1907 the King gave him permission to restore Garter mantles as the correct vestment for the Dean and Canons at Garter and obit services. Murrey cassocks (called Murrey after mulberry blue – an armorial colour of Edward IV, but veering over the years to a number of different shades from a reddish purple to rust-colour) were introduced for the choir in 1911, and bowing to the altar became an accepted practice. He introduced early communion services, and he gilded and restored the reredos behind the high altar.

In an attempt to get the patron saint of England better recognised in the Borough, he introduced a St George's Day service for local Boy Scouts, Church Lads Brigade and Navy League Lads.

The absence of King and Court was not the only reason why this was a less happy phase for the College of St George. Another was the presence of Canon John Dalton, a legendary figure in the life of the College, who 'constantly fought against the leadership of the Dean'.[2] Lord Stamfordham, George V's Private Secretary, told Eliot's successor, Dean Baillie that Dalton had made Dean Eliot 'an unhappy man for a quarter of a century.'[3]

It had become almost a tradition that at least one Canon made the life of the Dean difficult, and the Dean was frequently reminded that he was only 'primus inter pares'. When Dean Hamilton arrived in 1944, it was Canon Anthony Deane, who made his life 'miserable'. A later Canon, the magnificently bearded Alec Vidler, at Windsor from 1948 to 1956, explained the problem:

It is notorious that cathedral and collegiate chapters are prone to be quarrelsome. I once knew a Canon of Ely Cathedral (there were six of them then) who was said to be the only one on speaking terms with all the others. I came to understand at Windsor how that state of affairs could arise. Each member of a cathedral or collegiate chapter is likely previously to have been the head of some institution, whether a parish, a diocese, a college or a school, and so finds it very difficult to be in a subordinate position, to act as one of a team, and to bow to collegiate judgments. [4]

John Neale Dalton was born in 1839, ordained by Bishop Samuel Wilberforce and appointed a Canon in 1885, having been assistant curate at Whippingham Church, on the Isle of Wight, and later governor (tutor) to the Duke of Clarence and the Duke of York (the future George V) from 1871 to 1885 (accompanying them to Dartmouth and later to sea in HMS *Bacchante*). He served as Domestic Chaplain to George V from 1892 until his own death in 1931. Dean Baillie wrote of him:

Though Dalton's intellect was tremendous and his learning great, no one ever thought of going to him for enlightenment. He used his knowledge to correct or reprove, seldom to encourage. He was without disciples or followers.[5]

Dalton had extraordinary energy and vitality, and was known for his powerful and histrionic reading of the lessons. Canon Deane recalled how, when reading dialogue, he would 'attribute to one speaker a thunderous bass, the other would be made to answer in a high falsetto.' George V used to say: 'Let us go and hear the Canon roar!'[6] When a visitor commented to the Virger on the remarkable reading of a particular lesson, the Virger replied: 'Ah, sir, but you should hear him throw down Jezebel!'[7]

Significantly Dean Baillie devoted the five pages at the beginning of the Windsor section of his memoirs to the character of Canon Dalton, a brilliant essay which it would be more than tempting to re-print in full.[8] He found Dalton 'a man beyond the difficulties of whose character and personality I was not once able to penetrate.' He wrote of his vigour, vitality, force of mind, how 'intensely irritating' he was. He wrote: 'He approached every meeting determined to fight over the smallest details, only to prevent his colleagues, whom he despised, from having their way. This point of view in a strong man inevitably made his colleagues miserable.'

Baillie found that when he first arrived at St George's, Dalton had prejudiced the entire community against him, and it took more than two years before the Dean realised what had been going on. He concluded that he was an Elizabethan – his rollicking humour reminded him of an expurgated Rabelais, the gusto of his company at dinner of Falstaff.

Sir Edward Ford cited another difficulty with Dalton: 'He had the ear of George V'[9] or as *The Times* put it, the King was to him 'a friend who had a most special place in his affection,'[10] Dalton spending part of each summer holiday with him at Balmoral or Sandringham, which caused him to ignore 'the meaning or necessity of corporate responsibility'.[11] Walford Davies, the Organist of the Chapel, had an interesting theory about him,

Charles, 9th Duke of Marlborough, wearing Garter riband and star. He was appointed a KG by Edward VII in 1902, attended various Chapters of the Garter, but his cousin Winston Churchill had to appeal to the King that he be allowed to stay for luncheon as he was separated from his wife, Consuelo Vanderbilt and thus normally barred from court.

believing he had a total disregard of self:

Explosive behaviour in such men seems an accidental tribute of high spiritual vision. Possessed by the vision, they become reckless to all else, including the impression their words and voices may make. Canon Dalton explained to me one Sunday evening, in humblest fashion, that, when he read, his voice 'would go like that!' He intimated a child-like inability to improve it. Had he consciously, and for effect, used his whole unique vocal gamut of two octaves, from stentorian power to his almost uncanny, and even mischievous, whispering, he might have been a famous actor, but he never could have

An uncomfortable encounter. Edward VII, the Shah of Persia (Muzaffer-ed-Din) and Queen Alexandra on the royal yacht, *Victoria and Albert*, in August 1902, during the Shah's state visit. The King refused to give the Shah the Order of the Garter, causing something of a diplomatic incident. In this photograph all three are wearing Persian orders.

been the radiant, valiant, and unconscious influencer of such of his fellows as try to hold the fearless Christian faith which seemed to fashion his own life and words, and radiated from his reading of the Scriptures.[12]

* * * * *

Edward VII took an interest in the Order of the Garter, but not in relation to St George's Chapel itself. He never held a Garter ceremony there, but he revived the practice of appointing Ladies of the Garter, assigning a stall and banner to Queen Alexandra in 1901.

He created 24 Knights of the Garter, of whom 15 were members of the British or foreign royal families. Of the others appointed, five were Dukes, and the others prominent Marquesses and Earls. Perhaps the most interesting was Archduke Franz Ferdinand of Austria, who was assassinated at Sarajevo in 1914, and whose death precipitated the Great War.

Edward VII showed irate reluctance to create the Shah of Persia a Garter Knight when Lord Lansdowne invited him on a State Visit in 1902, luring him to Britain with the promise that the Order would be bestowed. Lansdowne even had some non-Christian insignia drawn up and thought that the King had approved these. The King was on board the Royal Yacht *Victoria and Albert* when the finished designs arrived and was so enraged that he threw them through a porthole. He refused to give the Shah the Garter, and the Shah duly departed in some umbrage. Later the King relented when Lansdowne threatened to resign, and sent Viscount

Edward VII's coffin in the Royal Vault after his funeral in May 1910. When Queen Alexandra died in 1925, his coffin was brought up to lie beside hers in the Albert Memorial Chapel. Both were later placed in a sarcophagus to the right of the High Altar.

The effigies of Edward VII and Queen Alexandra by the Australian sculptor, Sir Bertram Mackennal (1863-1931). At the King's feet Mackennal included the King's favourite dog, Caesar, who walked in his funeral procession.

Downe to Teheran to invest him on a Garter mission in February 2003. There were other Garter Missions during the reign – to Madrid, Württemberg and Tokyo.

The King held two Garter chapters at Windsor. In November 1906 he invested his son-in-law, King Haakon of Norway, and in November 1909, he invested King Manoel II of Portugal, then just 20 years old. The following year King Manoel was driven out of Portugal in a revolution. He settled at Fulwell Park in Twickenham, and took part in the four Garter ceremonies between 1911 and 1914, dying in 1932, aged 42.

Edward VII died at Buckingham Palace on 6 May 1910, like Queen Victoria, in the presence of Randall Davidson, by this time Archbishop of Canterbury. The funeral procession made its way to Windsor. Queen Emma of the Netherlands came over from Claremont to watch the procession from the roof of the Henry III Tower, where Prince and Princess Alexander of Teck (later the Athlones) had their apartments. Prince Alexander's three-year old daughter, May (later Lady May Abel Smith), was with them. As the gun carriage passed by, the little girl exclaimed: 'What! Uncle Bertie in a box?'[13]

The King's body was placed in the Royal Vault

after his funeral. The tomb bearing his effigy by Sir Bertram Mackennal, on which Sir Edwin Lutyens also worked as architect, was unveiled on the South Side of the High Altar in 1921. A particular touch was to depict Edward VII's dog Caesar, (who had walked so memorably in his funeral procession) at the King's feet, in the place where other kings have the heraldic lion.

Queen Alexandra lived on until 20 November 1925. Because the Quire of St George's Chapel was being restored, it had been impossible to have the funeral service there, to the great disappointment of Dean Baillie, who complained in the press that St George's Chapel was being sidelined. Instead the funeral service was held at Westminster Abbey, following a procession through the snow-covered streets of London.

On 29 November 1925 Queen Alexandra's coffin was committed in the Albert Memorial Chapel, in the presence of George V and Queen Mary, the King of Denmark, the King and Queen of Norway and other members of the Royal Family.

Just before Christmas that year, the coffin of King Edward VII was brought up from the Royal Vault, and the two coffins lay side by side in front of the altar, obscured from public view by the sarcophagus

ABOVE George V in Garter robes. During his reign the chapel was extensively restored.

RIGHT Queen Mary painted in Garter robes in 1914, a portrait by Sir William Llewellyn (1858-1941).

of the Duke of Clarence. The young Hector Bolitho saw the coffins in the Albert Memorial Chapel on 1 May 1926: 'The coffins were covered by old flags. It was a solemn moment, standing so near the dead King, unburied after almost sixteen years'.[14]

There the coffins remained until they could be placed in the sarcophagus by the altar in St George's on 22 April 1927. King George V and Queen Mary saw the tomb at Evensong the following Sunday, although the sarcophagus remained draped for some years until Queen Alexandra's effigy was ready.

GEORGE V (KING 1910-36)

There had not been a Garter ceremony at Windsor since the days of George III. One of the first things the new King did was to command one. On that day the Knights not only processed down the hill but

also back up again after the ceremony. It took place on 10 June, twelve days before the Coronation. The King and Queen Mary (now a Lady of the Garter) walked in the procession as did the Duke of Connaught, Prince Arthur of Connaught, and King Manoel of Portugal, in exile in England since the year before. George V invested his son, the Prince of Wales (later Edward VIII), but although the young prince took his stall in the chapel, he was not actually installed. There were similar annual Garter ceremonies of this kind in the next three years until the outbreak of the First World War.

War broke out in August 1914, and more parochially, a terrible row erupted at Windsor over the installation of electric light in the Quire. Being an enthusiast of electric light, Canon Dalton had introduced it into the Nave without complaints. In 1914 he wished to put it in large candelabra in the chancel, leaving the stall lights in the Quire as candles. Dalton got the King to agree to this, but Eliot was perturbed and asked for the King's approval in writing. An ambiguous answer was received from Lord Stamfordham indicating that the King had had second thoughts, and was not now prepared to 'sanction the general adoption of electric light in the choir.'[15]

Immediately after this came another communication from Stamfordham accusing the Chapter of negligence. John Fortescue, the Royal Librarian, had made a thorough inspection of the chapel fabric and discovered damage to the Oxenbridge Chantry, flaking in various works of art and that the Emmaus tapestry was badly crumpled. This fracas continued for some time, Eliot conceding that he wished to restore any damaged artworks so long as this was done in keeping, but rejecting the electric light experiment as giving too strong a light.

The Times had been pressing for the removal of the Garter banners of the Kaiser and his son since September 1914. In 1915 Queen Alexandra made a rare intervention in political matters writing to the King to urge him to sanction the removal of 'those hateful German banners in our sacred Church.' In earlier times, Knights of the Garter had been removed from the Order on account of treason. There were several such examples, some twenty Knights being degraded between 1387 and 1716, of whom six were reinstated. The most famous was Richard Nevill, Earl of Warwick (KG, 1460) – 'Warwick the Kingmaker', and the most recent, James Butler, 2nd Duke of Ormonde (KG, 1688), who originally supported William of Orange and was attainted as a supporter of James Stuart. He was degraded in 1716.

On 13 May 1915 George V reluctantly sanctioned the removal of the following eight banners:

Francis Joseph, Emperor of Austria, KG (1867)
William II, Emperor of Germany, KG (1877)
Ernest Augustus, Duke of Brunswick, KG (1878)
Prince Henry of Prussia, KG (1889)
Ernst Ludwig, Grand Duke of Hesse, KG (1892)
Crown Prince William of Prussia, KG (1901)

Edward, Prince of Wales (later Edward VIII, and following his Abdication, Duke of Windsor) in Garter robes, by Sir Arthur Cope, 1912.

Charles Edward, Duke of Coburg, KG (1902)
King William II of Württemberg, KG (1904)

Many of these Knights were closely related to the King. Four were grandsons of Queen Victoria. The Kaiser and his brother, Prince Henry of Prussia, were sons of Empress Frederick, her eldest daughter. The Duke of Coburg was a particularly unfortunate case being also the 2nd Duke of Albany, posthumous son of Prince Leopold, and brother of Princess Alice, Countess of Athlone. He had been brought up as an Englishman and then obliged to become a German when he was chosen to succeed his uncle, Alfred, Duke of Edinburgh, as Duke of Coburg, in 1900. As recently as June 1914 he had been a respected visitor to Britain, calling on his widowed mother, and being appointed an honorary

Prince Henry of Prussia, younger brother of the Kaiser, and a grandson of Queen Victoria. One of the Stranger Knights of the Garter, whose banners were removed from above their stalls during the Great War, in 1915.

DCL at Oxford, at which ceremony the Public Orator, A.D. Godley, had declared: 'Saxe-Coburg is hardly a foreign country . . .'[16]

The Grand Duke of Hesse was the son of Princess Alice, Queen Victoria's second daughter, and the Duke of Brunswick was 3rd Duke of Cumberland in the peerage of Great Britain. He was the son of the blind King George V of Hanover, and thus a great-grandson of George III. He was married to Queen Alexandra's sister, Princess Thyra of Denmark. Crown Prince William was the Kaiser's son and thus another grandson of Queen Victoria.

On 14 May, the day after the announcement, a gang of workmen entered the chapel in a private ceremony after Mattins. Garter King of Arms joined Dean Eliot, the Canons and Minor Canons, and the Governor of the Military Knights. The chapel was locked until the knightly achievements had been removed, but in a sensible gesture to modern times, the stall plates of the alien Knights were left in place for posterity.

There was a sequel to this. In 1959, Prince Louis of Hesse, the Grand Duke of Hesse's son, wrote to Lord Mountbatten, who had found his father's stall plate in the chapel:

Thank you very much for your letter about Papa's stall plate in St George's Chapel. I am astonished and pleased that it is still there, as he and all other German Knights of the Garter were officially deprived of the order during the First World War. This was brought on by Charley Coburg's idiotic act of sending back his British Orders and decorations after the declaration of war (so Papa told me). All the same Papa always considered himself as a Knight of the Garter as he had received it from Queen Victoria who had said to him 'Wear it as honourably as your father did' - and Papa thought that he had done so. I remember he had a talk about this with George V after the war and the King thought the whole thing rather ridiculous...[17]

In 1927, in discussion with the Foreign Office, some years after hostilities had ceased, when German relations and figures like King Boris of Bulgaria and Count Mensdorff were again being entertained at Windsor and Balmoral, George V reinstated them into the Royal Victorian Order, and reserved the right to do the same for ex-enemy Knights of the Garter, though in fact he never did reinstate any of them.

In 1917, in his eightieth year, Dean Eliot's health deteriorated sharply and on 25 August, after several heart attacks, he resigned the deanery. He died a few weeks later, on 1 November, and was buried, not at Windsor, but at Holy Trinity, Bournemouth. He was described as being free 'from any suspicion of narrowness or bigotry', and it was noted: 'Although he held so exalted a position he was no courtier. He lived a humble life amidst the surroundings of the greatest Court in the world and finished his life coincidentally on All Saints Day.'[18]

It was not unusual for a Canon of Windsor to succeed as Dean. Even though he was by then 78, Canon Dalton hoped that George V, who had once recommended him for the deanery of Westminster, might now grant him Windsor. But the King feared 'further discord' and the appointment went to

Albert Baillie. It was said that on learning the news, 'Dalton gave the King one of the worst hours he had ever spent.'[19]

ALBERT BAILLIE (DEAN 1917-45)

Albert Victor Baillie was a godson of Queen Victoria. His father, Evan Baillie, a diplomat, came from Inverness, and his mother, Lady Frances Bruce, youngest daughter of 7th Earl of Elgin and Kincardine (the man who saved the Parthenon marbles), was a Lady-in-Waiting to the Duchess of Edinburgh. His grandfather once danced with Queen Marie Antoinette. An aunt was the famous Lady Augusta Stanley, Lady-in-Waiting to the Duchess of Kent and Woman of the Bedchamber to Queen Victoria, and wife of Very Rev Arthur Stanley, Dean of Westminster. After she died in 1876, Baillie and his widowed mother lived with Dean Stanley at Westminster, where he encountered men such as Tennyson, Browning and Matthew Arnold. Later he knew and rather disliked Oscar Wilde.

Ordained in 1888, Baillie progressed to being Randall Davidson's chaplain when Davidson was Bishop of Rochester. In 1898 he was appointed Rector and Rural Dean of Rugby, was an honorary Canon of Worcester from 1905 to 1908 and in 1912 of St Michael's, Coventry. He moved to Windsor happily in 1917.

Baillie was no stranger to the castle, having been taken to visit his godmother, Queen Victoria, when a child. He had watched the passing show at Prince Leopold's wedding in 1882. He remembered Dean Wellesley, while Canon Hugh Pearson, at Windsor from 1876 to 1882, was a close family friend. When he arrived at Windsor, he noted Lord Stamfordham's warning about Canon Dalton, and Randall Davidson told him: 'Your great difficulty will be Canon Dalton.'[20]

Besides the Dalton problem, Dean Baillie's early years were made yet sadder by the illness of his wife, who after five years of suffering, died in 1924. After her death he was well looked after by a butler and other servants.

Once his colleagues had made up their own

Dean Albert Victor Baillie, Dean of Windsor from 1917 to 1945.

minds about Dean Baillie, they tended to like him. Canon Deane found him self-effacing, Sir Walter Parratt, the organist: 'a staunch and kindly friend.'[21] One of the features of his time as dean was his generous hospitality and his entertainment of theatrical figures and of the young. When new people arrived at the College, such as Walford Davies to be organist in 1927, or the Rev Harry Blackburne as Canon in 1931, the Dean was happy to take them in until their houses were ready for them, Davies staying with him for three months. It was said that many 'used him unsparingly.'[22]

The theatre was one of his great interests. Ivor Novello brought Alfred Lunt and Lynn Fontanne to lunch with him, as a result of which they put on a play for him in the Deanery. Eight guardsmen were regularly entertained to tea by the Dean. Boys from

Hungary (where he holidayed), including today one nonagenarian survivor, George Lane, stayed with him for long periods, and he all but adopted Hector Bolitho, who lived at the Deanery from 1926 to 1932. At first Bolitho was intimidated by the Dean, particularly on the telephone, when he was 'gruff and rude', but he learned that the Dean 'treated telephones as if they were vipers, to be dropped as soon as possible.'[23] Presently they collaborated on a number of excellent books.

One who knew the Dean well was Sir Edward Ford. He was at the bar in 1938 and went to see the Dean in his study to ask if his mother could rent a house in the Horseshoe Cloisters. The Dean, who was smoking a cigar, agreed and she lived there for some years. Ford recalled that the Dean cut an impressive figure. One evening he took them to the theatre, wearing an astrakhan coat, and to dinner at the Garrick, then back to Windsor in his car.[24]

Dean Baillie's most important achievement at Windsor was the extensive restoration work in the chapel between 1920 and 1930. The work cost £200,000 and only just averted disaster. The fabric had received little attention in the eighteenth century, and had not Sir Christopher Wren strengthened the roof in 1682, it might have been beyond repair.

A survey was carried out by the Chapel's architect, Sir Harold Brakspear, in 1918, which highlighted serious problems. The great tie-beams of oak, given by Bishop Beauchamp when the chapel was built, did not rest sufficiently on the walls; the deathwatch beetle had wrought its customary havoc; foundations were unsound, and the cracks in the roof were so alarming that there was danger of the vault caving in.

In 1920 Brakspear presented his report to the Dean and Canons. It ended with the ominous words: 'I therefore solemnly warn you that, in my opinion, unless the repairs are undertaken, serious consequences will result and that there is very grave danger of collapse.'[25] Not for nothing did Dean Baillie describe the work as 'possessed of quite exceptional perplexities.'[26]

Brakspear's report was based on his visual examination without the benefit of scaffolding, but proved sound. Originally it was hoped that the vaulting could be restored by grouting, undertaking two bays at a time, but when the work started, the situation revealed itself as considerably more serious than first realised.

The Chapel's wooden roof was in a state of decay. Some of the beams dating back to the reign of Edward IV needed replacing. They all needed to be lengthened and fixed more securely to the wall. As the men began their work, the cracks in the vaulting grew alarmingly and a platform had to be constructed the length of the Quire with shoring onto the vaulting itself.

Henry VII's builders had made no attempt to bond the springers into Edward IV's original walls. They had been built against the walls and were supported only by thin pilasters. It was remarkable that the vaulting had ever stayed up. By 1920 the walls were no longer vertical and the upper stonework had moved out of alignment by seven inches, and later the unsupported part of the roof by ten inches in the centre. 'A heritage of jerry-building,' declared the Dean.[27]

Worse was to follow. When the plaster was removed from the vaulting, two enormous cracks were discovered extending the length of the Quire. The entire vaulting had to be taken down and re-set. The flying buttresses had perished. The original stonework was seen to have been cemented over in the eighteenth century, while some of the buttresses were buckling. They were re-built. Cement had been used to cover the tracery of the windows in the eighteenth century.

The conclusion was that while Edward IV's builders had constructed a sound and secure building, the more recent additions and restorations in the times of Henry VII, Henry VIII, Christopher Wren, George III, and by Sir Gilbert Scott in the 1840s had all left much to be desired.

The roof was held up by four stone pillars, 3½ feet square and 55 feet high, and buttresses had to be built to support it. There was a chalk pit below

the whole of the west end of the chapel and the Beaufort Chapel needed proper foundations. The Urswick Chantry had also suffered due to the great weight of Princess Charlotte's memorial placed upon it. Since 1914 there had been scaffolding over both chapels. Some improvements were made and Dean Urswick's fine ironwork screen was re-placed in front of Princess Charlotte's memorial.

In 1929 the glass in the West Window was rearranged by Dr Montague James, Provost of Eton, who was the fount of knowledge on such matters, evidently improving still further on the 1841 reorganisation. He grouped the categories together and moved some of the better-preserved lights to the lower tiers of the window. Some more new glass went, but the Willement glass remained.

Other improvements were the moving of the two oak screens that previously stood in the bays where the tombs of Henry VI and Edward VII lay to act as screens and doors between the north and south Quire aisles. The heraldic bosses in the roof were re-enhanced. An altar was placed in the Rutland Chapel for services with small congregations, and the huge organ case was moved from the centre to the sides. This was done for practical reasons in connection with the working of the organ, but affords a much fuller view of the vaulting from both Nave and Quire.

Fundraising to meet the expenses was a complex matter. As has been seen, St George's Chapel is a collegiate church, the Chapel, cloisters and many houses around them being a freehold property within Windsor Castle. The 1867 Act of Parliament had left the Chapel in dire financial straits, unsupported by adequate funds. The College had surrendered its ancient lands and endowments in exchange for an annuity of £14,400. This figure remained fixed, while the ancient endowments were used to benefit the clergy in the country at large. Maintenance of the buildings and the cost of all the salaries were the sole responsibility of the Dean and Canons.

By the time of the 1920s restoration, large sums were required. The Dean felt unable to launch a public appeal since there had lately been one for Westminster Abbey. George V himself was an early donor. The First World War had placed the Knights of the Garter under financial strain.

However, they raised the first £25,000. Sir Campbell Stuart, of *The Times*, produced a man called Sydney Walton, who liked to remain in the background, but took pleasure from undertaking certain causes as labours of love. He had begun work as an office boy in Bishop Auckland, risen to work for Lord Rhondda in the First World War, and given voluntary assistance of great importance to a number of Government departments during the years of war. He was also a publicist.

Walton assisted the Dean by leading him to 'men who made money without yet having found a cause to interest them.' They had to be chosen with care, since there was a danger that some of the potential donors might prove to have made their fortunes in ways that would reflect ill on the appeal. Substantial contributions came from 1st Viscount Cowdray, a contractor, who had made a fortune in Mexico and later completed the Blackwall Tunnel and extended Dover Harbour, and who is commemorated near the North Door, and by Lord Woolavington, a well-known distiller and philanthropist, who twice won the Derby, and who gave £50,000 to the King for the restoration Both men received GCVOs.

Other benefactors assisted the College to raise £180,000. No money came to the Chapel from the Ecclesiastical Commission.

Walton led them to Frederick Minter, the London builder (F.G. Minter Ltd), who regularly made up the monthly deficit of £2,000. He placed new buttresses on the Bray and Rutland Chantries to add extra support. Furthermore he volunteered to make his own contribution, creating new King's Beasts (which had originally been on the roof until Wren removed them in an attempt to lighten the pressure) as a renewed counter-balance, visible on the skyline from miles around. The beasts were made in his own yard. Minter's son, who was also called Frederick (1887-1976), worked with him.

Some of the Queen's Beasts on the roof of St George's Chapel, a gift to the chapel by F.G. Minter.

Old Mr Minter died before the restoration was completed, but his son was created CVO in 1931 and KCVO in 1935, for his help with the restoration, and later GCVO in 1959 (for similar services to the Queen's Chapel of the Savoy).

Some time before the restoration was completed, an invitation had been received from the Canadian Education Society for the choir to tour Canada. In 1927, while their activities in the Chapel were curtailed by the ongoing work, the Dean and the Rev Edmund Fellowes took the Lay Clerks from the Chapel on this tour, accompanied by the choristers from Westminster Abbey and their organist, Dr Sydney Nicholson. Hector Bolitho went with them. The Dean held a church service in the dining saloon of the ship in mid-crossing, 'the discs of light through the port-holes, moving back and forth over the green baize table-covers, with the motion of the ship.'[28] In Winnipeg Cathedral, the choir sang – 'They looked like a flock of angels and gave no hint of the devilment they get up to on the train' – and Dr Nicholson coped well with a cinema organ, some of the stops of which were called 'Doorbell' and 'Steam tug whistle.'[29] The tour lasted 70 days and was a great success. Parliament in Ottawa suspended their sitting so that the choir could sing before them in Parliament House.

Three years later, when the Dean of Windsor returned from his annual European holiday, in September 1930, he was able to inspect the improvements in the Chapel. The scaffolding had been removed, and the Chapel was ready after ten long years of work. The Dean wrote:

I admit that it took my breath away. It seemed to be far more beautiful than I had remembered. I feel that I know the cathedrals of Germany and France and Spain and Italy fairly well, but I come back to Windsor and look upon St George's as possessing beauty unique of its kind. Of course, St George's is not of the type of a great cathedral. To say that it is more or less beautiful than Westminster Abbey would be ridiculous. Its beauty lies in its absolute completeness, in the richness of its detail, and in the wonderful finish of the craftsmanship in stone and wood and iron. Its dignity always gives me an idea of what the Perpendicular builders were striving for. In its conception mysticism seems to be giving way to reverence. When you compare our architectural development during the fifteenth century with the flamboyant development in foreign Gothic, I think you see, in buildings like St George's, the peculiar mental characteristics of Englishmen at that time. They seem to illustrate our religious history.[30]

On 4 November 1930 a Service of Thanksgiving was held in the presence of King George V and Queen Mary and many members of the Royal Family. The King decided 'for some stubborn reason'[31] that it was not an occasion for Garter robes, but the Archbishop of Canterbury, the Prime Minister (Ramsay MacDonald), the Lord Chancellor and the Ambassadors of those foreign Sovereigns who were Knights of the Garter were invited, along with the Knights Companions. The choirs of the Chapel Royal, Christ Church Oxford, Eton College, King's College Cambridge, Salisbury Cathedral, Westminster Abbey and Winchester Cathedral joined the St George's Choir that day to sing Wesley's great anthem, 'Ascribe unto the Lord'. At the time of the reopening, *The Times* declared:

> Perhaps nothing better could be wished for our land than that this material restoration should be quickly followed by a spiritual restoration of the ideals which such a place as St George's seems to affirm – the English temper of self-discipline and restraint, the spirit of unrestrained chivalry and of individual effort for the common weal, the courage which in the face of omens however dismal will send us into battle with stout hearts, to fight our dragons and, please God, to slay them.[32]

During the latter part of George V's reign, the College acquired the freehold of St George's School, and the school buildings were enlarged with financial assistance from Lord Wakefield (the locomotive oil tycoon), Sir Frederick Minter and Miss Violet Wills (of the Imperial Tobacco family). Then Lord Wakefield purchased some land where a disused brewery had stood and gave it to George V as a Silver Jubilee gift. The King gave it to the Chapter for use as a future school playground, and lived long enough to inspect the school and the site of the playground development. Edward VIII gave Wakefield a GCVO in 1936. Violet Wills was made a DBE in 1937.

One day in July 1931, Canon Dalton came to Evensong and read a Lesson with his habitual vigour. He returned to his house in the Cloisters, ate a large meal and died in his sleep. He was 91. It was the end of a reign of terror that had lasted since 1885. The College became an easier place in which to work. Of these times Sir Edward Ford recalled:

> Canon Deane did all the work, and wrote the 4th leader in *The Times* every Saturday and broadcast regularly, Venables was pompous, Ollard was nicknamed "Golf-bags" by Mrs Combe Tennant [their neighbour in the Horseshoe Cloisters], while Crawley and Deane disliked each other. Canon Crawley wanted to cut down the branch of a tree and Deane would not let him. One day Deane returned to find Crawley sitting on the branch to make it snap and called out of his window: "Stop! You can't do that!"[33]

* * * * *

A Garter ceremony was planned for Silver Jubilee year in 1935, but cancelled due to the strain this would impose on the King's health in a busy year.

George V paid his last visit to St George's Chapel in December 1935, when he attended the funeral of his sister, Princess Victoria. The King was already in poor health and had been deeply upset by his sister's death. His doctor, Lord Dawson of Penn, had hoped to see a draft of the service in advance, to 'secure its brevity.' Instead he found himself watching the King 'standing bent, weighed down in body and mind, for far too long a period.'[34] It was the King's last ceremony. King George V spent Christmas at Sandringham. He soon slipped into terminal decline and died on 20 January 1936.

Dean Baillie, a lone figure silhouetted in the Great West Door, awaiting the coffin of George V at his funeral in January 1936. He earned himself the nickname 'Albert the Magnificent' in ecclesiastical circles.

After Lying-in-State in Westminster Hall, his body was brought to Windsor for burial. Five trains bore the mourners from London, bringing statesmen including the Prime Minister Stanley Baldwin, Neville Chamberlain, Winston Churchill,

The effigies of George V and Queen Mary, sculpted by Sir William Reid Dick (1879-1961), on their tomb in the Nave.

Anthony Eden and the Ambassadors. The funeral train itself was delayed by half an hour. The train arrived at 1.09 pm and the bearer party prepared to pull the coffin – 150 men from HMS *Excellent*.

The funeral procession made its way to the foot of the West steps of the Castle, and the coffin was lifted off to the boatswain's piping. At the top of the west steps, waiting to greet it, was the lone figure of Dean Baillie. He had succeeded in getting his Canons out of the way in order to dominate the photographs in the papers the next day. In this ruse he was successful. Back at Westminster, the Archbishop of Canterbury's chaplain noted wryly: 'Not for nothing is he known as Albert the Magnificent.'[35]

A contemporary account described the scene from within the Chapel:

Presently there floated into the Chapel the faint thunder of the funeral march played by the massed bands of the Guards. It died away, and through the door came the shrill blast of the bosun's pipe as the coffin was 'piped over the side' at the foot of the steps. As it was borne up to the entrance the skirl of Highland pipes took up the mourning music, and to their high, exultant wailing the coffin passed through the door.[36]

Hector Bolitho noted that those in the Chapel were more personally involved with the late King than those who had processed outside:

The old, white haired virger [Evans] who waited by the west door was a sailor once and he had served in *Bacchante* under the King fifty-nine years before. They used to join in sailor talk whenever the monarch came here. One of the choristers who stood within the sanctuary sang here at the beginning of the century, when they brought Queen Victoria from Osborne on her last journey. There were others who had played their part in the life of the dead King. Near to the west door was the Dean, whose ancestors served the Royal Family in the time of George III. There were old ladies, dimly seen behind their veils, who used to dance in the Castle in the gay days before the war.[37]

When the coffin reached the bier above the lift into the Royal Vault, the symbols of kingship were removed – the Crown, the orb and sceptre, and

replaced with a mass of flowers by the Comptroller of the Household. At the appropriate moment in the ceremony, the coffin sank from view and King Edward VIII scattered earth onto it. Soon afterwards the service was over, and all that remained was 'the sweet incense of the masses of flowers' banked high against the walls of the Cloisters.[38]

The coffin of George V remained in the Royal Vault until his tomb was ready for a bay in the North Nave Aisle, near the Urswick Chantry. The sarcophagus was designed by Sir Edwin Lutyens, with an effigy by Sir William Reid Dick.

EDWARD VIII (KING 1936)

Edward VIII reigned for barely eleven months, during which time he created no Knights of the Garter. When he came to the throne, Dean Baillie suggested optimistically that the new King had always taken an interest in the chapel 'and I feel sure he will continue to do so'.[39] In his brief reign, he inspected the Scouts as they climbed the Great West steps on Scouts Sunday, 19 April, and on 1 May he came to the castle to receive the learned address from the Dean and Canons (one of the Privileged Bodies), and lunched at the Deanery. On

ABOVE LEFT The banners of George V and Queen Mary above their tomb.

ABOVE The Annual Scout Service on 19 April 1936 – the Scouts arrive on the West steps and salute King Edward VIII as they enter the chapel.

BELOW The Berkshire division of VADs marching past in 1936. The Princess Royal (sister of Edward VIII) took the salute at the Galilee Porch, and presented them with new colours. A service was held in the chapel.

1 October the King's sister, the Princess Royal, took the salute at the Galilee Porch, when the Berkshire division of VADs marched past on the day they received new colours.

A rare photograph of Edward VIII in the castle during his short reign. He is seen arriving at the Deanery for lunch with Dean Baillie on 1 May 1936, having come to the castle to receive Loyal Addresses from the Privileged Bodies.

Edward VIII made no impact on the chapel. In December 1936 he abdicated in order to marry a twice-divorced American, Mrs Wallis Simpson, following which he lived abroad in self-imposed exile. Dean Baillie dismissed the Abdication as follows: 'All the hopes with which we began last year have been frustrated. But this time our sadness has in it a note of tragedy.'[40]

There was further sadness in store in connection with St George's Chapel. The Duke of Windsor, as he became, paid for half his father's tomb. He knew that he would not be able to attend any dedication but asked Queen Mary to let him know if such an event took place. She did not do this, and he read about it in the newspapers. In the event he used this slight as an opportunity to release many pent-up feelings of antipathy to his mother, and after 1939, he answered none of her letters nor acknowledged her birthday. However, following the death of his brother, the Duke of Kent, in 1942, he resumed communication with her, and after the war he stayed with her several times at Marlborough House.

GEORGE VI (KING 1936-52)

The Abdication was a great shock to everyone, but to the delight of Dean Baillie, one of the first acts of the new King, George VI, was to command a Garter Ceremony to be held at Windsor, and this took place on 14 June 1937.

Because of the Coronation there were a lot of Knights to be invested and installed – the Earl of Clarendon, the Duke of Norfolk, the Marquess of Exeter, the Earl of Strathmore (the King's father-in-law), the Duke of Beaufort and Stanley Baldwin (Earl Baldwin of Bewdley). The Duchess of Sermoneta described the ceremony:

On this occasion the heralds who headed the procession looked like so many Knaves of Hearts, and the Knights of the Garter who followed wore long blue velvet cloaks that trailed behind them, and round hats trimmed with a profusion of white ostrich feathers. The Queen [Queen Elizabeth], very sweet in her robes, walked beside the King, and Queen Mary, splendidly dignified, swept along by herself. Except for the King and the Duke of Norfolk, all the Knights were very old, and the procession was held up by a Duke who could not be persuaded to remain at home and had insisted on taking part, though he leant on a stick and could scarcely toddle.[41]

The Duke was the 9th Duke of Devonshire, then

Princess Elizabeth and Princess Margaret, with other members of the Royal Family, watching the Garter procession from the balcony outside the Dean's study, 14 June 1937. With them was their maternal grandmother, the Countess of Strathmore.

in the last year of his life. The Duke of Argyll reported to a friend: 'Halifax said Devonshire nearly collapsed at the Garter Chapter. Against his doctor's orders he attended it & walked in two long processions through all the courtyards. His wife & nice daughter-in-law have a time of it with him as since his strokes his tempers have been dreadful.'[42]

George VI loved the Order of the Garter, and took a considerable interest in its appointments and ceremonial. In 1937 he appointed a non-clerical Chancellor of the Order, the Duke of Portland, severing it by Statute from the office of the Bishop of Oxford to whom it had been attached for 100 years. He redesigned the star, and a few days before he died in 1952 had designed some trousers that could accommodate the Garter below the knee.

The war intervened and the King was concerned about the fate of the Chapel. The fine stained glass windows were removed and the banners taken down, and many chapel treasures stored in safe places. During the war the last three surviving children of Queen Victoria died and their funerals were held in the Chapel – Princess Louise, Duchess of Argyll, in 1939 and the Duke of Connaught in 1942 (both aged 91) and Princess Beatrice (aged 87) in 1944. The King's brother, the Duke of Kent, was killed in a wartime flying accident and his coffin was lowered into the Royal Vault, where it remained until 1968.

ABOVE   King George VI and Queen Elizabeth walking back up the hill in the Garter procession, 14 June 1937.

BELOW   Princess Elizabeth and Princess Margaret walking up the hill after the Garter ceremony on 14 June 1937.

The Duke of Kent, brother of King George VI, killed in a wartime plane crash on 25 August 1942.

ABOVE The roof of the chapel, specially photographed to match the John Piper painting.

OPPOSITE PAGE TOP John Piper's wartime painting of the roof of St George's Chapel.

OPPOSITE PAGE BOTTOM A wartime painting of Windsor Castle with St George's Chapel in the background by John Piper (1903-92).

Once again hostilities provoked discussion about those alien Knights of the Garter whose banners should be removed. One victim was King Victor Emmanuel of Italy in 1940, another was Emperor Hirohito of Japan. Three other Stranger Knights were considered for removal but reprieved – King Leopold III of the Belgians, King Carol of Romania and Prince Paul of Yugoslavia.

In June 1944, just before he retired, Dean Baillie was due to preach in St George's Hall, where Mattins was held in wartime. The King sent a message to ask him to omit the prayer for Britain's enemies. As the King's Private Secretary, Sir Alan Lascelles, recorded: 'The Dean complied, but preached a sermon on the obligations of all Christians to forgive their enemies, and on the general duty of being a little blind to the faults of our neighbours at large, and of trying to see the good in them.' Lascelles found opinion divided over this 'somewhat personal attack, in the manner of John Knox,' but believed it would do no harm.[43] Lascelles was fond of St George's Chapel, its music

and its architecture, observing that its 'full beauty is very much dependent on the light.'[44] Both his daughters were married in the chapel.

Baillie resigned in September 1944. When he died in 1955, his successor as Dean described him as 'large-hearted and generous'.[45]

ERIC HAMILTON (DEAN 1944-62)

Eric Hamilton was the seventh son of the Rev Charles Hamilton, a scion of the Irish family of Hamiltons of Hamwood. Three of his elder brothers died as small children, while the oldest became a Lt-Colonel, another a vicar, and another,

Rt Rev Eric Hamilton, Dean of Windsor from 1944 to 1962, painted by Sir Gerald Kelly (1879-1972) – who spent years at Windsor Castle at work on the state portraits of George VI and Queen Elizabeth.

Sir George, a poet and writer. Young Eric studied art but this was not to be his life's work.

Hamilton was ordained in 1914. He served as Vicar of Knightsbridge, where he was known as 'the lovely Eric'[46] and afterwards as Bishop Suffragan of Shrewsbury and Rector of Edmond before succeeding Albert Baillie in 1944. Hamilton took up his appointment soon after his second son was killed serving in Italy in December 1943. As is traditional before such an appointment is made, he was invited to preach before the King and Queen, which he did on Sunday 6 May 1944. On the Monday following, the King instructed his Private Secretary to offer him the Deanery.

The new Dean tended to be formal, signing himself '+ Eric Hamilton, Bishop' even to close colleagues. Lionel Dakers, Assistant Organist from 1950 to 1954, called him 'remote, even to the extent of being quite unconcerned'[47] over how Dakers

would be housed after his marriage. 'A monkish figure,'[48] was another description, while Canon Alec Vidler wrote: 'He did all that was required of him as dean gracefully and efficiently, but there was not enough to employ all his talents and he would have been more happily and usefully employed as bishop of an urban diocese.'[49]

As children, Princess Elizabeth and Princess Margaret spent most of the years of the Second World War at Windsor Castle, which was fortified with barbed wire. This, as Princess Margaret pointed out: 'would never have kept the Germans out, but certainly kept us in'. King George and Queen Elizabeth spent the weekdays in London, and also retained the use of Royal Lodge, preferring that to the castle. This was the residence they first acquired in the early 1930s and which Queen Elizabeth used in widowhood as a weekend home.

In May 1946 the King had discussed the Garter with the new Labour Prime Minister, Clement Attlee, and told him he wanted it 'non-political and in my gift'. This appealed to Attlee since his party was generally against accepting honours. In July that year Attlee agreed that in future the King could confer the Garter, the Thistle, and the St Patrick without formal submission to the Prime Minister.[50] In December the King had held a Chapter of the Garter at Buckingham Palace, at which all the Knight Companions had been present except the 81-year-old Earl of Derby, and Lord Alexander of Tunis (who was in Canada as Governor-General). He told the assembled company that the Admonitions were ancient ones, and had been revived after many years of disuse. He emphasised the fundamental principles of the Garter and its Christian character.

In 1947 the King bestowed the Garter on Princess Elizabeth and the Duke of Edinburgh shortly before their wedding on 20 November. Princess Elizabeth was declared a Lady of the Garter by special statute on 11 November, and Prince Philip on 19 November, 'so that she will be senior to Philip,' as the King wrote to Queen Mary.

THE 1948 CELEBRATIONS

The full ceremonial of the Garter ceremony was revived on St George's Day 1948, the 600th anniversary of the founding of the Order. The King held an Investiture in the Garter Throne Room, a full Installation Service in St George's Chapel for the first time since 1805, and gave a luncheon in the Waterloo Chamber. It was a magnificent medieval revival of ceremonial in post-war Britain, at which both Princess Elizabeth and the Duke of Edinburgh were invested and installed, as well as a great number of new Knights of the Garter, many of them distinguished war leaders.

Originally it was intended to mark this anniversary with a fourfold celebration. Besides the Investiture and Installation of new Knights of the Garter, a performance of a play by John Masefield, the Poet Laureate, in the Nave, a Festival of Music, and a Thanksgiving Service. Due to post-war conditions of hardship and general financial crisis, the play had to be dropped.

The 1948 Garter Ceremony marked a high spot in the history of the Order with the King reviving ceremonies that had not taken place since the reign of George III. On St George's Day itself, he installed Princess Elizabeth, the Duke of Edinburgh and thirteen of the fourteen Knights of the Garter appointed since the 1937 ceremony. Only Lord Mountbatten was absent, serving as Viceroy of India.

The Times hailed the occasion as a 'Festival of Old England' on a perfect Spring day. Many of the new Knights were 'heroes of the late victory continuing the succession of the knights of Crécy and Poitiers, but headed on this occasion by the heiress-presumptive to the Throne and her consort.' The procession outside took its normal form – Military Knights, Officers of Arms and Knights of the Garter: 'The royal knights and ladies walked last – Princess Elizabeth and the Duke of Edinburgh

RIGHT Princess Elizabeth and the Duke of Edinburgh in Garter robes, both portraits painted by Sir Oswald Birley, 1949.

Princess Elizabeth and the Duke of Edinburgh, in the Garter procession, 23 April 1948, the day they were installed by King George VI.

in apparently merry conversation all the way, she showing with what unexpected harmony the beauty of modern girlhood can be framed in the "old look" of 1348, and then the Duke of Gloucester.'[51]

Queen Mary travelled down by car before the ceremony and took her place in the procession just inside the Great West Door. The service followed the traditional pattern and included the Vaughan Williams *Te Deum in G*.

The Festival of Music took place in the Nave in June, concentrating on cathedral music of English composers from the sixteenth century to the 1940s and on those composers particularly associated with St George's Chapel. Dr Edmund Fellowes, Minor Canon, and an expert on the English polyphonic music of the Tudor period, wrote:

> The intoning of the prayers, as well as of the versicles and responses, has also been a universal practice in Cathedral usage for four centuries. During this period a wonderful repertory of this class of music has been created by successive generations of English composers. Twentieth-century names are linked with those of the sixteenth in an unbroken chain; and all these musicians have been inspired by the same ideal, namely, that of contributing to the best of their ability something that may be found adequate as an offering of beauty in worship.[52]

A number of choirs joined the St George's Chapel choir and were conducted by distinguished figures such as Dr William Harris, the chapel organist, and Michael Tippett.

On the evening of 18 July the Thanksgiving Service for the 600th anniversary was held, attended by the King and Queen, Princess Elizabeth and the Duke of Edinburgh, the Duke of Gloucester and the Knights of the Garter in their robes. The King took the opportunity to install Lord Mountbatten immediately before the service, escorted to his seat by Lord Portal of Hungerford and Lord Addison. This time there was no procession through the castle, the Garter Knights robing in the Chapter Library and proceeding to the west steps to await the arrival by car of the King and Queen.

The procession into the chapel was much the same as usual – led by the Earl of Gowrie, Deputy Governor of the Castle, the Military Knights, but with no Officers of Arms.

In a short address the Archbishop of Canterbury spoke of Sir Gawain and his five virtues, 'generosity and love of his fellowmen and cleanness and courtesy that never failed and lastly pity that is above all other virtues'. He continued:

Our service here this evening celebrates both the Chapel of St George and the Noble Order which has here its spiritual home; celebrates the offering of prayer and worship made here day by day with all the perfection of music and song by the College of Priests and Military Knights for the Order and for all men, and celebrates also all the knightly virtues of faithful service which draw their power from that offering of prayer and worship. Each overlaps and locks with the other in an endless knot. And how greatly this generation needs to understand their interlocking. The world needs Christian character, the five virtues of Sir Gawain, quite desperately.[53]

The King would have liked to hold Garter ceremonies as annual events like the four his father had held before the First World War, but ill health intervened. There was a Garter ceremony in April 1950, and in May 1951 he was just well enough to install King Frederik IX of Denmark, along with three English knights, the King walking in the procession, but looking very drawn.

George VI continued to relish his association with the Order of the Garter until the end of his life. He died peacefully in his sleep at Sandringham on 6 February 1952, at the early age of 56. His funeral followed the same pattern as his father's. He was lowered into the Royal Vault, where he lay until 1969.

The King George VI Memorial Chapel was commissioned and built in the winter of 1968-9 and dedicated on 31 March 1969. On that day it was explained that 'King George VI was a sovereign whose reign needs special commemoration. Called unexpectedly to kingship, he led his people through fifteen difficult years of war and peace.' Furthermore, 'St George's Chapel was for him a place of regular worship and within its walls his faith was nourished and sustained.'[54]

He and Queen Elizabeth now lie there (re-united after 50 years), with the ashes of Princess Margaret, placed in the same grave.

SIX

The Present Reign

Q UEEN ELIZABETH II came to the throne with no weekend home near London. She and the Duke of Edinburgh decided to open up some rooms at Windsor Castle as an experiment, and liked it so well that they made it their home.

The Queen's grandmother, Queen Mary, died soon after the death of George VI, on 24 March 1953. She was buried in the Nave alongside her husband, George V. Her effigy had been sculpted along with his, after the King's death in 1936, because she reflected that her grandmother, the Duchess of Cambridge, and her aunt, the Grand Duchess of Mecklenburg-Strelitz, had lived to be over 90, and she was anxious not to be depicted as if she might have been his mother rather than his wife.

In the 1950s several of the older members of the Royal Family died, the Queen's cousin, Princess Marie Louise (daughter of Princess Christian, and a granddaughter of Queen Victoria) in December 1956, and Queen Mary's brother, the Earl of Athlone (Governor of the Castle 1931-57) in January 1957. The new procedure for such funerals was that the service was held in the chapel, and the burial then took place immediately at Frogmore without any descent into the Royal Vault. The Queen attended both services. A happier occasion was the marriage of the Athlones' granddaughter, Anne Abel Smith to David Liddell-Grainger in 1957, with the future Queen Beatrix of the Netherlands as one of the bridesmaids.

Spending weekends at Windsor brought the Queen and Prince Philip into close contact with Dean Hamilton, and the College of St George. They soon became aware of the somewhat moribund state into which the College had fallen on account

Queen Mary, the Queen's grandmother, who died on 24 March 1953. A portrait by Hay Wrightson.

of the war. The Duke of Edinburgh recalled: 'What was evident was that the finances were in a fairly difficult situation because there were too many canons, and it had just gone on as before and no one had really gripped it.'[1]

He also observed that Dean Hamilton was having problems with the Canons because of the Statutes.

There were other serious problems, as the Duke noted: 'As with so many other institutions, the normal process of change and development had been interrupted by the war, and both the economy of the College and the fabric of the Chapel and the Canon's Cloisters were in dire need of repair.'[2] He added: 'Dean Hamilton was a saint – but a traditionalist.'[3]

Dean Hamilton re-introduced an admission charge for tourists, which enabled the Dean and Canons to subsidize some of their poorer livings and to restore the Cloister buildings. It also slightly reduced the number of tourists. In 1958 the Queen allowed him to appeal to the Knights of the Garter for £200,000 in order to 'maintain the great traditions'[4] entrusted to the Dean and Canons. The Dean addressed the Knights in the Throne Room at the Garter ceremony on 16 June and they responded favourably. Prince Philip showed encouraging interest.

The Dean and Lord Halifax, Chancellor of the Order of the Garter, put together an appeal, which was essentially private due to 'the particular relationship to the Crown in which the Chapel stands, set as it is within the precincts of Windsor Castle and occupying its own particular extra-Diocesan status.'[5] They pointed out that the 1867 annuity of £14,400 and the turnstile income of £18,000 were inadequate to meet demands. The 1959 costs were listed as follows:

Immediate repairs to the Chapel	£65,000
Restoration of the Horseshoe Cloister	£50,000
Repairs to the Deanery and Canons' Cloisters (in danger of collapse)	£56,000
Repairs to the Dean's Cloister	£6,000
Repairs to the Curfew Tower and Chapter Library	£2,500
Roadway north of the Chapel, surface water drainage, Chapter staff quarters	£8,000
Standard Surveyors' Fees for all excepting Item 1	£12,500
Total:	£199,750

£63,952 was raised immediately, and the admission charge was raised to 2/- for adults, and 1/- for children. But by November 1959, the flow of contributions had practically ceased. Nevertheless this enabled the Chapter to engage a skilled stonemason and to start the urgent repairs on the Horseshoe Cloister. As there was still a long way to go to reach the necessary targets, a professional fundraiser, Captain R.J.B. Kenderdine, RN, was employed. Lord Halifax died suddenly. The Dean wrote: 'We are much the poorer for the loss of his wisdom, experience and charm, perhaps most of all for his sheer goodness of heart. He was one of the truly great men of the century.'[6] A new appeal chairman was appointed, Field Marshal Earl Alexander of Tunis, KG, who lived nearby at Winkfield.

By January 1961 the Private Appeal had still not reached the halfway point and when the appeal finally achieved £120,000, a further £160,000 was needed.

Hamilton faced the traditional problem of difficult relations in Chapter. In Hamilton's day, Duncan Armytage (Canon from 1947 to 1954) assumed the mantle of Canons Dalton and Deane in this respect. Alec Vidler described him as 'tiresomely obstreperous and uncooperative, and liable to sulk if he did not get his way.' He noted that 'the inevitable tensions in the Cloisters . . . ceased to trouble after Duncan Armytage's sudden death in February 1954' when he was succeeded by Charles Ritchie, 'the most amiable of colleagues.'[7]

During Hamilton's time in office, the Beaufort Chapel was restored.

Sir Winston Churchill had been appointed a Knight of the Garter in 1953 in time to wear the robes at the Queen's Coronation. He was installed in 1954. Sir Anthony Eden was appointed in 1954 and installed with the Earl of Iveagh and another former Prime Minister, Earl Attlee, on 19 June 1956.

This proved an uncomfortable ceremony since Lord Iveagh was obliged to sit next to Sir Winston Churchill in the Garter stalls. The two men (both born in 1874) loathed each other and were observed to cold shoulder each other. There was an historical reason for this. They had been childhood neighbours and playmates in Dublin when

The stall plate of Rupert, 2nd Earl of Iveagh, KG (1955).

Churchill's grandfather, the 7th Duke of Marlborough was Lord Lieutenant of Ireland. The Guinness estate, Farmleigh, was next door to the Lord Lieutenant's residence. One day they were playing horses, and Churchill was playing jockey. He struck the then Rupert Guinness with a cord. An over-zealous nurse applied carbolic acid to the small injury, causing a scar that Iveagh bore on his forehead throughout his life.

Lord Iveagh, head of the Guinness family, was perhaps an unusual choice as a Garter Knight in 1955, being neither a distinguished politician nor war leader, though he was a patron of many charities and had made a considerable contribution to agriculture, converting his Suffolk sporting estate into a fruitful agricultural unit. He was interested in the production of germ-free milk and was one of the first producers in Britain to obtain a licence to sell Grade A milk. He was also the brother-in-law of

Lord Halifax, then Chancellor of the Order. Lord Iveagh was to prove a considerable benefactor.

Dean Hamilton travelled to Southern Rhodesia to represent the Universities' Mission at the inauguration of the new Central African Province in 1955. His other achievements included restoration of the daily Eucharist and his institution of addresses in Holy Week and the Three Hours Devotion on Good Friday. It was his idea to place an altar in the Nave, greatly increasing the religious significance of St George's to the visiting tourists.

On 1 October 1961, in failing health, Dean Hamilton announced his intention to retire, ending his last letter to the Friends: 'Forgive my shortcomings as your friend and Dean.'[8] As it happens he died in the Deanery during the night of 20/21 May 1962.

While Robin Woods, his successor as Dean, described Hamilton as 'generous of heart and saintly of character',[9] it was hard for colleagues to assess his influence, much of which was not accessible to the outside world. Mention was made of his charm and kindness, his deep faith and goodness, and the trouble he took in worship irrespective of the size of the congregation. Sir Michael Adeane, the Queen's Private Secretary, acknowledged that his 'poor health prevented him from doing as much as he would have liked.'[10]

Dean Woods was more categorical: 'Appointed during the war, he served King George VI and Queen Elizabeth and their young family with quiet ability, but financial difficulties over the chapel and the independent attitude of the canons, together with increasing ill health, had made his latter years a burden.'[11]

ROBIN WOODS (DEAN 1962-71)

Robin Woods was a robust successor and during his nine years at Windsor he was at his most influential. Woods hesitated for some time before accepting the appointment, determined to use it to the full if he took it on. In retirement he said: 'If I took the job, it was made clear that I would be expected to turn everything upside down.'[12]

Woods was powerful and energetic. He understood finance and was full of initiative and reforming zeal. He hit St George's Chapel like a whirlwind though even he was surprised and frustrated to find that 'ecclesiastical change comes slowly.'[13] In particular he regretted the adherence to tradition and to the Statutes by Canon Bryan Bentley, and the inevitable reminders about the Dean being 'Primus inter pares'.

Bryan Bentley was a particularly interesting figure at St George's. A scholar at King's College, Cambridge, who had gained a first in both the Classical and Theological Tripos, and won the Carus Greek Testament prize, he was a keen theologian and tackled issues of changing sexual morality. He influenced the government to adopt the concept of irretrievable breakdown of marriage as the primary justification for divorce, as opposed

Rt Rev Robin Woods, Dean of Windsor from 1962 to 1971, with the Queen after the service of thanksgiving for the 50th anniversary Jubilee of the Royal Air Force and dedication of RAF candlesticks (in the Nave) on 8 December 1968.

to that of marital offence. He addressed the question of women taking holy orders years before this was adopted and wrote many letters of high intellectual content to *The Times* on theological matters.

Bentley had been devoted to Eric Hamilton and was not in sympathy with the new Dean, nor later did he prove to be an easy colleague. Even the Duke of Edinburgh registered him as difficult.

Woods inherited Dean Hamilton's problems over the restoration of the medieval buildings attached to St George's, and the re-accommodation of the

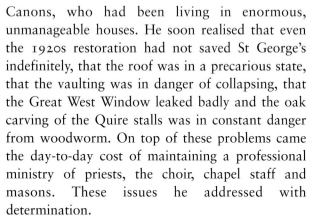

The stall plate of Charles, Prince of Wales, created a Knight of the Garter in 1958, and installed in 1968.

Princess Marina, Duchess of Kent, who died aged 61, on 27 August 1968. A photograph by Cecil Beaton.

Canons, who had been living in enormous, unmanageable houses. He soon realised that even the 1920s restoration had not saved St George's indefinitely, that the roof was in a precarious state, that the vaulting was in danger of collapsing, that the Great West Window leaked badly and the oak carving of the Quire stalls was in constant danger from woodworm. On top of these problems came the day-to-day cost of maintaining a professional ministry of priests, the choir, chapel staff and masons. These issues he addressed with determination.

More than his recent predecessors, Robin Woods relished his connection with the Royal Family. There was a popular story that he once said: 'There is too much name-dropping going on in the castle. The Queen and I don't like it.' At Woods's memorial service at Worcester Cathedral in 1997, Archbishop Carey pointed out that a similar story had been told of Randall Davidson.

Dean Woods was something of a family friend and mentor to Prince Charles (taking him out for Sunday excursions), and to a lesser extent to Princess Anne. He was influential in the decision that Prince Charles should go to Trinity College, Cambridge, his old college. In 1964 he christened Prince Edward and in June 1968 his voice rang with emotion when he read the prayers at the Garter ceremony at which Prince Charles was installed. Later that summer he took part in the funeral of Princess Marina, Duchess of Kent, who had died of a brain tumour aged 61. After the service he entertained the Royal Family, including the Duke of Windsor, at the Deanery, since the Queen's apartments were closed for the summer.

He presided over the building of the King George VI Memorial Chapel between a buttress of the North Quire Aisle and the Rutland Chantry. This was the first structural addition to the exterior of St George's since the chapel was completed in 1528.

Originally the King George VI Memorial Chapel was to contain eight lancet windows with plain

LEFT The funeral of Princess Marina, Duchess of Kent, 30 August 1968. The Queen and the Duke of Edinburgh (front) with Robin Woods, Dean of Windsor (left), the Queen Mother, Prince Charles and Princess Anne, Princess Margaret and the Earl of Snowdon, with Sir Philip Hay (hidden), Lady Rachel Pepys, Major Peter Clarke, the Duchess of Gloucester, the Duke of Windsor, Prince Richard of Gloucester, the Earl and Countess of Pembroke, and Madame Zoia Poklewska-Koziell.

BELOW The King George VI Memorial Chapel in the North Quire Aisle. The grave of King George VI and Queen Elizabeth, the memorial to Princess Margaret, and bas reliefs of Princess Margaret, Queen Elizabeth and King George VI.

glass. But the Knights of the Garter (including Royal and Stranger Knights, amongst them the Duke of Windsor and Prince Paul of Yugoslavia) responded to a plea from the then Chancellor of the Order, the 5th Marquess of Salisbury, to contribute

The John Piper windows and the ceiling of the King George VI Memorial Chapel.

presided over by Alec Naylor, the son of a long-serving lay clerk. Their present captain, only their third, John Handcock, has served since the start.

A concert of Brahms, Bach and César Franck in St George's Chapel at which Yehudi Menuhin and his sister Hephzibah played the violin and piano in the presence of the young Prince of Wales in November 1967, inspired Woods to create the Windsor Festival. This opened on 17 September 1969 with Menuhin and William Walton conducting the combined bands of Coldstream and Welsh Guards in the Lower Ward, followed by fireworks, which impressed everyone except, perhaps inevitably, Canon Bentley, since, again perhaps inevitably, one of the fireworks exploded in his garden.

In that first Festival the Menuhin Festival Orchestra performed more than once in St George's Chapel; Yehudi and Hephzibah Menuhin and Maurice Gendron played Beethoven and Tchaikovsky in St George's Hall, and there was a glorious evening of Beethoven, conducted by Yehudi Menuhin in the Waterloo Chamber, on the last night, 27 September. At that concert Menuhin conducted and also played the solo part in the *Violin Concerto in D Major*.

ST GEORGE'S HOUSE

Perhaps Woods's greatest achievement was the creation of St George's House as a place where spiritual and temporal could combine. This came about due to the reorganisation of the accommodation of the houses of the clergy. At St George's House, leaders and people of influence in public life could step back to discuss and ponder on matters of significance concerned with human well being, and where the clergy could reassess their vocation in the mid-term of their careers, in much the same way as officers passed through staff college. He was not concerned with training would-be clergy, but 'bringing in incumbents, rural deans and specialist clergy to a period of refreshment and instruction.'[15]

This necessitated another fundraising campaign,

donations of £2,500 in order that John Piper might be commissioned to design stained glass to enhance these windows. The sum was easily achieved and Patrick Reyntiens made the windows. In thanking the Knights, Lord Salisbury wrote of George VI: 'He was, I feel, though so humble, – and perhaps in a way because he was so humble – a really great man.'[14]

In March 1969 the coffin of George VI, still covered by the Royal Standard which had been used at his funeral in 1952, was brought from the Royal Vault, and buried in the new chapel. A service of dedication was held a few days later, on 31 March, in the presence of the Queen, the Queen Mother and the Royal Family and the Knights of the Garter, including Prince Paul of Yugoslavia.

In 1966 Robin Woods instituted the Lay Stewards to assist at Sunday services and the larger services such as the Garter Ceremony, and at royal marriages and funerals. This voluntary group was

which proved more successful than the one instigated by Hamilton and Halifax. The new Dean addressed the Knights of the Garter at the Garter ceremony on 15 June 1964. But the one Knight of the Garter who could help them more than any was absent – the 90-year-old Earl of Iveagh, who had last attended such a service in 1960.

A month later, the Duke of Edinburgh wrote personally to Lord Iveagh: 'The Queen and all the Knights were very sorry not to see you at Windsor for the Garter Service this year and I am sure they would all like me to send you their good wishes ...' [16] He went on to outline the new plans:

> Briefly the situation is that the Canons', minor Canons', and singing clerks' houses are all rather too big and many of them are almost falling down from lack of repair. The Dean's idea is that the houses should be modernised and redivided into smaller and more easily managed units. With the space gained from this reconstruction he wants to establish the necessary rooms and facilities to accommodate about thirty-five visitors, either lay or clerical or a combination of both, for a series of courses to be run by the Chapter of St George's. The courses would be

The Queen with Robin Woods, Dean of Windsor, and the Military Knights of Windsor, at the Opening of St George's House, 23 October 1966. In the foreground, left to right, Major Thomas Garnett, Lt-Colonel Richard Penfold and Brigadier William Robinson, and in the background, Major Henry Clough (then in his 90th year).

> refresher periods for the clergy, and for the laity they would be designed to help senior executives in industry, commerce and administration to understand the relevance of Christianity to their daily work.[17]

Prince Philip mentioned an initial cost for repair and reconstruction of £175,000, though the sought figure was £350,000. This resulted in Robin Woods going to see Lord Iveagh on 29 July 1964. Iveagh wrote back to Prince Philip to say: 'I was extremely sorry that I had to miss the Garter Service at Windsor this year . . .' He then told Prince Philip that the Dean 'came to see me today and explained his scheme to me. I found it most interesting. We are going to keep in touch and I will see what I can to do to help.'[18]

In turn, Robin Woods reported to Prince Philip: 'You will be glad to know, Sir, that as a result of your letter to Lord Iveagh, I had a very good talk with him and with his financial advisers, and now hope for the best.'[19] Woods later recalled that at that meeting, or possibly a subsequent one, the old Earl asked him: 'How much should I give?' '£35,000'. To which the earl replied: 'Done!' and a tenth part of the funds was raised at a stroke.[20] According to the records, the figure was in fact £10,000 up front, and a further £21,000 later, thus £31,000 in all.

In what the Duke of Edinburgh later described in a memo to his Private Secretary as 'the most professional piece of fund raising I've ever come across',[21] some £250,000 was raised in four months, and a further £100,000 followed soon afterwards. Subscribers included the Queen, the Queen Mother and other members of the Royal Family (including the Duke of Windsor), Knights of the Garter and large corporations, figures such as Paul Mellon, J. Paul Getty and Sir Frederick Minter, but also Military Knights, Percival Bridger (Lay Clerk), H.W. Wollaston (son of a Garter King of Arms), Sir Austin Strutt, a Lay Steward, and Marguerite D'Janoeff (who painted the portrait of Dean Woods in St George's House).

Two Minor Canons were duly re-housed, and St George's House came into being. It was dedicated and opened in the presence of the Queen and the Duke of Edinburgh on Sunday 23 October 1966, at which, according to the Dean, Canon Bentley 'confessed his early misgivings and non-cooperation in the development of collegiate life, he pointed out that a turbulent priest had been brought in as Dean: but then to our astonishment, before the Queen and a large congregation thanked God for the new venture and for my leadership.'[22] Lord Iveagh made his last appearance in the chapel at this service, in a wheelchair, then aged 92, and with the help of his nurse and a male attendant, gallantly rose from it for the National Anthem.

The first consultation, 'The Role of the Church in Society Today' had taken place the evening before with contributions from Lord Caccia, then Provost of Eton, the Marquess of Salisbury, and the Duke of Edinburgh. From the start, the Dean's 'mission' to include people connected with business and professional ethics, and relations between people in large organisations was central to its development. One idea was to bridge gaps between different groups, young and old, unions and managers, and scientists and theologians.

St George's House now forms a crucial part in the life of the College of St George. The Duke of Edinburgh still plays a key role in its work and for many years presided over the annual St George's House lecture, instigated by Michael Mann, when he was Dean, which has featured many speakers of international importance.

Dean Woods was forever striving for change, but, as he wrote in his memoirs, it took him five years to redefine the wider usage of St George's Chapel and its collegiate foundation.

As the 1960s gave way to a new decade, the Dean's view was that St George's Chapel and the College of St George now required a prolonged period of consolidation. This coincided with an offer to him to become Bishop of Worcester, which led to much soul-searching since he relished every aspect of life at Windsor. Woods accepted Worcester, and left Windsor early in 1971, Canon Bentley immediately removing his chair at Chapter in over-zealous adherence to the Statutes.

Worcester was a fairly senior bishopric. Woods implied in his memoirs that he may well have hoped for a more senior promotion in due course, but this was his last ecclesiastical appointment. He retired in 1981, and died aged 83 in 1997.

LAUNCELOT FLEMING (DEAN 1971-76)

Dean Woods took a key role in the appointment of his successor, and it was decided that a bishop was needed as having the necessary authority and qualities of leadership to oversee the various gatherings of laymen and women from spheres of government, and commercial organisations at St George's House. Woods was delighted to hand over to Launcelot Fleming, the retiring Bishop of Norwich.

The funeral of Prince William of Gloucester in August 1972. On the steps the Duchess of Gloucester, Prince and Princess Richard of Gloucester, the Lord Chamberlain (Lord Maclean), the Dean's Virger (Roy Read), the Queen and the Duke of Edinburgh and other members of the Royal Family.

Fleming was a much loved man, whose varied career had included accompanying the three-year British Graham Land Expedition to the Antarctic; being a wartime naval chaplain; director of the Scott Polar Research Institute; taking a keen interest in education and the environment and Outward Bound activities; and having helped Prince Philip with the foundation of the Duke of Edinburgh's Award Scheme in the 1950s.

When he was consecrated as Bishop of Portsmouth in 1949, Archbishop Fisher had expressed reservations about him: 'He has had no parochial experience at all, there is a doubt about his power to administer and exercise discipline or to temper his enthusiasm by considered judgment.'[23] But Fleming rose to be Bishop of Norwich – sometimes known as 'the Dead See' – which brought him into contact with the Royal Family when they were at Sandringham.

He was installed on 16 July 1971 in the presence of the Queen, the Queen Mother, Princess Margaret and Prince William of Gloucester, at whose funeral he presided the following year: the Prince was killed when his plane crashed in the Goodyear Air Race at Wolverhampton in August 1972.

St George's Chapel was fully in the focus of the nation for several days following the death of the Duke of Windsor in Paris on 28 May 1972. The

The Lying-in-State of the Duke of Windsor, in the Nave, June 1972.

Duke's coffin was flown to RAF Benson and then brought by hearse to Windsor Castle, where for two days it lay in state in the centre of the Nave of the chapel, completely empty except for the bier. The spot where the ex-King's coffin lay is now marked with a black marble plaque in the floor.

On the evening of Saturday 3 June, the Duchess of Windsor came to see it, after the chapel was closed to the public, accompanied by Lord Mountbatten and by Prince Charles, who walked down from the castle. Mountbatten recorded:

> At the end she stood again looking at the coffin and said in the saddest imaginable voice, "He was my entire life. I can't begin to think what I am going to do without him, he gave up so much for me and now he has gone. I always hoped that I would die before him".[24]

The funeral took place on Monday 5 June, and was attended by the Duchess of Windsor, the Queen, the Queen Mother, King Olav of Norway and most of the Royal Family. In the congregation were many who had played their part in the Abdication crisis, Lord Brownlow, Lady Alexandra Metcalfe, Lady Diana Cooper and the photographer, Cecil Beaton. Of all those present, he left the most vivid account of the service:

> The vaulted chapel rather beautiful and the music good. Then a clank as the trumpeters arrived. Then the louder clank, clank, clank could be heard as the procession started with the Governor of Windsor Castle and the Military Knights in their scarlet uniforms, medals clinking, all marching with a loud stamp-shuffle ...
>
> Then the coffin borne by eight sturdy Welsh Guardsmen, arms linked and heads bowed. On the Duke's personal standard a huge, trembling mass of Madonna lilies, followed by a group of male Royalty.
>
> The coffin passed in front of the altar, the service began with the hymn, 'The King of Love my Shepherd is'. Some of the verses seemed rather poignant: 'Perverse and foolish oft I strayed' ...
>
> The service was short, and entirely noble. It even

The plaque marking the spot where the Duke of Windsor lay in state in the Nave between 2 and 3 June 1972.

gave a departed nobility to a young man who once had such charm that everyone considered he was the ideal choice. But he lived on to keep his charm and little else, and one wondered how lucky we all were that even for such an unsuitable reason as the hard, brash, wise-cracking American, he had stepped down to make way for the Queen Mother, and now the very admirable and remarkable Queen.

Wonderful as the service was, I was not moved by the death of this man who for less than a year had been our King. History will make his love story into a romance. In fact, for us so close, it is hard to see that. Wallis ... is a good friend to all her friends. There is no malice in her. There is nothing dislikeable. She is just not of the degree that has reason to be around the Throne ...

The most moving sight was to see carried on cushions the orders that now in death he [the Duke of Windsor] had to give up – the diamond embroidered Garter. These of such inherent grandeur, such dignity, that one was reminded of Shakespeare's Kings and Princes, and they made one feel that the fair-haired Prince had not been the stuff of history ...[25]

Beaton concluded that he felt 'great emotion that the strength of the monarchy was something that could not in spite of all today's rebels be overthrown. It is as important an ingredient in the life of Britain as ever it has been, or so this simple service gave me the conviction.'[26] In the afternoon, the Duke's coffin was buried at Frogmore.

Dean Fleming also played his part in the military

The stall plate of Emperor Hirohito of Japan, created a Knight of the Garter in 1928, removed from the Order in 1942, and reinstated in 1971, prior to his State Visit to Britain.

funerals of the Duke of Gloucester in 1974 and Field Marshal Viscount Montgomery of Alamein in 1976, the Quincentenary celebrations in 1975, which involved a Thanksgiving Service on St George's Day at which the Queen, most of the Royal Family and the Knights of the Garter were present, and following which the Queen entertained the entire College of St George to luncheon in the State Apartments. The summer passed with concerts, an exhibition and other celebrations.

Emperor Hirohito of Japan was reinstated into the Order of the Garter prior to his State Visit to Britain in October 1971. This reinstatement had first been mooted as early as 1952, and there had been some concerns in diplomatic circles when young Crown Prince Akihito visited the chapel to lay a wreath for Queen Mary, while on his visit to Britain to represent the Emperor at the Queen's Coronation. The diplomats were worried that he might notice that his father's banner was not displayed in the chapel, but fortunately he did not.

In 1971 there was some controversy in the press about Emperor Hirohito's banner going up again. Some people complained when in according to tradition the dying Emperor was prayed for in chapel services, in sickness and again after his death on 7 January 1989. This was nothing as compared to the aggression which the media stirred up in May 1998, when, in correct accordance with diplomatic tradition, Hirohito's son, Emperor Akihito was given the Garter on his State Visit to Britain.

Emperor Haile Selassie of Ethiopia walked in the 1972 Garter procession, escorting the Queen Mother. Dean Fleming led the service at which his banner was presented, following his deposition and murder in Ethiopia in 1975. This service was notable for the presence of many Rastafarians.

At St George's House, which Fleming much enjoyed, he instituted courses for senior churchmen from all Christian churches, not just Anglican, and made sure that environmental issues were discussed. At one inter-faith conference the Dalai Lama was present.

A biography of Fleming published in 2003 suggested that he had achieved little during his time as Dean. The Canons conspired against him, in particular Bryan Bentley and James Fisher. His successor, Michael Mann, claimed that he 'was not well and had only five years to before retirement . . . By this stage Launcelot was too tired and was there far too short a time to have the energy to take on what was a formidable consortium, so the Chapel and the Castle community went into "suspended animation" during his Deanship.'[27] A Military Knight told the same author: 'Dean Fleming was like a stone dropped into a pool which made no ripples.'[28]

This was a calm period, seemingly free from machination – at least on the part of the Dean. Launcelot Fleming retired in 1976 and died in 1990. In his obituary, he was described as 'a retiring,

gentle man, kind and courteous, in a different mould both from the energetic Dean of Windsor who preceded him and the rather politic one who followed him.'[29]

MICHAEL MANN (DEAN 1976-89)

Michael Mann had been involved with St George's House under Robin Woods, when he was Director of the Missions to Seamen. Launcelot Fleming had appointed him a Canon of Norwich in 1969 and the Bishop's Advisor on Industry. Then Woods took him to Worcester as Bishop of Dudley in 1974, because of the St George's House connection, and believing him to have 'the right ideas about the way in which the patterns of ministry should develop.' When he went to Windsor in 1976, Woods noted: 'We had shared the hopes and aspirations of Windsor together for many years, and I certainly did not grudge losing him so quickly to that sphere of work.'[30] As all Deans are, Mann was Chairman of the Council of St George's House.

Fleming's biographer mentioned that Mann put Mattins into the Nave (it has now returned to the Quire), adding: 'Not for nothing had he been a Colonel of Dragoons.'[31] In order to achieve this, when services were conducted in the Nave, he used to ask that all those present should be counted, including choir and Military Knights – an interesting way of collating statistics to political advantage. Of the varied activities in Mann's early life, the significant phase was what he learned in the Army and at Harvard Business School. He applied these techniques to the Chapel, which was competently run during his Deanship, if at times an uncomfortable phase for some of those who lived through it.

In his early years at Windsor, in the Harvard Business School tradition, he encouraged the retirement of most of those who had been there longer than himself. Mann was also a military historian. From 1981 to 1986 General Sir Hugh Beach was Warden of St George's House. Some said that they thought Mann was the general and Beach the bishop. Mann also enjoyed a close association with Prince Philip, who admired his administrative skills, and he secured Prince Philip's agreement to publish their correspondence on a number of religious issues, including the possible conflict between science and religion.

Thanks to considerable efforts on his part, Michael Mann arranged the burial in Jerusalem of Princess Andrew of Greece, Prince Philip's mother, whose body had lain in the Royal Vault since her funeral in 1969. Princess Andrew had been born in Windsor Castle, almost in the presence of her great-grandmother, Queen Victoria. After a life of wars, separations, illnesses and other disasters, not to mention heroism on her part, she had returned to London from Greece in 1967 and spent her last days living with the Queen and Prince Philip at Buckingham Palace, where she died in December 1969.

On a visit to the Royal Vault, Dean Mann was surprised to find her coffin resting there and was instructed that it was his job to fulfil her long-held wish to be buried in Jerusalem. The negotiations lasted from 1976 until August 1988, when he finally overcame all the obstacles, political, religious and otherwise, and the Princess's coffin was placed in a vault under the Church of St Mary Magdalen on the Mount of Olives in Jerusalem.[32]

The Dean had from time to time offered prayers for the Duchess of Windsor at services during her long illness, and had kept in touch with news of her health in Paris, as best he could. In April 1986, he presided over her funeral, a private service, attended by the Queen and members of the Royal Family, and the Duchess's few surviving friends, at which the press noted that her name was not mentioned once during the service. This occurred due to an overly strict adherence to the instruction to give her the same funeral as the Duke, but omitting the reading out of his styles and titles. The tradition in the Book of Common Prayer is not to name the deceased, though in St George's Chapel some mention of the name is normally made. The Duchess was buried next to the Duke at Frogmore.

The Silver Jubilee was celebrated in 1977, old Canons left and new Canons arrived; the Chapter Clerk and the Virger retired; the annual St George's House lecture was instated in 1978, with the American Ambassador, the Hon Kingman Brewster, speaking on Power and Responsibility in the Eighties; the occasional services of the Royal Victorian Order took place in the chapel, and new choir stalls were placed in the Nave.

In 1982 Canon Bentley retired, though he continued to live in the Canon's Cloister as an honorary Canon until his death in 1996. In 1986 the Queen celebrated her 60th birthday with a large Service of Thanksgiving in the chapel.

Michael Mann was in charge when the Choir School was revamped at the cost of a million pounds, and the Queen opened its new extension in June 1988. He finally retired in July 1989 after what for him had been 'thirteen of the most wonderful and happy years at St George's', adding that the post of Dean of Windsor had been described as 'the best job in the Church of England!'[33]

PATRICK MITCHELL (DEAN 1989-98)

Patrick Mitchell's phase was seen by many as a happy time for St George's Chapel, particularly in the pastoral sense. He was formerly at Wells, and was described by Canon Trevor Beeson, of Westminster Abbey, as 'the elegant Dean of Wells' and 'highly thought of.'[34] He came to Windsor with his second wife, Pamela, both having been widowed at about the same time. They arrived at a moment when the Deanery's joists and floorboards needed substantial work due to the deathwatch beetle.

A tall man and a kind one, he made a point of getting to know all the extended community in turn, and once registered, he never forgot a name. He always had time for the community, and travelled overseas with the Friends of St George's. Most memorably, he led a highly successful pilgrimage to the Holy land and Jordan, with 36 Friends of St George's, mustered by their honorary

Very Rev Patrick Mitchell, Dean of Windsor from 1989 to 1998.

secretary, Tim O'Donovan with the help of Any Event Ltd.

Patrick Mitchell did not attempt to emulate the energetic style of leadership of his predecessor. St George's House was not his prime interest, nor did he primarily concern himself with matters of finance. He contributed greatly to the historical understanding of the chapel's past, inviting the British Archaeological Association to hold a conference about Windsor in 1998.

During his years as Dean, there was the first royal wedding in the chapel for many years when the Duke of Kent's daughter, Lady Helen Windsor married Tim Taylor in July 1992. Over the years a number of members of the Royal Family had been confirmed in the chapel. In the spring of 1997, Prince William was confirmed there, an occasion attended by the Prince of Wales and his former wife, Diana, not long before her tragic death.

Repairs and improvements continued apace, chapel lighting was improved, the vaulted ceiling of the Quire was cleaned, and a new fabric advisory committee was established with the Duke of Gloucester as one of its members. His philosophy was declared in his last letter to the Friends: 'Worship must always come first,' but he did not forget 'all those self-effacing people who work tirelessly behind the scenes to keep the wheels turning.'[35]

DAVID CONNER (DEAN FROM 1998)

With the present Dean, the 64th in the history of the College, history merges into the working life of the College today. Dean Conner was formerly Bishop of Lynn, having previously served as Chaplain at Winchester College and as Vicar of St Mary the Great, Cambridge.

He has presided over a particularly active phase in the life of the College. It was, as so often in its long history, another time of difficulty, the money needed for the fabric, not to mention the running costs, having become an issue of crisis. Claude Hankes-Drielsma, who had been involved with St George's House for over 20 years, secured £5 million for the House, to honour the 80th birthday of the Duke of Edinburgh in June 2001. He was then persuaded to mastermind a special appeal to mark the Queen's 80th birthday in April 2006. He completed the task entrusted to him, securing substantial donations and pledges for the College of St George from a range of benefactors, including members of the Royal Family, Companions of the Garter, and generous private sponsors, who recognised the significance and implications of the occasion. He was made a KCVO in the Queen's Birthday honours of 2006.

Under the inspiration of Sir Michael Hobbs, Governor of the Military Knights, the College created a Foundation to support its economic needs. This was the first time since its constitution in the fourteenth century that the Chapter had established an entirely separate fund-raising body including significant lay participation.

The Dean presided over a wedding and four funerals. In 1999 Prince Edward chose St George's Chapel for his wedding to Sophie Rhys-Jones. Since then the Earl and Countess of Wessex have been great supporters of the chapel, attending concerts and other events there. In 2006 the Earl of Wessex became Patron of the Windsor Festival.

Princess Margaret had attended Dean Conner's installation at a time when she was already in indifferent health. She died in February 2002, and her funeral took place in the chapel on 15 February, by coincidence the 50th anniversary of the funeral of her father, King George VI. The Queen Mother flew from Sandringham at the age of nearly 102 to attend the service, which proved to be her last ever official outing. She died a few weeks later at Royal Lodge on 30 March and though her funeral was held in Westminster Abbey on 9 April, it fell to David Conner to pronounce the blessing at her interment, on which occasion the ashes of Princess Margaret were placed beside the coffins of her parents in the King George VI Memorial Chapel, it having been her express wish to be near her parents in death.

In October 2004 Princess Alice, Duchess of Gloucester, who came regularly to Christmas Mattins at St George's Chapel until she was 93, died at Kensington Palace, aged 102, and her funeral was held at the chapel. On Boxing Day the same year, Rt Hon Sir Angus Ogilvy, husband of Princess Alexandra (both regular attenders of the annual St George's House lecture) died in hospital and his funeral took place in the chapel. Both were buried at Frogmore.

A few months later, on 9 April 2005, the Prince of Wales married Mrs Camilla Parker Bowles in the Guildhall, Windsor, and the service of blessing took place in the chapel in the presence of the Queen, members of the Royal Family, friends and many celebrity guests who support the Prince's Trust and other similar charities.

The present Dean combines his work at St George's with the arduous role of Bishop to the Forces, necessitating many travels overseas so that

The present Dean of Windsor, Rt Rev David Conner, Dean since 1998.

in 2005 the Chapter revived the office of 'locum tenens', calling it Vice-Dean. The senior Canon, John White, holds this position.

The integrity of the College and its future as a place where, in faithfulness to its statutes, the opus dei is daily maintained, is the heart of David Conner's view of his Deanship. He has also striven to bring the wider membership of the College of St George closer together.

As senior residents of the castle, the Queen and the Duke of Edinburgh continue to take a keen interest in the life of the College. Both chose to celebrate their 80th birthdays with family and friends at St George's Chapel, Prince Philip in June

LEFT The bust of the Queen, sculpted by Angela Conner, a gift to the Queen from the Companions of the Garter on the occasion of her 80th birthday. The commission was inspired by the late Duke of Devonshire, KG.

OPPOSITE PAGE Choristers in the Dean's Cloister.

2001, and the Queen in April 2006.

St George's Day, 23 April 2008, marks the 60th anniversary of the installation of the then Princess Elizabeth and the Duke of Edinburgh into the Order of the Garter, the day on which King George VI revived the full ceremonial of the Order, with investitures and installations.

And so the long association between the Chapel, the College of St George, the Order of the Garter and the British monarchy continues as strongly in the twenty-first century, albeit with contemporary priorities, as ever it did in its long history.

PART TWO

THE LIVING CHAPEL

SEVEN

'A good Quire of voices'

ONE OF THE most outstanding contributions made by the College of St George over 600 years of history has been its musical tradition. This was particularly marked in the period immediately after the Reformation when the new form of Common Prayer was developed and enriched musically at St George's.

The tradition has continued up to the present day. Sir George Elvey, Sir Walter Parratt, Dr Edmund Fellowes, Sir Walford Davies, Sir William Harris and the distinguished musicians who have followed them have made contributions of great value.

* * * * *

In June 1833, shortly before the arrival of George Elvey, the diarist, Thomas Creevey was staying with Colonel Ferguson in Canon Stopford's house, and noted:

> There never was such a passion for actual beauty, and the most striking and charming associations ... Then I could hear the organ of St George's Chapel whilst I was dressing, and had not fifty yards to go to be present and hear the Anthem in it before I went to the Races ... I never spent two more agreeable days in my life.[1]

The College continues to inspire new compositions. An important commission came in 1958 when the Duke of Edinburgh asked Benjamin Britten to compose for the chapel, originally hoping he might create 'a complete service.'[2] Prince Philip had got to know Britten when staying with his cousins, Prince and Princess Louis of Hesse, at Wolfsgarten in Germany. One day he approached Britten with the idea and Britten replied that he was 'extremely excited by this suggestion.'[3] The result was a *Jubilate*, which has often been sung in the chapel since 1961, and formed a part of Prince Philip's 80th birthday service in the chapel in June 2001.

The choir has been an integral element of the College of St George, predating the present chapel by a century. The Statutes of 1352 ordained that 'one of the said Vicars more learned than the rest in instructing grammar and singing shall be bound diligently to instruct the said Chorister boys of the same Chapel in grammar and singing'.[4] There were only six boys at first, but the number was raised to thirteen in 1475. Now there are 12 men and 23 boys.

Ever since its foundation, the choir has sustained the daily worship in the chapel and takes part in services on royal occasions and for the Order of the Garter.

In early days the boys were trained in the complexities of the liturgy with its three vital elements – text, chant and ceremony. They were given general education too but remained choristers 'for the time only during which they [were] endued with fullness of voice.'[5] Plainsong gave way to a polyphonic musical form, introduced in the mid fourteenth century, which depended largely on men's voices.

By the time the present chapel was built, the choir was fully capable of performing music in the flowing polyphonic style. There was an organ in the old chapel at St George's as early as 1406. Accommodation for the choir was somewhat scratchy until 1520 when the choristers were comfortably installed in Denton's Commons, the new dwellings being built by Canon Denton at his own expense.

The choir survived the vicissitudes of the Reformation, and was looked on favourably by successive monarchs. Queen Elizabeth I ordained:

> Whereas our Royal College of St George hath in the days of our father been well furnished with singing men and children. We willing it should not be of less reputation in our day, but rather augmented and increased ... [we] will and charge that no singing man or boy shall be taken out of the said Chapel, by virtue of any commission not even from our household Chapel [the Chapel Royal] ...[6]

Elizabeth I encouraged the choirboys to take part in plays by Richard Farrant and other dramatists, in which they acted the female roles.

During the Civil War of 1642 when the Dean, Canons and other members and servants of the College were expelled from the Cloisters, the disbanded choirs from St George's and Eton College were given an hour's daily practice in sacred music (vocal and instrumental) in the rooms of Thomas Weaver at Eton. After the Commonwealth period, at the Restoration in 1660, the full College of St George was re-established. Some six years later Samuel Pepys sat in the Quire to hear an anthem sung, recording: 'It is a noble place indeed and a good Quire of voices.'[7]

Several organists appear as Benefactors of the College, including John Marbeck, organist at the time of the Reformation. He was thought to have been a chorister, and later he was Master of the boys and organist. In 1544 he was condemned to suffer burning at the stake for having denounced the mass in writing, but the Bishop of Winchester obtained a royal pardon for him, it is said, on account of his musical talents. Marbeck was a theologian as well as a musician and composer. He brought out the first Concordance of the English Bible.

William Child, organist at the time of Charles II, is celebrated as one of the chapel's benefactors. For many years King James II failed to pay his salary, to the point that he allowed the Dean and Canons to recover the debt from the King. He settled with

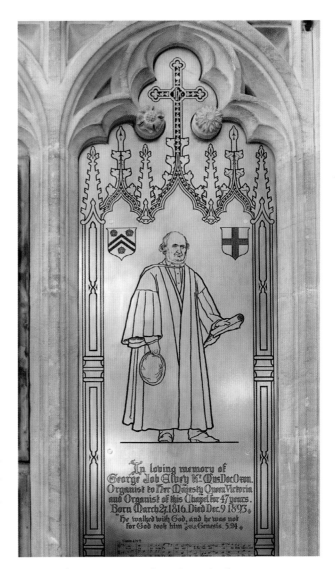

Memorial to Sir George Elvey, Organist from 1835 to 1882, a brass tablet in the Rutland Chantry.

them for £5 and some wine. But then James II discharged the debt direct to him. Child lamented his ill fortune, and the Dean and Canons released him from his bargain on condition that he paid for the paving of the Quire. This he did happily, and there were still funds left over.

It took two centuries to overcome the havoc wreaked by the Civil War, despite the help of other benefactors. It was not until the reign of Queen Victoria that the choirboys were given an all-round education in the Victorian sense of the concept. Besides a purely musical training, they had always

Most of his best works were composed for St George's Chapel services between 1856 and 1860, the Prince Consort being a particularly sympathetic patron. He composed his anthem, 'Wherwithal shall a young man cleanse his way?' for the confirmation of Prince Edward of Saxe-Weimar, Queen Adelaide's nephew. Later he conducted the music at the wedding of the Prince of Wales (later Edward VII) in 1863, for which he wrote 'Sing unto God', and in 1871 a festal march for the wedding of Princess Louise.

Elvey was married four times, three of his wives predeceasing him. He retired in 1882, soon after the wedding of the Duke of Albany, rather feeling that he had been dismissed, despite being 84 at the time. Just before his death in December 1893, he conducted the St George's Chapel choir at the annual concert they gave at the Albert Institute in Windsor.[8]

SIR WALTER PARRATT (ORGANIST 1882-1924)

Walter Parratt succeeded Elvey. He was a Huddersfield man, and music was his love from early childhood. At the age of four, he would crawl under his father's feet at the organ and create music by putting the pedals down with his hands. At the age of 12 he could play Bach's fugues from memory, and being very small, walked over the pedals as he could not reach them from the seat. After several previous appointments he became Organist of Magdalen College, Oxford in 1872, when he was 31. Ten years later, on Elvey's retirement, Parratt was lured to Windsor by Queen Victoria's son, Prince Leopold, and by Dean Wellesley.

Elvey predicted 'a fine row'[9] about the organ that would confront the new organist, since it was hopelessly out of date. There was no possibility of playing Bach fugues on it – but Parratt put his trust in the Dean and Canons. 'I shall get what I want, I

been taught to read and given some element of classical education. Now they were given an organized routine, a schoolmaster to attend to their academic needs and a matron to take care of their health and appearance.

SIR GEORGE ELVEY (ORGANIST 1835-82)

George Elvey took over as Organist and Choirmaster in 1835 and, for the next 45 years, the College made giant strides in its musical life. Elvey was born in Canterbury in 1816 and chosen by William IV and Queen Adelaide to be organist at Windsor, aged 19. To the general public he was known for his setting of a popular harvest hymn, and as the composer of anthems. He favoured old English church music and also loved the works of Handel.

suppose,' he wrote to his wife, 'and this will bind me to this place.'[10]

The organ was rebuilt and the manuals placed on the south side from where the organist had a clear view into the Nave, which he found useful on state occasions. From Elvey he inherited a good choir, which he soon pulled into fine shape, being extremely critical of any form of slackness, conceit or vulgarity. There was an extensive repertory of works from Thomas Tallis to S.S. Wesley, to which he added the work of new young church musicians. Many of C.V. Stanford's works were performed at St George's before publication. Before long some 450 anthems were in regular performance.

Elvey bequeathed him the Windsor and Eton Madrigal Society, a hundred strong, who combined with the St George's Choir, especially in performances of the St Matthew Passion. He founded the Windsor Orchestral Society. During Parratt's time as organist, Canon J.N. Dalton converted the choir school into a preparatory school and the present St George's School was thereby established in 1893.

Parratt created a distinctive style of organ-playing, known in the musical world as 'The Parratt School'. An extraordinary number of his choristers and pupils emerged as successful musicians in their own right, mainly as organists, including Sir Walford Davies and Sir William Harris, both organists at Windsor, and Dr Henry Ley, at Eton. As recently as December 2006, his last surviving chorister, John Denison died at the age of 95. He had sung at the Westminster Abbey wedding of the Duke and Duchess of York (later George VI and Queen Elizabeth) in 1923 and went on to be Director of South Bank Concert Halls (formerly General Manager, the Festival Hall) in London. At John Denison's memorial service at St George's, Hanover Square, some members of the St George's Choir sang under the direction of Timothy Byram-Wigfield, with Roger Judd at the organ.

Under Parratt, the services at the Chapel became the focal point for organists throughout Britain. He was also professor of the organ at the newly founded Royal College of Music. He composed the anthem, *Confortare*, for the Coronation of Edward VII, as well as music for Garter ceremonies early in the reign of George V, and the Investiture of the Prince of Wales at Caernarvon Castle in 1911. For recreation he played chess, in which he gained some notoriety.

In the First World War, most of the Lay Clerks being on active service, the choir was inevitably depleted. Parratt had scarcely had time to pull the choir together again after the war when St George's was closed in 1920 for the major restoration of the building. It was fortunate that Parratt had never been a noisy organist, for had he been, the vibrations might have brought the roof down. During the restoration, the organ was dismantled and Canon Dalton fulfilled a long-held wish to replace it with a new one, with pipes divided in two sections. This gave a splendid effect from the Nave, but, at the time, there were those who worshipped in the Quire, who appeared to regret the change, missing 'the dominating figure of the organ from the east end, not hiding, but pointing with graceful fingers at the superb fan-tracery of the roof', as Parratt's son, Geoffrey, put it. He concluded: 'To many the Chapel is converted into a tunnel.'[11] Parratt did not live long enough to judge the effect.

For seven years the East End of the Nave was boarded up and there were services in the Nave, for which a small organ was used. Parratt could be seen at the keyboard. By this time he was failing in health and sometimes merely started a processional hymn with one note on his pitch-pipe and left the choir to sing unaccompanied. His son, Geoffrey, noted that the only advantage was that the voices were better heard in the Nave. 'In the choir the banners and carved woodwork mopped up the sound like a blanket, and the muffling effect could always be heard when a processional hymn was sung and the voices entered the choir.'[12]

Sir Walter Parratt died on 27 March 1924 and his ashes were placed in the North Quire Aisle near the organ steps and opposite a tablet to his daughter, Amy, who predeceased him in 1917.

Dr Fellowes, Minor Canon since 1900, took over the work of the choir during the vacancy, while for a short while a former chorister, G.S. Kitchingman, acted as organist, and later Malcolm C. Boyle (another pupil of Parratt's, and later organist of Chester Cathedral). Walford Davies, who had originally declined the Chapter's offer to be organist, finally accepted and arrived in 1927.

SIR WALFORD DAVIES (ORGANIST 1927-32)

Walford Davies was born in Oswestry in 1869. He arrived at Windsor in 1882 to have his voice tried by Sir George Elvey, and served as chorister under him and also under Parratt. When his voice broke in 1885, he became an assistant organist at the chapel. His fellow assistant in the organ loft was Hubert Hunt.

In order to give Davies employment, Dean Davidson appointed him his secretary, a task at which he proved poor, 'untidy, forgetful and given to scrawling letters in an unformed hand.'[13] Davies soon gave up being Davidson's secretary and became organist of the Royal Chapel in Windsor Great Park until 1890, when he was accepted into the Royal College of Music.

As his career progressed, he became organist of the Temple Church in London. He composed for the Three Choirs Festival and Leeds Festival and served as Professor of Music at Aberystwyth University. He became fascinated by broadcasting music, which resulted in his career expanding on many fronts. It was his old Windsor boss, Randall Davidson, by then Archbishop of Canterbury, who first proposed Davies for the Windsor organship. Davies declined on the grounds that he was too busy, and the Dean and Canons heeded the Archbishop's advice to keep the options open, especially while services were still being held in the Nave. In the Michaelmas term of 1927, he was persuaded to come to Windsor.

The Quire was still being restored, whilst Davies presided over the rebuilding of the organ, a large four-manual instrument with 63 speaking stops with a pedal organ having 13 stops. There was a difference of opinion over a plan to have two consoles, side by side, and Davies won over the Dean and Canons by offering to pay the extra costs

Choristers rehearsing in the Quire.

which so alarmed them. (He was eventually refunded).

As an organist, he was a bit out of practice due to his many public duties, and an operation in 1926 had slowed him down, while causing him to put on weight. His ambition was to make the music at St George's an inspiration to all church musicians. He invited numerous other choirs to join in their endeavours, and at the reopening service in 1930 an impressive number of magnificent cathedral choirs took part. In 1932 he initiated a festival of church music.

During his time at Windsor, which ended in 1932, he became a tremendous hero to the choirboys, who enjoyed his open hospitality. Occasionally he found his concept of church or cathedral music in conflict with the ancient statutes laid down by Edward III. As one of his biographers put it: 'Sadly, the five years he was to spend there were not without conflict, partly because of his radical opinions about the restoration of the organ, and partly because of his over-liberal views on the form of the services.'[14]

For the reopening service in November 1930 Davies composed a *Te Deum* for double choir and orchestra, which earned the accolade of 'perfect' from George V. Two years after leaving Windsor, Davies was appointed Master of the King's Musick, which involved him in the musical aspects of the Silver Jubilee celebrations and the Coronation of George VI and Queen Elizabeth, for which he composed the *Confortare*. He died of a heart attack on 11 March 1941, and his ashes were placed in the garden of Bristol Cathedral. At Windsor, his musical arrangements are still performed regularly, a popular favourite being his setting of 'God be in my Head' (composed in 1908), which was sung at the funeral of George V.

SIR WILLIAM HARRIS (ORGANIST 1932-61)

Davies's successor at Windsor was Charles Hylton Stewart, but he died on 14 November 1932 after six months in the post. The next organist was Dr William Harris. Born in 1883, he was another of Sir Walter Parratt's pupils, while Walford Davies was a considerable influence, teaching him composition, Harris being his assistant organist at the Temple Church. He spent most of his life in collegiate churches. After being assistant organist at Lichfield Cathedral, he was successively organist at New College (during which time he played the organ at the funeral of Lord Oxford, formerly Prime Minister, H.H. Asquith, at Sutton Courtenay Church in 1928) and then Christ Church, Oxford. In 1933 he came to Windsor, where he found an outlet for his talents in the great ceremonial services he conducted there and the festivals he organised. He remained as organist until 1961. He was well known for the composition of anthems such as 'Faire is the heav'n', 'Bring us, O Lord God', and the beautiful 'King of Glory, King of Peace' (1925) (this last based on the hymn with words by his favourite poet, George Herbert), being perhaps the best known.

Whilst at Windsor, Harris taught the Queen and Princess Margaret to play the piano. The King's Private Secretary, Sir Alan Lascelles, particularly liked to come to the organ loft during Evensong, and relished the playing of the organ. Looking down on the choirboys during an anthem in 1942, he reflected: 'they were probably thinking of whether there would be buns for tea and similar mundane matters, and were quite unconscious that, for those of us up aloft, they were the authors of a volume of sound of transcendent beauty.'[15] During his time at Windsor, Harris sent six choristers to sing at the Queen's wedding in Westminster Abbey in 1947.

A connoisseur of organ-playing, H.J. White, the Dean of Christ Church, compared Harris to the Eton College organist, H.J. Ley, stating: 'When Ley plays it's like Liszt extemporizing on the piano: when Harris plays it's like Bach playing his own fugues.'[16] Ley himself judged that few could rival 'Doc H' (as he was known to the choristers) in knowledge, skill or experience.

In the early 1950s his assistant organist was Lionel Dakers. He recalled:

> He was as original and at times venturesome in much of his composition as he was instinctively traditional in his organ playing. To him the then fashionable and relatively new pursuit of Baroque interpretation was anathema and was facetiously summed up by him and others as 'tinkle, tinkle' or 'bubble and squeak' sounds. He was an avid performer of the organ music of Bach, invariably commencing a fugue using the diapasons. Feeling skittish one day he suddenly pulled out the 4ft Principal as well and chucklingly proclaimed 'Aha – Baroque!' as he set off.[17]

Dakers also recalled that Harris used to test him out, announcing that he would not be at Evensong, but then listening from some distant corner of the Nave.

Alastair Sampson, one of Harris's choristers and later Organist of Eton College Chapel, wrote of him:

> As an organist Harris had inherited from Parratt a wonderful sense of restraint, in complete contrast to

Dr Henry Ley, the much celebrated organ-playing Eton Precentor, just down the road. During my five years as a chorister, I doubt if I heard the Tuba stop drawn as many times, whereas I have little doubt that Etonians were hearing theirs as many times in a week. Nor have I ever heard psalms accompanied with such subtle yet gentle imagination.[18]

Harris retired in 1961 and died aged 90 in 1973.

DR SIDNEY CAMPBELL (ORGANIST 1961-74)

His successor, Dr Sidney Campbell was born in 1909. He began his working life in local government and had no professional teaching until he trained for and obtained his FRCO in 1931. He was organist at St Peter's, Wolverhampton, and Sub-Warden of the Royal School of Church Music, Canterbury, before becoming successively organist of Ely, Southwark and Canterbury Cathedrals, coming at last to Windsor in 1961.

Hardly had Sir William Harris retired than the organ collapsed and Campbell oversaw its reconstruction. The new organ was dedicated in the presence of Queen Elizabeth the Queen Mother in 1965, and he relished playing it in 'his extremely individual style of panache'.[19] While at Windsor, he arranged settings for litanies and other liturgical music and composed the music for a *Jubilate Deo* for the dedication service for the opening of St George's House in 1966.

Besides the *Jubilate*, a rich selection from across the centuries was in evidence at the St George's House service. There was the 'Vivat Regina' and 'O Pray for the Peace of Jerusalem' from Hubert Parry's Coronation anthem, 'I was Glad', the music for the four hymns were respectively by Orlando Gibbons (1583-1625), Henry Smart (1813-79), Thomas Tallis (ca 1505-85), and R.H. Prichard (1811-87), while the chant for Psalm 67 was composed by Sir William Harris.

During Campbell's time as organist, Robin Woods introduced the idea of choral and organ scholarships. The Dean and Canons invited applications from Reading University to fill three

Dr Sidney Campbell, Organist from 1961 to 1974, outside his house, 23 The Cloisters.

postgraduate choral scholarships, offering accommodation for men to join the Lay Clerks singing in the choir. They also offered two organ scholarships for organists at the Royal College of Music to reside at Windsor, accompany the services, and help with training the choir, while continuing their studies at Windsor. These initiatives were created to strengthen the musical tradition of the chapel in particular and the heritage of English Church music in general. The endowment of all the five scholarships was estimated to cost £30,000.

Robin Woods described Campbell as 'a superb musician, competent composer and imaginative planner', but added that he was 'highly temperamental'. There was a well remembered incident when he came down from the organ loft to conduct an eight-part Tudor anthem and gave the choir a note to sing unaccompanied only to find the trebles notoriously astray. In a rage he tore the score into shreds and threw it at the boys. The Minor Canon broke the silence by intoning 'Let us Pray'. An hour later Campbell offered his resignation to the Dean who calmed him down and would hear of no such thing. 'Is there not always an emotional price to pay for good music?' concluded the Dean.[20]

Richard Russell, Headmaster of St George's School, described Campbell as 'a crusty old character' who 'could be acid: he did not like officialdom; he did not like poor singing.' But he added: 'Beneath the crust, however, there appeared a lonely man, and I found that he had a dry sort of wit and could be very funny.'[21]

Dr Campbell had a self-deprecating sense of humour, once relating his irritation at a woman tourist who posed for a photograph outside his kitchen window, at 23 The Cloisters, a part of the College which should have been devoid of tourists. As he explained it, he happened to have a pan of cold water in his hand and the window was open. He did not look up but shortly afterwards he was aware of her walking away, somewhat taken aback, rubbing the back of her legs.[22]

Not especially noted for his sartorial elegance, Campbell adopted the polo-neck shirt in the 1960s when 'in mufti', as he liked to call it. This was noticed by Canon Bentley, with whom he was on good terms, and from then on the Canon eschewed the starched dog collar under his cassock in favour of a white polo-neck jersey.

Amongst the organ scholars who came during Campbell's time were John Morehen and John Porter. Francis Grier, now a noted composer, was one of his choristers and who later had the present Director of Music, Tim Byram-Wigfield, as one of his pupils.

One summer day in June 1974 Sidney Campbell failed to turn up at early morning choir practice. He had died unexpectedly in the night, aged only 64.

CHRISTOPHER ROBINSON
(ORGANIST 1975-91)

After a short period during which John Porter acted as organist, Christopher Robinson arrived. There were many changes, Sung Mattins being dropped except on Sundays, Saint Days and other special occasions. Christopher Robinson was a generation younger, and first and foremost a choirmaster, whereas Campbell had been an organist before everything else. The Headmaster of St George's School, Richard Russell, noticed a change. He observed that a 'distinct polish was being rubbed

onto it.' The boys worked harder, which concerned some of the parents, but there were rich rewards. In 1975 they joined the London Bach Choir at the Festival Hall in 1975 to perform William Mathias's 'This World's Joie' for the first time. The performance was followed by an EMI recording in 1976.

The choir appeared in many cathedrals and on the continent. Evensong was regularly broadcast from St George's by the BBC and Christmas Mattins televised every third year. Six choristers sung the grace in the film, *Chariots of Fire*. One of his pupils, Martin Denny, a chorister from 1981-6, became Director of the Windsor Festival in 2001.

JONATHAN REES-WILLIAMS (1991-2004)

In 1991 Christopher Robinson was succeeded by Jonathan Rees-Williams, who came from directing the choir at Lichfield Cathedral. He introduced new works into the repertoire and confirmed the daily choral tradition as the heart of the chapel choir's fundamental purpose. Between 2001 and 2002 the chapel organ was completely refurbished, having been played at nearly 13,000 services since the 1965 restoration. This was largely paid for by the Friends of St George's in response to a Millennium appeal.

In April 2002 the St George's Chapel choir sang in Westminster Abbey with the Abbey choir and the choir of King's College, Cambridge, at Princess Margaret's memorial service, to fulfil her known wishes.

TIMOTHY BYRAM-WIGFIELD
(DIRECTOR OF MUSIC FROM 2004)

In 2004 Rees-Williams was succeeded by the present Director of Music, Timothy Byram-Wigfield, who was born in 1963, trained at the Royal College of Music, and was organ scholar at Christ Church, Oxford. Before coming to Windsor, Byram-Wigfield had been sub-organist of Winchester Cathedral, then Master of the Music at St Mary's Episcopal Cathedral, Edinburgh, and immediately Director of Music at Jesus College, Cambridge.

RIGHT Tim Byram-Wigfield in the Dean's Cloister.

LOWER RIGHT Roger Judd, Assistant Organist since 1985, seated at the console of the organ.

At the 80th birthday service for The Queen, on St George's Day, April 2006, Byram-Wigfield conducted 'The Golden Rule' arranged by Sir Peter Maxwell Davies, Master of the Queen's Music, with words by Andrew Motion, the Poet Laureate. He has made several recordings with the choir and is keen to take them to perform outside the walls of Windsor Castle so that more people can enjoy hearing 'a choir of excellence.'[23]

In September 2006 they flew to New York to perform at the British Memorial Garden on the 5th anniversary of 9/11 in the presence of the Duke of York and relatives of the United Kingdom citizens who died in the tragedy. They undertook further engagements in New York in support of the New York Downtown Hospital. In October 2007 there was another such trip to the United States.

The expenses of running the choir have risen over the years and now cost about £450,000 a year. A very significant donation was received from Mr and Mrs Donald Kahn to help secure the future of the choir.

In July and August 2007, the Dean (Rt Rev David Conner) and the Chapter Clerk (Charlotte Manley) walked 250 miles from Shere (seat of Sir Reginald Bray, KG, the benefactor whose bequest completed the building of the chapel) to Winchester, Stratfield Saye, Oxford and on to Windsor. Their walk took in the homes of past and present Knights of the Garter, and some of the fifty churches linked historically to St George's Chapel (Hartley Wespall, Sutton Courtenay, Rotherfield Greys and others). They raised a considerable amount of money to create a choral bursary. By walking through that historical countryside, they linked physical reminders of aspects of the chapel's history with the fine choral tradition of the College.

EIGHT
The Military Knights of Windsor

THE MILITARY KNIGHTS are an integral part of the College of St George. They were formed by Edward III in 1348. In the constitution of the College provision was made at first for 24 and later for 26 Knights, who had been prisoners of the French and had become impoverished as a result of

the payment of heavy ransoms. They were then called 'Poor Knights' or 'Alms Knights' and were offered a small pension and accommodation in Windsor Castle. This provision was 12 pence a day, which was increased in the reign of James I to 24 pence with 40 shillings a year for other needs.

Edward III was keen that they should live 'in proper knightly estate'. Their 'beads-man' role was essential to the foundation. They had to be unmarried in order to fulfil their religious duties. They were required to pray daily for the Sovereign and the Knights of the Garter and if one of them failed to do so, their daily allowance was shared amongst the other knights.

Until the Reformation there were never more than three Knights at any given time. Only eight were appointed before 1400, for example, the first recorded knight of some 648 Military Knights (to date) being Robert Beverle (Beverley), who received payment as a Poor Knight between May and July that year. John Kiderowe (possibly Clitheroe) was the sole Poor Knight between 1429 and 1431. Sometimes the statutes were abused, and civilians were admitted by royal favour.

It was Henry VIII who put matters in order. He amended their statutes, confining them to 13 in number, provided adequate financial backing to pay their stipends, and allocated an extra £3.6s.8d a year for one to be their Governor. James Crane was appointed in 1558, but died soon afterwards, to be

The Governor of the Castle, Air Chief Marshal Sir Richard Johns, leading the Garter procession down the West steps – the Military Knights led by their Governor, Major-General Sir Michael Hobbs.

The houses of the Military Knights in the Lower Ward, photographed from the roof of St George's Chapel.

succeeded by John Acton. These plans were ratified in Henry's will and honoured by his daughter, Queen Mary. In 1557 she built new accommodation for them in the walls of the castle, and rebuilt what is now called the Mary Tudor Tower, where the Governor of the Military Knights now lives. This tower is the only place in the United Kingdom where Mary I's arms appear alongside those of Philip II of Spain.

Elizabeth I continued to take an interest after she succeeded her sister, and she issued new statutes, defining the knights as to be 'unmarried Gentlemen brought to necessity after active military service'. They were given a red gown and a blue and purple mantle with the cross of St George on the left shoulder.

During the period of the Commonwealth between 1649 and 1659, the Military Knights were not ejected from the castle and they were paid out of the confiscated Chapter livings, unlike the Dean and Canons, who were removed because they were a reflection of a papist past. In 1656 Sir Francis Crane appointed five officers to a new Foundation (later called the Lower Foundation) and thus there were 18 Poor Knights present at Cromwell's funeral

in 1658 (5 on Crane's and 13 on the Royal Foundation). The Lower Foundation continued to exist until as late as 1921, when it lapsed and the number of Military Knights became 13 again.

Most of the Poor Knights were worthy figures, but some were colourful and controversial figures. In their latest Roll, Major Richard Moore (MK number 637) recounts stories of ancient misdemeanours, of one seventeenth century Governor being described as 'no gentleman and no soldier' and of fights and fisticuffs between individual knights. As recently as 1905, Major Charles Strutt, appointed in 1901, was found to have engaged in a devious financial scam to defraud a brother officer and had his conduct severely criticized in the Chancery Division. There were discussions as to whether he could be dismissed as a Military Knight, but it was found that he had not offended against the Elizabethan Statutes. However, Letters Patent were introduced to the effect that a Military Knight held office and could be dismissed at the Sovereign's pleasure. Strutt stayed on, dying in 1908.

The Military Knights photographed on the West steps of the Chapel by Sir Benjamin Stone in 1899. They include veterans from the Crimean War, the Siege of Sebastopol, the Charge of the Heavy and Light Brigade, and the Indian Mutiny.
Front row, left to right: Major Richard Molesworth, Major Robert Dickens, Captain John Pickworth, Colonel Francis Maude, VC, and Captain William Maloney (Governor 1896-1905).
Back row: Major Henry Bolton, Captain Maurice FitzGerald, Colonel Dunbar Muter, Colonel Henry Somerset, Colonel Frederick Swinfen, and Lt-Colonel Montagu Battye.

Many Poor Knights suffered grievously fighting for their country, for example Major Roger Thornton, appointed in 1693, who had 'served in the wars all the time of the unhappy Rebellion to the ruin of a very considerable fortune to which he was born and is now aged and infirm.'[1]

On 17 September 1833 William IV officially granted the Poor Knights the style of 'The Military Knights of Windsor' their previous title being deemed rather demeaning. He ordained that they

should wear the red uniform of an officer on the Unattached List with their badge the cross of St George and their buttons embossed with the Garter star. They did so for the first time on Christmas Day 1833. This has remained their uniform ever since, except that in 1907 Edward VII gave them the white crossbelt adorned with a brass plate bearing the Garter star, and added a black belt to be worn over the red sash.

Throughout their long history, Military Knights have been veterans of most of the important campaigns and battles. For instance, nineteen of them fought at Waterloo. In the 1890s and early 1900s, the great traveller, photographer, politician and philanthropist, Sir Benjamin Stone, visited Windsor Castle. Loving more than anything to record history with his camera, he photographed eleven Military Knights as a group on the West steps of the Chapel. These included three survivors of the Crimean War (Colonel Swinfen, having been in charge of the Heavy Brigade at Balaclava), while others had been present at the Sieges of Delhi,

The Military Knights of Windsor, 1966.
Front row, left to right: Major H.K. Clough, Brigadier E.K.B. Furze, Major-General Sir Edmund Hakewill Smith (Governor), Lt-Colonel R.F. Squibb, Brigadier W.P.A. Robinson.
Back row: Major T.W. Garnett, Lt-Colonel H.G. Duncombe, Lt-Colonel G.F.G. Turner, Lt-Colonel L.W. Giles, and Brigadier A.A. Crook.

Lucknow, and at the Fall of Sebastopol. Amongst them was Colonel Francis Maude, VC, one of only two VC holders amongst the Military Knights, who won his Victoria Cross at the siege of Lucknow. The other was Lt Colonel Bryan Lawrence, VC, who won his at Essenboch, South Africa. He was appointed in 1934 but resigned a few years later and retired to Kenya.

Colonel Maude had served in the Crimean War and used to delight the choristers by reciting Tennyson's 'The Charge of the Light Brigade'. 'We were always thrilled to hear him recount what he had seen with his own eyes', wrote Russell Thorndike, actor brother of the actress, Dame Sybil, a chorister of the 1890s.[2] Maude was at the centre of a dispute with the Dean and Canons when he was forbidden promotion within their ranks due to being bankrupt. This led to the Military Knights petitioning the Commander-in-Chief, HRH the Duke of Cambridge, and writing to Queen Victoria. Worse still an attack on the way the Dean and Canons operated found its way into the press.

In 1905 Edward VII decided that their Governor should be a Major-General and transferred their governance from the Dean to the Constable and Governor of Windsor Castle, there having been considerable arguments between the Dean and Military Knights.

The role of the Military Knights has always been to attend services, to pray for the Sovereign, the Sovereign's family and for the Knights of the Garter. As such the Military Knights used to sit in the front row of the Garter stalls at the level of the aisle. There are occasional accounts of them. The young Marquess of Lorne (later 9th Duke of Argyll and husband of Queen Victoria's fourth daughter,

Major H.K. Clough, Military Knight of Windsor from 1932 to 1970.

Princess Louise), recalled that when he was at Eton in the 1860s, he used to sit behind one of them in the Garter stalls:

> I remember one of these old gentlemen who excited my wonder ... for he had a bullet wound on both sides of his bald skull, and to all appearance the shot must have either traversed or made the circuit of that hard head with remarkable care, for he was a knight of Windsor for many decades after the French had hit him with a bullet large enough to kill him.3

Russell Thorndike remembered the Military Knights as 'some half-dozen old and distinguished-looking officers in long military coats. On a ledge beyond their hassocks they had placed their cocked hats, resplendent with cock's feathers.'4

Their number have always included memorable castle figures – Lt-Colonel 'Toddy' Hodgson, who was banned from fishing at Frogmore after Queen Mary heard him swearing; Major 'Billy' Clough, who served in the South African War, and who was surrounded by loving ladies until his dying day; and more recently, Brigadier John Lindner, who rode his motor scooter through the Home Park to his allotment at Frogmore, when aged 90, causing the Queen to send a message that he need not salute her, since she was anxious he might fall off.

It was only from Easter Day 1927, following the reintroduction of services into the Quire after the 1920s restoration that the Military Knights

ABOVE Major-General Sir Michael Hobbs, Governor of the Military Knights since 2000.

BELOW Military Knights' houses and the Mary Tudor Tower, where their Governor lives.

Major-General Sir Michael Hobbs, leading the Military Knights out of Mattins on a Sunday morning.

Major Peter Bolton, Military Knight since 1990, and Brigadier Timothy Hackworth, Military Knight since 1992, in the Dean's Cloister before marching into Sunday Mattins.

marched into chapel in procession. In 1942, following a petition to the Governor, it was decided that the Military Knights would give obeisance to the altar, and a further request was made for better seats, the front row, which they then occupied, being what Brigadier-General Pelly called 'very uncomfortable and . . . not made for grown men.'5 Lord Wigram, the Deputy Constable, approved the idea, Dean Baillie approached King George VI and he gave his sanction on 13 November 1942. From then on, they were allocated their own seats in the row immediately in front of the Garter stalls.

They have additional ceremonial duties beyond Sunday Mattins. They lead the annual Garter procession led by their Governor and in front of him the Governor of Windsor Castle (unless he is a Knight of the Garter, in which case he processes with the other K.G.s. In recent years, the Earl of Athlone, Viscount Slim and Lord Elworthy have all been Governors of the Castle, but also Knights of the Garter. Mary Downward, wife of the then Governor of the Military Knights, was watching the procession pass the Galilee Porch. As Sir Peter Downward recalled: 'The Queen Mother, no longer able to take her place in the procession was standing nearby and as we came past at our usual slow pace, said to Mary: "Here come the old darlings!"'6 The Queen Mother was 99 at the time.

In addition to their regular Sunday attendance at Mattins, they process in the chapel on Christmas Day, Easter Day, at Evensong on St George's Day, at the quarterly obit services, at the installations (and funerals) of Deans, Canons and fellow Military Knights, and at other special services, including the Royal Victorian Order service. They stand vigil over the coffins of members of the Royal Family immediately before the funeral.

They play a particular part in the presentation of Garter banners of deceased Garter Knights, leaving their seats in the Quire during the service (usually Evensong) at a chosen point, in order to escort their Governor as he collects the banner, and then carries it through the Quire to the altar rail, where he hands it to the Dean who lays it on the high altar. They provide a Guard of Honour at state visits to Windsor Castle, which have become popular since the late 1960s (to avoid traffic jams in London, which annoy the Londoners, while Windsorians take these things more in their stride).

The Military Knights also give an annual dinner with five guests – always the Constable, the Dean, the Keeper of the Privy Purse and the Castle Superintendent and a guest of honour, invariably a Garter Knight. Amongst those who have attended

The Military Knights in the Garter procession of 2006.

are Prince Philip, The Princess Royal, the Duke of Norfolk, and Lord Carrington. Major-General Sir Peter Downward considered these dinners as 'the highlight of the year in the Military Knights' calendar.'7 Their most recent guest was Lady Soames, a Lady of the Garter.

Today the Military Knights also support the College of St George in many other ways, for example, Colonel David Axson who had served as Honorary Secretary to the Guild of Stewards at the College since 2003, took over as Clerk to the Friends and Companions (of the College of St George) in 2006, and Lt Colonel Stuart Watts, a former Director of Army Music, is Concert Manager.

Military Knights are not allowed to wear their uniforms outside Windsor Castle without the Sovereign's permission. They did so at the wedding of the Prince of Wales to Lady Diana Spencer at St Paul's Cathedral in 1981, at the Royal Hospital, Chelsea, for the Army Benevolent Fund Parade in 1993, and twice at Buckingham Palace in 2002, the year of the Golden Jubilee – for the presentation of Loyal Addresses, and again at the Parade of the Royal Companies.

Today new Military Knights are expected to be married and must be under the age of 65 when appointed. They must be soldiers of officer rank. Their seniority is measured from the date of their appointment as a Military Knight, irrespective of rank.

In the past the Military Knights have described themselves – in a petition to Charles I for money owed them as 'so many decayed old Gentlemen who have spent the best part of their lives in the service of our country.' Today they are considerably less decayed. If they get too infirm to fulfil their duties, then they tend to 'retire', becoming 'super-numerary'.

The Military Knights are an integral part of the life of the College of St George, and it is a fine sight to them emerging from the houses in the castle wall, and making their way over to chapel, wearing the uniform designated for them by King William IV.

NINE

The Year at St George's

THERE IS CONTINUOUS worship at St George's, as there has been, more or less without a break, since the College of St George was established in 1352. The statutes declare that members of the College must 'wait eternally upon the Lord.'

In St George's Chapel there is a minimum of three services every weekday with four services on some days including Sundays. In term time the choir sing services six days a week. Even on Garter Day, when there is the Thanksgiving Service in the afternoon, the three other services are still held.

On weekdays there is Mattins at 7.30am, Holy Communion at 8am and Sung Evensong at 5.15pm. On Fridays only, Holy Communion is also said at 11.30. On Sundays, there is Holy Communion at 8.30, Sung Mattins with sermon at 10.45, Sung Eucharist at 11.45, and Choral Evensong at 5.15.

There are quarterly Obits, in March, June,

ABOVE The Queen and the Duke of Edinburgh with David Conner, Dean of Windsor, arriving for Easter Mattins 2007.

BELOW 'Is she coming?' Flowers for the Queen after Easter Mattins 2007.

ABOVE The Quire open for tourists.

BELOW A group of schoolchildren by the Great West Door in the Nave.

September and December. The most significant is the September Obit, when members of the College come together to remember the Founder and Benefactors at a special Sunday morning Eucharist. The other Obits take place at the time of Evensong. These are Days of Obligation, when those who are members of the College are obliged to attend, unless they are granted leave of absence for a well-stated reason. These members include the Dean, Canons, Minor Canons, Military Knights, Lay Clerks and Choristers, the Organist and Master of Choristers (Director of Music), the Clerk of Works, and the Master of Grammar (the Headmaster), the Chapter Clerk and the Virger. The Warden of St George's House is admitted to the College but as his is not an ancient post the holder is not installed as a member.

Until recently the September Obit was sometimes attended by the Lord Chancellor as the Visitor, but early in 2007 the Visitorship was transferred to the Sovereign.

The December Obit is celebrated at the time of Evensong with the Obit of Henry VI, at which the Provost of Eton is present. Lilies and roses are laid on the King's grave by two pupils of Eton College – lilies for Eton and roses for King's College, Cambridge.

January is traditionally the time of year for cleaning the chapel, and some years the Quire is closed, with all services taking part in the Nave. Epiphany is celebrated with a Sung Eucharist.

Easter falls in March or April, the beginning of Lent (Ash Wednesday) being marked by Sung Mattins at 9am, and Evensong with the Allegre *Misere*. On Palm Sunday there is the blessing of

palms at all the morning services. During Holy Week there is a rhythm of quiet services for members of the Community, often with periods of music and meditation late in the evening. Maundy Thursday includes the Eucharist of the Lord's Supper, followed by the watch (when members of the community keep a presence in the Chapel through the night).

On Good Friday there is the liturgy for Good Friday in the morning and then readings and

The Albert Memorial Chapel with the Deanery on its right.

prayers every 20 minutes in the Chapel throughout the afternoon. Because it is Good Friday, the state apartments are closed, and entrance to the Castle precincts that day is free, so invariably a huge number of visitors come to the chapel, which is open as a place of worship. Many enter initially as tourists but once inside, they find no lights, an altar

A stonemason at work on the west front of the chapel.

Flower arranging under the organ screen.

stripped bare to the wood, and quietness throughout, except for the regular rhythm of prayer, readings and hymns. Many stay for a long time, moved by the experience, and even those who do not stay respect the atmosphere.

The Vicar's Hall (the former Chapter Library, where Shakespeare's *The Merry Wives of Windsor* is said to have received its first performance. Below it are the Archives of St George's Chapel.

The Horseshoe Cloister, where the Lay Clerks live.

Easter Eve Vigil includes the first Communion of Easter. On Easter Day itself, there are four services. In contrast to the austerity of Lent, the chapel is transformed. The bare altar is lavishly covered, the darkness is broken by the Easter fire and the lighting of the Paschal candle. There is a profusion of flowers and an Easter garden.

The Queen and the Duke of Edinburgh, and any of their immediate family who are staying with them, attend Easter Day Mattins. (Normally, when the Queen is at Windsor, she worships at the Royal Chapel in the grounds of Royal Lodge, which is more private, and away from the gaze of tourists). The Easter term ends after Evensong, which means the choir is on holiday and the Military Knights do not march into chapel for Sunday Mattins.

It is perhaps worth pointing out that only very few of the annual services involve the Albert Memorial Chapel, which is not under the jurisdiction of St George's Chapel. For many years it was in the care of the Ministry of Works and is now maintained by the Royal Household. Because the floor is made of inlaid marble and can easily be damaged, the Albert Memorial Chapel is no longer open to the general public, but tourists can usually look into it through the open doors during visiting hours.

THE NATIONAL SCOUTS' SERVICE

The National Scouts' Service takes place each year in the chapel on the Sunday closest to St George's Day, and is attended by new Queen's Scouts and Gallantry Award Holders, who come from across Britain and sometimes from abroad. Adults whose good service to the Scouting Movement has been recognised by St George's Day Awards attend Mattins in the chapel. There is also a parade of Queen's Scouts in the Quadrangle of the Castle, at which the Queen or another member of the Royal Family, the Duke of Kent as President or a Vice-President of the Scout Association takes the salute.

A form of Scouts Service was begun at the time of Dean Eliot, but lapsed in the 1920s. The present Scouts Service was the brainchild of Canon Harry

Blackburne, who was convinced that Lord Baden-Powell had had the concept of the Order of the Garter in mind when he founded the Scouting movement. King George V took the salute at the first ever parade, and the Dean of Windsor gave the address at the first service, with the mighty sword of Edward III in his hand.[1]

In his short reign in 1936, Edward VIII was present at a Scouts' Service.

THE ROYAL VICTORIAN ORDER

The Royal Victorian Order service takes place every four years in the chapel, very often in April during the Easter Court.

Since 1937 the Chapel of the Royal Victorian Order had been the Savoy Chapel in London, and

The Queen and the Duke of Edinburgh with Rt Rev Michael Mann, Dean of Windsor, after the first Royal Victorian Order service held in the chapel on 7 December 1978. The Queen Mother is to the left. Back left – Sir John Johnston, then Assistant Comptroller of the Lord Chamberlain's Office, and back right – Hugo Vickers as Lay Steward.

The Officers of Arms in the Garter procession of 2006.

Royal Victorian Order, she was never invested with a GCVO. In 2007, following the death of Queen Elizabeth the Queen Mother in 2002, the Princess Royal was appointed Grand Master of the Order. There is a procession of Knights and Dames Grand Cross in their robes, and members of the Order are seated together, regardless of rank, though the senior recipients in each degree tend to be placed in the Quire.

* * * * *

In May Ascension Day and Pentecost are celebrated, and there is a confirmation service in the chapel. If, as at present, the Dean of Windsor is a Bishop, he confirms the candidates, who come from St George's School or the Royal Chapel in the Great Park, having been prepared by the school chaplain (one of the Minor Canons) or the Canon who is Chaplain in the Great Park.

THE GARTER CEREMONY

The Garter Ceremony is the most colourful of all the annual services in the Chapel, being rich in ceremonial. It is part of the Solemnity of St George, which includes the Renewal of Intention on Sunday, the Thanksgiving service (which is very often also an Installation service) on the Monday afternoon, and a Solemn Requiem for departed members of the Order of the Garter on Tuesday evening (at which

over the years three services for the Order were held there, the last being in November 1958, at which 240 recipients were present. It was the Duke of Edinburgh who suggested that St George's would be a more appropriate place, largely because it could seat over 1,000 people.

Therefore the Queen decided to hold a service in December 1978, and this has now become a regular feature, followed, since 1983, by a reception for the recipients in St George's Hall. In the congregation for the first such service was Lt-Col Gerald De Courcy-Ireland, who had been appointed MVO, 4th class as far back as 1917 for commanding the Guard of Honour when George V visited the Army in France.[2] At the 1991 service, the 97-year-old Earl of Southesk, KCVO (1923) was present.

On these occasions the Royal Family wear their GCVO or KCVO stars, but the Queen does not, on the grounds that apart from being Sovereign of the

Carriages waiting to convey members of the Royal Family back up the hill after the Garter Ceremony.

several Companions are present, wearing their Garter stars).

For the Garter Ceremony the chapel is closed for a few days for preparation, the chairs in the Nave turned to face inwards to observe the procession passing, and the lawns outside the chapel are filled with stands for spectators. If there is an Investiture of new Companions, this takes place in the Garter Throne Room in the morning. There is a luncheon in the Waterloo Chamber, and then the procession forms to walk down the hill from the State Apartments to the Horseshoe Cloister, up the steps to the Great West Door and into the chapel.

The procession is led by the Governor of Windsor Castle (unless he is a Knight of the Garter), followed by the Governor of the Military Knights, the Military Knights marching, the Officers of Arms in their tabards, then the Companions of the Order of the Garter, the royal Knights and Ladies, the Officers of the Order, and then the Queen and the Duke of Edinburgh. The procession ends with a detachment of the Yeomen of the Guard.

ABOVE The Queen and the Duke of Edinburgh after the Garter ceremony. Amongst the Companions on the steps – Lord Kingsdown, the Duke of Wellington, Lord Ridley, Baroness Thatcher, The Duke of Abercorn, Field Marshal Lord Inge, and the Prelate, the Bishop of Winchester.

BELOW The Yeomen of the Guard leaving St George's Chapel.

ABOVE The Duke of Kent, the Princess Royal, and the Prince of Wales leaving the Garter ceremony, followed by the Chancellor (Lord Carrington) and the Prelate (the Bishop of Winchester).

BELOW The Garter procession in the year of the Golden Jubilee. In the procession Grand Duke John of Luxembourg, the Queen of Denmark, the Duke of Gloucester and the Duke of Kent, the Princess Royal and the King of Norway.

The Laying-up of the banner of Admiral of the Fleet Lord Lewin in 1999.

The Australia window in the Dean's Cloister.

If there are new Companions to be installed, the Queen waits beside her stall, gives her instruction for the installations to take place, and the Chancellor of the Order, Lord Carrington, calls out their full names and style, and the new Knight or Lady is conducted to a Garter stall.

The service always includes a solemn *Te Deum* and an anthem, and after the Blessing, the procession re-forms and leaves the chapel by the Great West Door. The Queen and the Royal Family leave by carriage, the Companions by car, and others on foot.

LAYING UP OF GARTER BANNERS

In January 1952, a month before his death, King George VI approved the simple ceremony whereby, after a Knight of the Garter dies, his banner is laid up on the High Altar. This usually takes places at Evensong, though occasionally it has been part of a funeral service or at an afternoon memorial service. When Lord Longford died, the Countess of Longford, being in her 90s, the banner was laid up during Mattins on a Sunday morning.

Evensong proceeds as usual, and towards the end of the service, the Governor of the Military Knights leads the Military Knights out of the North Quire Aisle door. Escorted by Military Knights, he carries the banner down the North Quire Aisle and into the Quire. There is silence but for the marching feet of the Military Knights, and the banner is then given to the Dean of Windsor who raises it up and lays it on the altar. The banner is then returned to the family of the deceased Knight and they find a suitable resting place for it. The 10th Duke of Beaufort's is in St Michael and All Angels Church, Badminton; the 7th Earl of Radnor's in Salisbury Cathedral; Field Marshal Earl Alexander of Tunis's in the Guards Chapel, London; Queen Elizabeth The Queen Mother's in the hall at Clarence House.

From notification of the death until the laying up ceremony, the Knight's stall is cordoned off and a laurel wreath is placed in it, bearing his name. His banner, helm and crest are taken down, as is the half-drawn sword above the stall. The crest is returned to the College of Arms. The stall-plate remains in perpetuity, some of these plates being so old that they came from the earlier chapel.

* * * * *

ABOVE Canon John White, the Vice-Dean.

ABOVE Canon Dr Hueston Finlay.

BELOW Canon John Ovenden.

BELOW Charlotte Manley, the Chapter Clerk.

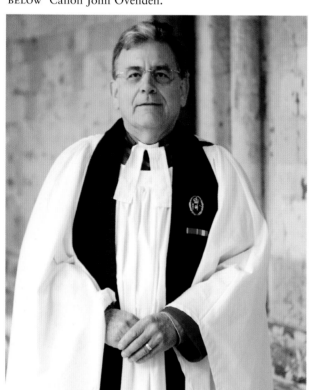

The Vestry.

A Feast of Title (The Visitation) is celebrated with a Sung Eucharist on 2 July. Between the end of July and the middle of September, when the choir is on holiday, many visiting choirs come to sing in the chapel, sometimes staying for as long as a week. This is always a particularly busy time with the tourist season at its height.

In late September, there are Windsor Festival concerts in the chapel. Since the Festival began in 1969, many great artists have performed there. In 2007 the Academy of St Martin in the Fields performed, and as a finale to the Festival, the St George's Chapel choir joined the City of Birmingham Symphony Chorus and Orchestra for a magnificent performance of Elgar's *Dream of Gerontius*, conducted by the chapel's former organist, Christopher Robinson.

In October a Feast of Title (Edward the Confessor) is celebrated with a Sung Eucharist, All Saints Day is observed with a Sung Eucharist and All Souls with a Solemn Requiem. On the Sunday closest to 11 November, Remembrance Sunday is observed in the chapel, with the traditional two minutes silence. In Advent there is an Evensong with music and readings and there are several carol services – for St George's School, the Community and on Christmas Eve, the traditional Nine Lessons and Carols. A crib is placed in the chapel.

On Christmas Eve, there is a midnight Eucharist, and on Christmas Day, there are four services, the most popular ones being Sung Mattins with sermon and Evensong with a procession. In the 1960s until the 1980s, the Queen and the Royal Family used to spend Christmas at the castle, and there was a large contingent of royalty present at Christmas Mattins. For some years the late Princess Alice, Duchess of Gloucester used to attend Christmas Mattins, before visiting her husband's grave at Frogmore.

OPPOSITE PAGE The Nave seen from under the organ screen.

RIGHT The Christmas crib in the Nave.

The Duke of Kent and his family came one year, and sometimes Princess Alexandra attends this service. (The most regular attender of St George's Chapel services was the late Princess Margaret, who invariably came to Sung Eucharist on Sunday mornings if she was staying at Royal Lodge).

The College term ends on Christmas Day and commences again early the next January. Meanwhile the busy life of the chapel continues, with the regular daily services as there have been since 1348. The chapel is open to visitors, all days except Sundays when it welcomes those who wish to attend the act of worship. This fine building continues to fulfil the duties laid down in the original statutes, while forever adapting to the new demands of modern times.

St George's Chapel is a masterpiece of medieval architecture, which can be seen from miles around, reaching elegantly above the battlements of Windsor Castle, held in great affection at the heart of the nation, and it maintains a thriving religious and choral tradition.

Acknowledgements

Sir Claude Hankes has been this book's godfather from the start. One of the book's aims is to celebrate those benefactors who have supported St George's Chapel so generously in past centuries and who continue to do so today.

At the College of St George I am grateful to Canon John White for his meticulous editing of the text. As editor of the Monograph series, he is a wise and knowledgeable expert. Charlotte Manley, the Chapter Clerk, has been unfailingly helpful, guiding many an early morning photography session and also providing the facts for the last chapter. Jane Tippett dug out an extraordinary amount of historical material for me, working in the London Library.

His Royal Highness The Duke of Edinburgh spoke to me about the College of St George in the present reign, and I also interviewed the late Sir Edward Ford and the late Sir John Johnston. Sir Richard and Lady Johns kindly allowed Elizabeth to photograph the chapel from the Norman Tower. Major Richard Moore helped me in respect of the Military Knights. I would also like to thank Rt Rev David Conner, Dean of Windsor, Tim Tatton-Brown (Archaeological Consultant to the Dean and Canons of Windsor), Dr Eileen Scarff, Richard Wragg, Enid Davis and Eleanor Cracknell (at the St George's Chapel Archives), Dame Anne Griffiths (The Duke of Edinburgh's archivist), Bridget Wright (Royal Library), John Handcock, Tim O'Donovan, Nigel Jaques, Brigadier Sir Miles Hunt-Davis (Private Secretary to HRH The Duke of Edinburgh), the late Hugh Montgomery-Massingberd, Rish Durka, Maggie Burns (the Heritage Centre, Birmingham Central Library), and Leslie Grout (1981 Mastermind champion). Sir Michael Hobbs and Georgie Grant Haworth have been supportive of the project since its conception.

For considerable help in the past, though not specifically for this book, I would like to record my gratitude to the late Very Rev Robin Woods, the late Dr Sidney Campbell, and the late Roy Read.

We would also like to thank all those who agreed to be photographed for the book either formally or while going about their daily work.

HUGO VICKERS

CREDITS FOR PHOTOGRAPHS AND OTHER ILLUSTRATIONS

Unless otherwise stated, all photographs are © Elizabeth Vickers/The Dean & Canons of Windsor, 2008.

Albert Memorial Chapel photographs © Her Majesty Queen Elizabeth II, 2007: pages 18 (lower); 80 (upper); 81; 91; 95; 96.

King George VI Memorial Chapel photographs © Her Majesty Queen Elizabeth II, 2006: pages 129 (lower); 130.

The Royal Collection © 2007, Her Majesty Queen Elizabeth II: pages 60; 74; 76; 84; 104 (right); 105; 119 (both); 121 (both).

St George's Chapel Archives: page 92 (both).

The Heritage section, Birmingham Central Library: photographs by Sir Benjamin Stone: pages 62; 79 (lower); 85; 97; 98 (both); 100; 103 (left); 154.

© British Library Board. All rights Reserved (Shelfmark HARL Ms 3749 Norden), pages 44-5.

Plans drawn by Christopher Chaplin, pages 11; 33.

Elizabeth Vickers photographs © Elizabeth Vickers: pages 138; 152; 158; 159 (both lower); 164 (both); 165 (both); 166 (both).

Hugo Vickers photographs © Hugo Vickers: pages 9 (right); 99 (left); 167 (left).

Hugo Vickers Collection: pages 9 (left); 18 (upper); 19 (lower); 26 (both); 32 (lower); 34 (lower); 42; 46 (lower); 51 (lower); 52 (both); 54; 55; 57; 59; 64; 90; 99 (right); 101; 102; 104 (left); 106; 107; 114 (upper); 115 (right, upper and lower); 116 (both); 117 (all); 122; 124; 127; 128; 129 (upper); 131; 132; 134; 144; 149; 155; 156 (left); 163.

Bibliography

BOOKS

Anon, *Crowns & Crests* (CPD Print & Design Ltd)
Hail and Farewell (The Times, 1936)
Memoirs of the Last Two Years of the Reign of King Charles I (G & W Nicol, 1815)
The Quincentenary Handbook (Oxley & Son, 1975)

Ashmole, Elias, *The Institution, Laws and Ceremonies of the most noble Order of the Garter* (Nathaniel Brooke, 1672)

Aspinall, A. (ed), *The Letters of George IV, Volume iii* (Cambridge University Press, 1938)
The Letters of the Princess Charlotte, 1811-1817 (Home and Van Thal, 1949)

Athlone, HRH Princess Alice, Countess of, *For My Grandchildren* (Evans Bros, 1966)

Baillie, Albert Victor, *My First Eighty Years 1864-1944* (John Murray, 1951)
St George's Chapel, Windsor Castle & Its Precincts, A Short Guide (Oxley & Son, 1930)

Baldwin Smith, Lacey, *Henry VIII* (Granada, 1973)

Barret, Charlotte (Ed), *Diary and Letters of Madame D'Arblay, Volume III* (Macmillan, 1905)

Beeson, Trevor, *Window on Westminster* (SCM Press, 1998)

Begent, Peter J., *The Romance of St George's Chapel* (Windsor, 2001)

Begent, Peter J., & Chesshyre, Hubert, *The Most Noble Order of the Garter* (Spink, 1999)

Bell, G.K.A., *Randall Davidson, Volume 1* (Oxford University Press, 1935)

Belsham, William, *Memoirs of the Reign of George III, Volume 1* (Hurst, Robinson, 1824)

Beltz, George Frederick, *Memorials of the Most Noble Order of the Garter* (William Pickering, 1841)

Blackburne, Haidee, *Trooper to Dean* (J.W. Arrowsmith, 1955)

Blackburne, Harry W., *The Romance of St George's Chapel, Windsor Castle* (Raphael Tuck & Sons, 1933)

Bland, Olivia, *The Royal Way of Death* (Constable, 1986)

Bolitho, Hector, *Edward VIII* (Eyre and Spottiswoode, 1937)
My Restless Years (Max Parrish, 1962)
The Romance of Windsor Castle (Evans Bros, 1946)

Bond, Maurice, *St George's Chapel, Windsor – The Quincentenary Souvenir Book of Photographs* (Windsor, 1975)
The Inventories of St George's Chapel 1384-1667 (Oxley & Son, 1947)

Bond, Shelagh M., *The Monuments of St George's Chapel, Windsor Castle* (Oxley & Son, 1958)

Boothroyd, Basil, *Philip* (Longmans, 1971)

Bothwell, J.S., *Edward III and the English Peerage* (Boydell Press, 2004)

Bray, William (ed), *Diary of John Evelyn Esq, FRS* (Bickers and Son, 1879)

Brooke, John, *King George III* (Constable, 1972)

Brown, Sarah, *A History of the Stained Glass of St George's Chapel, Windsor Castle* (Windsor, 2005)

Chesshyre, Hubert, *Garter Banners of the Nineties* (Windsor, 1998)

Clive, Mary, *This Son of York* (Macmillan, 1973)

Colles, H.C., *Walford Davies* (Oxford University Press, 1942)

Cunningham, Peter (ed), *The Letters of Horace Walpole, Earl of Orford, Volume IX* (Richard Bentley, 1859)

Dakers, Lionel *Places Where they Sing* (The Canterbury Press, Norwich, 1995)

Davenport, Hester, *Writers in Windsor* (Cell Mead Press, 2005)

Deane, Anthony C., *Time Remembered* (Faber and Faber, 1945)

De-la-Noy, Michael, *Windsor Castle – Past and Present* (Headline, 1990)

Dictionary of National Biography (various editions)

Dobson, Austin (ed), *Diary & Letters of Madame D'Arblay (1778-1840), Volume 5* (Macmillan, 1905)

Dorment, Richard, *Alfred Gilbert* (Yale University Press, 1985)
Alfred Gilbert – Sculptor and Goldsmith (Royal Academy/Weidenfeld & Nicolson, 1986)

Downward, Peter, *Old Yourself, One Day* (privately printed, 2004)

Edinburgh, HRH The Duke of, *A Windsor Correspondence* (Michael Russell, 1984)
Survival or Extinction (Michael Russell, 1989)

Falkus, Gila, *Edward IV* (Weidenfeld & Nicolson, 1981)

Fellowes, Edmund H., *Memoirs of an Amateur Musician* (Methuen, 1946)

Memoranda Concerning King Charles I (Oxley & Son, 1950)

The Knights of the Garter 1348-1939 (SPCK, 1939)

The Military Knights of Windsor 1352-1944 (Oxley & Son, Windsor, 1944)

The Vicars and Minor Canons of His Majesty's Free Chapel of St George, Windsor Castle (Oxley & Son, 1945)

Fellowes, Edmund H., & Poyser, Elisabeth, *The Baptism, Marriage & Burial Registers of St George's Chapel, Windsor Castle* (Oxley & Son, 1947)

Fraser, Flora, *Princesses – The Six Daughters of George III* (John Murray, 2004)

Frith, William Powell, *A Victorian Canvas* (Bles, 1957)

Galloway, Peter, Stanley, David & Martin, Stanley, *Royal Service, Volume 1* (Victorian Publishing, 1996)

Gardiner, Rena, & Bond, Maurice, *History in St George's Chapel, Windsor Castle* (Workshop Press, 1966)

Gash, Norman, *Mr Secretary Peel* (Longmans, 1961)

Gaskell, Martin, *St George's House – A Celebration of Forty Years* (privately printed, 2006)

Geddes, Jane, *Medieval Decorative Ironwork in England* (Society of Antiquaries, 1999)

Gore, John (ed), *Creevey* (John Murray, 1948)

Gunn, S.J., & Lindley, P.G., *Cardinal Wolsey – Church, State and Art* (Cambridge University Press, 1991)

Hart-Davis, Duff (ed), *King's Counsellor* (Weidenfeld & Nicolson, 2006)

Heald, Tim, *The Duke – A Portrait of Prince Philip* (Hodder & Stoughton, 1991)

Hedley, Olwen, *Windsor Castle* (Robert Hale, 1967)

Hibbert, Christopher, *The Court at Windsor* (Longmans, 1964)

Queen Victoria in Her Letters and Journals (John Murray, 1984)

Holmes, Grace, *The Order of the Garter – Its Knights & Stall Plates* (Windsor, 1984)

Holmes, Richard, *Edward VII – His Life & Times* (Amalgamated Press, 1910)

Queen Victoria (Boussod, Valadon & Co, 1897)

Hughes, Jonathan, *Arthurian Myths and Alchemy* (Sutton, 2002)

Hunt, Giles, *Launcelot Fleming: A Portrait* (Canterbury Press, Norwich, 2003)

James, M.R., *The Woodwork of the Choir* (Windsor, 1933, revised 1985)

Jekyll, Joseph, *The Correspondence of Mr Joseph Jekyll with his sister-in-law, Lady Gertrude Sloane Allaby, 818-1838* (London, 1894)

Jesse, Edward [surveyor of Her Majesty's Parks and Palaces], *Summer Day at Windsor and a Visit to Eton* (John Murray, 1843)

Knight, Charles, *Passages of a Working Life, Volume 1* (Bradbury & Evans, 1864)

Knighton, Lady, *Memoirs of Sir William Knighton, BART, GCH, Keeper of the Privy Purse During the Reign of His Majesty King George the Fourth, Including his Correspondence With Many Distinguished Personages, Volume 1* (Richard Bentley, London, 1838)

Kurtz, Harold, *The Empress Eugénie* (Hamish Hamilton, 1964)

Lee, Albert, *The Story of Royal Windsor* (Jarrold & Sons, London, 1910)

Longford, Elizabeth, *Victoria R.I.* (Weidenfeld & Nicolson, 1964)

Lorne, KT, Marquis of, *The Governor's Guide to Windsor Castle* (Cassell, 1896)

Maas, Jeremy, *The Prince of Wales's Wedding* (Cameron & Tayleur, 1977)

McAllister, Isabel, *Alfred Gilbert* (A & C Black, 1929)

Moore, Major Richard, assisted by Moore, Mrs Jennifer, *The Roll of the Alms (Poor) Knights of Windsor and The Military Knights of Windsor 1368-2006* (unpublished)

The Military Knights of Windsor – Brief History and Personal Profiles 1946-2006 (privately printed, 2006).

Morshead, Sir Owen, *Windsor Castle* (Phaidon Press, 1951)

Mortimer, Ian, *The Life of Edward III, Father of the English Nation* (Jonathan Cape, 2006)

N., J., *A Perfect Catalogue of all the Knights of the Most Noble Order of the Garter* (London, 1661)

Ollard, S.L., *Fasti Wyndesorienses – The Deans and Canons of Windsor* (Oxley & Son, 1950)

Ormrod, W.M., *The Reign of Edward III* (Yale University Press, 1990)

Pain, Nesta, *George III at Home* (Eyre Methuen, 1975)

Papendiek, C.L.H., *Court and Private Life in the Time of Queen Charlotte, Volume 2* (London, 1887)

Peel, George, *The Private Letters of Sir Robert Peel* (John Murray, 1920)

Pimlott, Ben, *Hugh Dalton* (Jonathan Cape, 1985)

Pope-Hennessy, James, *Queen Mary* (Allen & Unwin, 1959)

Pote, Joseph, *The History and Antiquities of Windsor Castle and the Royal College, and Chapel of St George: with the Institutions, Laws, and Ceremonies of the Most Noble Order of the Garter* (Joseph Pote, Eton, 1749)

Richmond, Colin & Scarff, Eileen, *St George's Chapel, Windsor, in the Late Middle Ages* (Dean & Canons of Windsor, 2001)

Rose, Kenneth, *King George V* (Weidenfeld & Nicolson, 1983)

Ross, Charles, *Edward IV* (Eyre Methuen, 1974)
  Richard III (Eyre, Methuen, 1981)
Rowse, A.L., *Windsor Castle in the History of the Nation* (Weidenfeld & Nicolson, 1974)
Russell, Richard, *Headmaster* (privately printed, ca 1984)

St John Hope, W.H., *The Stall Plates of the Knights of the Order of the Garter 1348-1485* (Archibald Constable & Co, 1901)
  Windsor Castle, 3 volumes (Country Life, 1913)
Scofield, Cora L., *The Life and Reign of Edward the Fourth* (Longmans Green, 1923)
Sermoneta, The Duchess of, *Sparkle Distant Worlds* (Hutchinson, 1947)
Stoughton, John, *Notices of Windsor in the Olden Time* (David Bogue, 1844)
Stow, John, *Annales* (London, 1631)
Stratford, Lawrence, *Edward the Fourth* (Sir Isaac Pitman & Sons, 1910)
Sutton, Anne F. & Visser-Fuchs, Livia with Griffiths, R.A., *The Royal Funerals of the House of York and Windsor* (The Richard III Society, 2005)
Symons, Christopher, *Sir Henry Walford Davies* (Oswestry & District Civic Society, 2003)

Tatton-Brown, Tim, *The Deanery, Windsor Castle* (The Antiquaries Journal, Society of Antiquaries of London, 1998, Volume 78)
Taylor, Joseph, *Relics of Royalty or Remarks, Anecdotes & Conversations of His Late Majesty George III* (A.H. Newman & Co (1820)
Thomson, Mrs A.T., *Memoirs of the Court of Henry the Eighth* (Longman, etc, 1826)
Thorndike, Russell, *Children of the Garter* (Rich & Cowan,1937)
Tighe, Robert Richard & Davis, James Edward, *Annals of Windsor, Volume II* (Longman Browen Green, Longmans and Roberts, 1858)
Tillyard, Stella, *A Royal Affair* (Chatto & Windus, 2006)

Tovey, Sir Donald & Parratt, Geoffrey, *Walter Parratt* (Oxford University Press, 1941)

Vickers, Hugo, *Alice, Princess Andrew of Greece* (Hamish Hamilton, 2000)
  Elizabeth The Queen Mother (Hutchinson, 2005)
  The Kiss (Hamish Hamilton, 1996)
  The Unexpurgated Beaton (Weidenfeld & Nicolson, 2002)
Vidler, Alec, *Scenes from a Clerical Life* (Collins, 1977)
Vulliamy, C.E., *Royal George* (Jonathan Cape, 1937)

Warburton, Rev W., *Edward III* (Longmans, Green, 1876)
Wardle, Ralph M. (ed), *Collected Letters of Mary Wollstonecraft* (Cornell University Press, London 1979)
Watson, Francis *Dawson of Penn* (Chatto & Windus, 1950)
Wheatley, Henry B., *The Diary of Samuel Pepys, MA, FRS* (George Bell & Sons, 1895)
Wheeler-Bennett, John, *King George VI* (Macmillan, 1958)
White, John A., *Spoken Light – Images of St George's Chapel* (Windsor, 2007)
Windsor, the Dean of, & Bolitho, Hector (eds), *Letters of Lady Augusta Stanley* (Gerald Howe, 1927)
Woodham-Smith, Cecil, *Queen Victoria – Her Life and Times, Volume One 1819-61* (Hamish Hamilton, 1972)
Woods, Robin, *An Autobiography* (SCM Press, 1986)
Wridgway, Neville, *The Choristers of St George's Chapel* (Chas Luff & Co, 1980)

Ziegler, Philip (ed), *From Shore to Shore* (Collins, 1989)

PAMPHLETS, MAGAZINES AND NEWSPAPERS

Annual Reports of the Society of the Friends of St George's (1936-2007); programmes for the Garter Ceremony 1965 to 2007;
Country Life; Daily Telegraph; Etoniana; Gentleman's Magazine; London Gazette; The Times; Windsor & Eton Express;

Sources

ONE – 'ST GEORGE FOR ENGLAND!'
(Pages 17-42)

1. Geddes, p. 157.
2. Pote, p. 131.
3. Pote, p. 26.
4. Davenport, pp. 1-2.
5. Lander, J.R., *The Historical Background to St George's Chapel in the Fifteenth Century* (Quincentenary Handbook), p. 9.
6. Lander, *op. cit.*, p. 10.
7. Sutton & Visser-Fuchs, p. 21.
8. Derived from Falkus, *The Life and Times of Edward IV*.
9. *Excerpta Historica* [quoted in Ross, *Edward IV*, p. 418].
10. Geddes, p. 262.
11. Lorne, p. 65.
12. Stoughton, p. 97.
13. Stoughton, p. 98.
14. Stratford, pp. 316-7.
15. Stoughton, p. 99.
16. Late Sir John Johnston to author, 22 June 2006.
17. Stow, p. 449.
18. Rowse, p. 41.
19. Derived from Ross, *Richard III*, p. 136.
20. Quoted in Lorne, p. 65.
21. Article on Sir Reginald Bray in *Dictionary of National Biography, Vol II*, p. 1146.
22. Mitchell, Patrick, *Bishop Oliver King and his work at Windsor and Bath Abbey* (Friends' Report, 1996-7), p.342.
23. Pote, pp. 195-6.
24. Pote, p. 27.
25. Lorne, p. 80.
26. Lindley, P.G., *Italian Renaissance Sculpture*, in Gunn & Lindley, p. 279.
27. Rowse, p. 57.

TWO – THE YEARS OF NEGLECT
(Pages 43-54)

1. Quoted in Rowse, p. 74.
2. Aubrey, *Brief Lives*.
3. Derived from Lee, pp. 183-4.
4. Morshead, Owen, *St George's Under the Commonwealth* (Friends' Report, 1958), p. 26.
5. *Memoirs of the Last Two Years of the Reign of Charles I*, p. 195 to end.
6. Derived from *Memoirs (op.cit)*, p. 195 to end.
7. Hedley, p. 102.
8. Report of Sir Henry Halford (Nichols, Son & Bentley, 1813), quoted in Fellowes, *Memoranda Concerning King Charles I*, p. 15.
9. Derived from Frith, *A Victorian Canvas*.
10. Some derived from Tatton-Brown, Tim, *Destruction at St George's Chapel* (Friends' Report, 1995-6), pp. 295-8.
11. Bray, p. 52.
12. Derived from Tatton-Brown, Tim, *The Deanery, Windsor Castle* (Antiquaries Journal, 1998, Vol. 78), p. 357.
13. Ashmole, p. 498.
14. Jesse, pp. 30-1.
15. Hibbert, *The Court at Windsor*, p. 80.
16. Entry for 26 Feb 1665-6 - Wheatley, pp. 234-5.
17. Entry for 26 April 1667 - Wheatley, pp. 288-9.
18. Entry for 26 March 1670 – Bray.
19. Pote, p. 62.
20. Pote, p. 52.

THREE – 'A SCENE OF LIGHTNESS AND GRACES'
(Pages 55-74)

1. *Gentleman's Magazine*, June 1786.
2. Tighe & Davis, p. 101.
3. Papendiek, p. 97.
4. Barret, p. 84.
5. Barret, pp. 431-3.
6. Brooke, pp. 285-6.
7. Mary Wollstonecraft to Jane Arden, Windsor, *post* 1780 [quoted in Wardle, p.65].
8. Letter to Miss Berry, Strawberry Hill, 9 Oct 1791 [quoted in Cunningham, *Vol IX*, p.357].
9. Letter as above [quoted in Cunningham, *Vol. IX*, pp. 356-7].
10. *The Times*, 7 Sept 1787.
11. *The Times*, 7 Sept 1787.
12. Barret, pp. 173-4.
13. 22 July 1799 – Barret, pp. 438-9.
14. Brooke, p. 287.
15. Knight, p. 65.
16. Taylor, pp. 150-3.

17. Derived from Vulliamy, pp. 288-9.
18. Pain, p. 155.
19. Belsham, p. 394.
20. Tillyard, p. 331.
21. Quoted in Brooke, p. 386.
22. Letter, 9 Nov 1811 - Aspinall (ed), *Letters of Princess Charlotte*, p.12.
23. Bland, p. 116.
24. Bland, p. 118.
25. Diary, 2 Dec 1818 – Dobson, p. 380.
26. Morshead, *Windsor Castle*, p. 5.
27. Taylor, pp. 177-94.
28. Fellowes & Poyser, *Registers of St George's Chapel*, p. 249.
29. *The Times*, 2 Feb 1818.
30. Aspinall (ed), *The Letters of George IV, vol iii*, p. 1097.
31. Letter, Royal Lodge, 20 Jan 1827 – Knighton, *Vol 1*, pp. 358-60.
32. Letter, 21 Jan 1827 – Peel, p. 92.
33. Letter, 21 Jan 1827 – Peel, p. 93.
34. Letter, 21 Jan 1827 – Peel, p. 94.
35. Letter, 21 Jan 1827 – Peel, p. 95.
36. Gash, p. 425.
37. *The Times*, 16 July 1830.
38. Jekyll, pp. 242-3.
39. *The Times*, 16 July 1830.
40. *Extracts from the Diary of Miss Margaretta Brown* (Etoniana, no 69 ff).
41. *The Times*, 7 August 1834.
42. *Dictionary of National Biography, Vol VIII*, p. 1211.
43. Queen Victoria's Journal, 21 August 1836.
44. Woodham-Smith, *Vol One 1819-61*, pp. 126-7.
45. *The Times*, 10 July 1837.

FOUR – QUEEN VICTORIA
(Pages 75-98)

1. Queen Victoria's Journal, 1837.
2. *The Times*, 28 Nov 1838.
3. Baillie, A.V. (Friends' Report, 1944), p. 14.
4. Ollard, p. 53.
5. *The Times*, 2 Oct 1840.
6. *The Times*, 2 Oct. 1840.
7. Tighe & Davis, *Vol II*, p. 657.
8. *The Times*, 9 Sept 1841.
9. Tighe & Davis, *Vol II*, p. 657.
10. *The Times*, 24 Oct 1842.
11. Derived from *The Times*, 3 Aug 1841; 9 Sept 1841; 18 May 1842; 24 Oct 1842; & 11 Sept 1843.
12. *The Times*, 11 Sept 1843.
13. *London Gazette*, Nov 1849.
14. Battiscombe, Georgina, *Gerald Wellesley* (Friends' Report, 1963, p. 126).
15. Bell, *Vol 1*, p. 77.
16. Bell, *Vol 1*,
17. Battiscombe, *Gerald Wellesley* (Friends' Report, 1963, p. 128).
18. Battiscombe, *Gerald Wellesley* (Friends' Report, 1963, p. 134).
19. Windsor, Dean of, & Bolitho, p. 285.
20. Windsor, Dean of, & Bolitho, pp. 285-6.
21. Cuthbert, Elizabeth H., *The Last King of Hanover* (Friends' Report, 1990-1991, pp. 285-6).
22. Kay, Julian, review of Holt-Wilson, Sandy, Lecture: *The Life of Prince Alamayu Teodros in the UK* [Anglo-Ethiopian Society website].
23. Kay, *op. cit.*
24. Queen Victoria's Journal, 14 November 1879 - Langton, Jane, *Alamayou, Prince of Abyssinia* (Friends' Report, 1987-1988, p. 390).
25. Derived from Langton, Jane, *Alamayou, Prince of Abyssinia* (Friends' Report, 1987-1988, pp. 382-90).
26. Queen Victoria's Journal, 30 Nov 1870 – Hibbert, *Queen Victoria in her Letters and Journals*, p. 223.
27. Derived from Cuthbert, Elizabeth, *A Monument to the Prince Imperial* (Friends' Report, 1977-1978, pp. 383-90).
28. Empress Eugénie to Col Arthur Bigge, quoted in Kurtz, p. 323.
29. *The Times*, 28 April 1882.
30. Baillie, *My First Eighty Years*, pp. 171-2.
31. Bell, *Vol I*, p. 69.
32. Longford, p. 326.
33. Queen Victoria to Archbishop of Canterbury, 4 May 1883, quoted in Bell, *Vol I*, p. 69.
34. *The Times*, 2 May 1883.
35. Bell, *Vol 1*, p. 69.
36. Queen Victoria to Archbishop of Canterbury, 4 May 1883, quoted in Bell, *Vol I*, p. 69.
37. Queen Victoria's Journal, 9 Dec 1882, quoted in article on Randall Davidson, *Dictionary of National Biography, 1922-30*, p. 241.
38. Bell, *Vol I*, p. 69.
39. Letter from Richard Cecil Grosvenor to *The Times*, 25 July 1883.
40. *The Times*, 20 Aug 1888.
41. Bell, *Vol I*, p. 70.
42. Derived from Cuthbert, E.H., *Prince Leopold, Duke of Albany* (Friends' Report, 1983-1984, pp. 188-920).
43. Bell, *Vol I*, p. 82.
44. Bell, *Vol I*, p. 388.
45. Baillie, *My First Eighty Years*, pp. 87-8.
46. Bond, Maurice, *Philip Frank Eliot* (Friends' Report, 1966-67, p. 314).
47. Queen Victoria's Journal, 3 May 1891, quoted in Bond, Maurice, *Philip Frank Eliot* (Friends' Report, 1966-67, p. 319).
48. Bond, Maurice, *Philip Frank Eliot* (Friends' Report, 1966-67, p. 315).

49. Baillie, *My First Eighty Years*, p. 172.
50. McAllister, p. 129.
51. Dorment, *Alfred Gilbert*, p. 150.
52. McAllister, p. 132.
53. Dorment, *Alfred Gilbert – Sculptor and Goldsmith*, p. 154.
54. Bond, Maurice, *Philip Frank Eliot* (Friends' Report, 1966-67, p. 329).
55. Bell, *Vol I*, p. 356.
56. *Windsor & Eton Express*, 2 Feb 1901.
57. Bell, *Vol I*, p. 356.
58. Bolitho, *My Restless Years*, p. 132.
59. Bell, *Vol I*, p. 357.

FIVE — RESTORATION AND RENEWAL
(Pages 99-123)

1. Fellowes, *The Military Knights of Windsor*, p. lii.
2. Baillie, *My First Eighty Years*, p. 172.
3. Baillie, *My First Eighty Years*, p. 173.
4. Vidler, pp. 139-40.
5. See Baillie, *My First Eighty Years*, p. 173.
6. Pimlott, p. 21.
7. Deane, p. 211.
8. Baillie, *My First Eighty Years*, pp. 173-7.
9. The late Sir Edward Ford to author, London, 5 July 2006.
10. *The Times*, 29 July 1931.
11. Baillie, *My First Eighty Years*, p. 176.
12. *The Times*, 31 July 1931.
13. Athlone, p. 126.
14. Bolitho, *My Restless Years*, p. 127.
15. Bond, Maurice, *Philip Frank Eliot* (Friends' Report, 1966-7), p. 323.
16. *The Times*, 25 June 1914.
17. HRH Prince Louis of Hesse to Earl Mountbatten of Burma, 19 March 1959 [Broadlands Archives].
18. *The Times*, 2 Nov 1917.
19. Rose, p. 287.
20. Baillie, *My First Eighty Years*, p. 173.
21. Tovey & Parratt, p. 135.
22. *The Times*, 4 Nov 1955.
23. Bolitho, *My Restless Years*, p. 127.
24. Sir Edward Ford to author, 5 July 2006.
25. *Country Life*, 8 Nov 1930.
26. Baillie, *My First Eighty Years*, p. 180.
27. *Country Life*, 8 Nov 1930.
28. Bolitho, *My Restless Years*, p. 155.
29. Bolitho, *My Restless Years*, p. 156.
30. *Country Life*, 8 Nov 1930.
31. Bolitho, *My Restless Years*, p. 156.
32. *The Times*, 4 November 1930.
33. Sir Edward Ford to author, 5 July 2006.
34. Watson, p. 274.
35. Diary of Rev Alan Don, 29 Jan 1936 [Lambeth Palace Library].
36. *Hail and Farewell*, p. 89.
37. Bolitho, *Edward VIII*, p. 248.
38. *Hail and Farewell*, p. 91.
39. Dean Baillie's Letter, Friends' Report, 1935.
40. Dean Baillie's Lettter, Friends' Report, 1936, p. 5.
41. Sermoneta, p. 139.
42. 10th Duke of Argyll to Bartholomew Hack, 17 June 1937 [Hugo Vickers papers].
43. Hart-Davis, p. 239.
44. Hart-Davis, p. 392.
45. Friends' Report, 1955, p. 3.
46. Obituary of Canon G.B. Bentley, *The Times*, 20 Sept 1996.
47. Dakers, p. 86.
48. John Handcock to author, 31 Oct 2006.
49. Vidler, pp. 138-9.
50. Wheeler-Bennett, p. 757.
51. *The Times*, 24 April 1948.
52. Friends' Report, 1948.
53. Archbishop of Canterbury's address, 18 July 1948.
54. Description of King George VI Memorial Chapel (by Robin Woods), contained in Dedication service sheet, 31 March 1969.

SIX — THE PRESENT REIGN
(Pages 124-140)

1. HRH The Duke of Edinburgh to author, Buckingham Palace, 7 Nov 2006.
2. Foreword by HRH The Duke of Edinburgh, in Woods, p. vii.
3. Duke of Edinburgh to author, 7 Nov 2006.
4. Friends' Report, 1959, p. 5.
5. Dean Hamilton, St George's appeal document, enclosed with letter from Hamilton to Duke of Edinburgh, 5 January 1959 [Duke of Edinburgh papers, BP].
6. Dean's Letter, Friends' Report, 1959, p. 5.
7. Vidler, pp. 139-40.
8. Friends' Report, 1961, p. 41.
9. Friends' Report, 1962, p. 75.
10. Woods, p. 41.
11. Woods, pp. 136-7.
12. Heald, p. 194.
13. Woods, p. 143.
14. 5th Marquess of Salisbury to HRH Prince Paul of Yugoslavia, 2 Dec 1968 [Prince Paul papers, Bakhmeteff Archive, Rare Book and Manuscript Library, Columbia University, NY].
15. Woods, p. 139.
16. Duke of Edinburgh to Earl of Iveagh, 21 July 1964 [copy in Duke of Edinburgh papers, BP].
17. Duke of Edinburgh to Iveagh, 21 July 1964 [copy in

Duke of Edinburgh papers, BP].

18. Iveagh to Duke of Edinburgh, 29 July 1964 [Duke of Edinburgh papers, BP].

19. Woods to Duke of Edinburgh [copy in Duke of Edinburgh papers, BP].

20. Woods to author, ca 1991.

21. Duke of Edinburgh memo to Rear-Admiral Christopher Bonham Carter (undated, but March 1966) [copy in Duke of Edinburgh papers, BP].

22. Woods, p. 139.

23. Fisher to the Prime Minister, 18 June 1949 [Archbishop Fisher papers, Lambeth Palace Library].

24. Ziegler, pp. 254-5.

25. Vickers (ed), *The Unexpurgated Beaton*, pp. 255-6.

26. Vickers (ed), *The Unexpurgated Beaton*, pp. 257.

27. Hunt, p. 242.

28. Hunt, p. 243.

29. Hugo Vickers tribute to Rt Rev Launcelot Fleming, *Daily Telegraph*, 1 Aug 1990.

30. Woods, p. 219.

31. Hunt, p. 241.

32. For a full account – see Vickers, *Alice, Princess Andrew of Greece*, pp. 399-405.

33. Friends' Report, 1987-88, pp. 376-7.

34. Beeson, p. 278.

35. Friends' Report, 1997-1998, p. 363.

SEVEN – 'A GOOD QUIRE OF VOICES'
(Pages 142-151)

1. Gore, p. 343.
2. HRH The Duke of Edinburgh to author, 7 Nov 2006.
3. Boothroyd, p. 186.
4. Statutes, quoted by Michael Mann in Wridgway, p. ix.
5. Statutes 17 (p. 9), quoted in Wridgway, p. 3.
6. Wridgway, p. 32.
7. Entry for 26 Feb 1665-6 - Wheatley, pp. 234-5.
8. Derived from *The Times*, 11 Dec 1893.
9. Tovey & Parratt, p. 59.

10. Tovey & Parratt, p. 149.
11. Tovey & Parratt, p. 131.
12. Tovey & Parratt, p. 132.
13. Colles, p. 17.
14. Symons, p. 24.
15. Hart-Davis, p. 77.
16. Article on Sir William Harris, *Dictionary of National Biography, 1971-80*, p. 383.
17. Dakers, p. 73.
18. Sampson, Alastair, *William Harris (1883-1973): Anthems* (Sir William Harris – Anthems – CD – 2006).
19. *The Times*, 6 June 1974.
20. Woods, pp. 144-5.
21. Rusell, p. 31.
22. Late Dr Sidney Campbell to author, ca 1969.
23. Tim Byram-Wigfield to author, Windsor Castle, 8 May 2006.

EIGHT – THE MILITARY KNIGHTS OF WINDSOR
(Pages 152-158)

1. Moore, Richard, *The Roll of Alms (Poor) Knights of Windsor*, p. 26.
2. Thorndike, p. 9.
3. Lorne, p. 60.
4. Thorndike, p. 51.
5. Moore, *op.cit.*, p. 85.
6. Downward, p. 511.
7. Downward, p. 490.

NINE – THE YEAR AT ST GEORGE'S
(Pages 159-171)

1. Blackburne, Haidee, p. 80.
2. Galloway, p. 57.

Index